The Political Economy of Government Subsidised Housing in South Africa

This book unpacks the political economy of government subsidised housing programmes in South Africa.

Exploring government policy towards subsidised housing in South Africa, this edited collection analyses various programmes, their shortcomings and potential options to address these weaknesses in the context of a country experiencing an exponential demand for housing in the face of insufficient supply. *The Political Economy of Government Subsidised Housing in South Africa* looks at the complex and contested nature of subsidised housing in post-apartheid South Africa, stimulating debate and knowledge sharing on housing programmes, and proffering solutions to the issue. The book explores the issue from both practical and intellectual standpoints, exploring the relationship between historical institutional legacies and contemporary power structures, and their role in the provision of housing for the growing population of South Africa.

This book will be of great interest to students of urban and regional planning, political economy, development studies and African studies.

Sithembiso Lindelihle Myeni is a Lecturer in Housing and Planning at the University of KwaZulu-Natal, South Africa. He is a Cannon Collins Educational Trust and Ford Foundation Alumnus. He is the Principal Investigator for the Sustainable Human Settlements Decision Support Tools and the Municipal Innovation Maturity Index Research Projects. Both are funded by the Department of Science and Technology.

Andrew Emmanuel Okem is a Science Officer in the School of Life Sciences, University of KwaZulu-Natal, South Africa. He is a Co-Principal Investigator of the Sustainable Human Settlements Decision Support Tools funded by the Department of Science and Technology.

Routledge Studies on the Political Economy of Africa

1 **The Political Economy of Energy in Sub-Saharan Africa**
Edited by Lucky E. Asuelime and Andrew E. Okem

2 **The Political Economy of Land and Agrarian Development in Ethiopia**
The Arssi Region since 1941
Ketebo Abdiyo Ensene

3 **The Political Economy of Livelihoods in Contemporary Zimbabwe**
Edited by Kirk Helliker, Manase Kudzai Chiweshe and Sandra Bhatasara

4 **The Politics of Economic Reform in Ghana**
Edited by Richard Aidoo

5 **The Political Economy of Government Subsidised Housing in South Africa**
Edited by Sithembiso Lindelihle Myeni and Andrew Emmanuel Okem

The Political Economy of Government Subsidised Housing in South Africa

Edited by
Sithembiso Lindelihle Myeni
and Andrew Emmanuel Okem

Routledge
Taylor & Francis Group
LONDON AND NEW YORK

First published 2020 by Routledge

2 Park Square, Milton Park, Abingdon, Oxon OX14 4RN
605 Third Avenue, New York, NY 10017

Routledge is an imprint of the Taylor & Francis Group, an informa business

First issued in paperback 2021

Publisher's Note

The publisher has gone to great lengths to ensure the quality of this reprint but points out that some imperfections in the original copies may be apparent.

British Library Cataloguing-in-Publication Data
A catalogue record for this book is available from the British Library

Library of Congress Cataloging-in-Publication Data
A catalog record has been requested for this book

ISBN: 978-1-138-36491-2 (hbk)
ISBN: 978-1-03-217750-2 (pbk)
DOI: 10.4324/9780429431043

Typeset in Times New Roman
by Wearset Ltd, Boldon, Tyne and Wear

Contents

Contributors vii

Introduction: setting the scene – an overview of government subsidised housing in South Africa 1
SITHEMBISO LINDELIHLE MYENI AND ANDREW EMMANUEL OKEM

1 **Sustainable Development Goals and the New Urban Agenda: a South African experience** 12
OLIVER MTAPURI AND SITHEMBISO LINDELIHLE MYENI

2 **A historicity of housing policies in apartheid South Africa** 28
ANDREW EMMANUEL OKEM, SITHEMBISO LINDELIHLE MYENI, OLIVER MTAPURI AND SIPHO NKAMBULE

3 **An assessment of the National Development Plan in the actualisation of government subsidised housing in South Africa** 39
SITHEMBISO LINDELIHLE MYENI AND ANDREW EMMANUEL OKEM

4 **Apartheid housing and urban livelihoods in apartheid South Africa** 52
SIPHO JONATHAN NKAMBULE

5 **A demand-driven subsidised housing policy for South Africa** 60
JUDITH OJO-AROMOKUDU, MICHAEL SAMUEL AND RUBBY DHUNPATH

6 **Assessment of stakeholders' participation in the implementation of Cornubia Housing Project in eThekwini Municipality** 80
NDWAKHULU TSHISHONGA

7 **Enhanced women's participation in state subsidised housing programmes: a case of Federation of Urban Poor in iNanda, Durban** 97
VINCENT MYENI AND PHUMELELE KHUMALO

8 **Citizenship, gender and the technologies of governance: an interrogation of the low-income housing programme in KwaZulu-Natal** 112
SITHEMBISO LINDELIHLE MYENI AND TAFADZWA CHIBVONGODZE

9 **Revisiting land challenges in housing urban poor people in post-apartheid South Africa: an insight into Durban** 128
LOVEMORE CHIPUNGU AND KNOWLEDGE ZUNGU

10 **Housing for individual sovereignty through innovations in policy and practice** 147
SITHEMBISO LINDELIHLE MYENI AND OLIVER MTAPURI

11 **A gendered discourse on women's access to housing in South Africa** 160
CLAUDINE HINGSTON

12 **Climate change and housing: implications for urban poor people in South Africa** 173
ANDREW EMMANUEL OKEM, MDODA DAVISDON ZONDO, SIYABONGA NTOMBELA AND SARAH BRACKING

Index 188

Contributors

Andrew Emmanuel Okem is a Science Officer in the School of Life Sciences, University of KwaZulu Natal, South Africa. He holds a doctorate in Policy and Development Studies from the same institution. He is a co-Principal Investigator for the Sustainable Human Settlements Decision Support Tools.

Dr Claudine Hingston currently works at the Management College of Southern Africa (MANCOSA) where she heads the MANCOSA Centre for Women Leadership and also serves as an academic lecturer. She is also actively engaged in research work and has written and published a number of articles on women, leadership and gender issues.

Danford Tafadzwa Chibvongodze is reading for a PhD in Development Studies at the University of KwaZulu-Natal. His research interests are in urban theory, urban poverty, governance, spatiality and gender. He has five years of work experience in the field of development, in which he has coordinated community projects in the areas of health promotion and poverty mitigation. Danford has hands-on experience in project management, HIV advocacy, social research, food security and urban agriculture.

Judith Ojo-Aromokudu is an Architect, lecturing at the School of Built Environment and Development Studies at the University of KwaZulu Natal Durban. Her research interest is in informality in the Built Environment and Urban Vernacular Architecture of the 21st century.

Knowledge Zungu is a doctoral candidate at the University of KwaZulu-Natal. He holds a Master's Degree in Housing, Postgraduate Diploma in Law (Forensic Investigation and Criminal Justice), and a Bachelor of Social Science Degree. His research interests are in land, low-income housing, fraud and corruption.

Dr Lovemore Chipungu holds a PhD in Town and Regional Planning. He is currently a Senior Lecturer at the University of KwaZulu-Natal. He has published widely in peer-reviewed journals and books; and his areas of interest are housing policy, urban land and urban design.

Mdoda Davidson Zondo is pursuing his doctoral studies in the Development Studies programme at the University of KwaZulu Natal. He has a keen interest in environmental issues.

Michael Samuel is a Professor in the School of Education, University of Kwa-Zulu-Natal. His research interests include teacher professional development, postgraduate higher education studies and lifehistory research. His recent books are *Teacher education in Mauritius* and *Disrupting higher education curriculum: Undoing cognitive damage.*

Ndwakhulu Tshishonga is a lecturer in the school of Built Environment and Development studies at the University Kwazulu-Natal. He holds a BA, BA (Hons) in Development Studies (UNISA); an MA in Applied Anthropology (Goldsmith College, University of London), MM in Public Development and Management (WITS) and MPA-Public Administration (UWC), Advanced Diploma (UWC-Adult Education) and Social Reconstruction and Development Certificate (SADEP-UWC). His interests are in citizenship and local government and local governance, Intergovernmental Relations, Social Movements and Protests, etc. His teaching interests range from Alternative Models of Development, Project Management and Development Planning to Micro Level Strategies in Economic Community Development, Co-operatives. His current research is on Intergenerational poverty, Inclusive and Exclusive Citizenship and Local Governance, Youth and Gender development as well as poverty issues and food security, politics of service delivery & social movements, Indigenous knowledge systems. His research output entails scholarly conference presentations and publication in journals such as Journal of Public Administration, Agenda, African Journal of Public Affairs, and Journal of African & Asian Local Government Studies. He has published more than 20 book chapters and journal papers nationally and internationally.

Oliver Mtapuri has a PhD in Development studies (University of KwaZulu Natal) and an MBA degree from the University of Zimbabwe. He is an Associate of the Institute of Chartered Secretaries and Administrators. Before joining the academe, Oliver worked for 12 years in the Government of Zimbabwe as a Labour Economist/Researcher in the Ministry of Labour and Social Welfare. Oliver's areas of research interest include poverty, redistribution and inequality, innovation, food supply, community-based tourism, public employment programmes, research methodologies, structural equation modelling, financial management, climate change and project management. Recently he has taken a keen interest in the nexus between the environment and poverty particularly in light of the many 'poverties' and 'inequalities' afflicting contemporary societies. Oliver is the Academic Leader of Research for the School of Built Environment and Development Studies at UKZN. He is the Interim National Research Foundation SARCHI Chair in Applied Poverty Reduction Assessment and facilitates Poverty and Inequality and Development Management Modules in the Discipline of Development Studies.

Phumelele Khumalo is a professional Town Planner but practicing as a Project Manager in the private sector. She is a PhD candidate in the School of Built Environment and Development Studies at UKZN in the discipline of Housing.

Rubby Dhunpath is the Director of Teaching & Learning at the University of KwaZulu- Natal. A former senior research specialist at the HSRC and Rockefeller Research Fellow, Rubby is also a Fulbright and Spencer Alumnus. His recent publication is an edited volume: Disrupting Higher Education Curriculum: Undoing Cognitive Damage.

Professor Sarah Bracking is Professor of Climate and Society in the School of Global Affairs, King's College London.

Sipho Jonathan Nkambule lectures in the Discipline of Housing, University of KwaZulu Natal. He holds Doctor of Philosophy from Rhodes University, South Africa.

Sithembiso Lindelihle Myeni is a Lecturer in Housing and Planning at the University of KwaZulu-Natal (UKZN). Before this appointment, he was a former post-doctoral fellow with South African Research Chair Initiative in Applied Poverty Reduction Assessment at UKZN. Myeni is also a Cannon Collins Educational Trust and Ford Foundation Alumnus. He serves as a Principal Investigator for the Sustainable Human Settlements Decision Support Tools and the Municipal Innovation Maturity Index Research Projects. His research interests are gender and housing, Science, Technology and Innovation as well as rural development.

Siyabonga Pherison Ntombela is a lecturer in International & Public Affairs cluster School of Social Sciences at the University of KwaZulu-Natal. He is also a Research Fellow in Monitoring and Evaluation at the Maurice Webb Race Relations Unit.

Vincent Myeni is a Lecturer and researcher in the discipline of Housing. He is based in the School of Built Environment and Development Studies, at the University of KwaZulu-Natal. His research interest includes, the use and conservation of natural resources, the role of housing delivery in poverty alleviation. Climate change and sustainable housing and livelihoods. He is a housing practitioner and has passion for teaching project management modules.

Pumulele Xabindlo [illegible] professional Town Planner but practising as a Project Manager in the private sector. She is a PhD candidate in the School of Built Environment and Development Studies at UKZN in the discipline of Housing.

Rubby Dhunpath is the Director of Teaching & Learning at the University of KwaZulu-Natal. A former senior research specialist at the HSRC and [illegible] Fisher Research Fellow, Rubby is also a Fellow of [illegible] and Science. Amongst his recent publications is an edited volume, *Disrupting Higher Education Curriculum: Undoing Cognitive Damage*.

Professor Sarah Bracking is Professor of Climate and Society in the School of [illegible]

[illegible]

Introduction

Setting the scene – an overview of government subsidised housing in South Africa

Sithembiso Lindelihle Myeni and Andrew Emmanuel Okem

Introduction

South Africa was liberated from its repressive governance system with the general elections of April 1994 marking a new phase in the country's history. Over the past 25 years of democratic rule, the political rationality of self-help housing through government subsidised housing has been debated by the government in formulating a unified national policy for Africans. This has significantly increased the number of government subsidised housing beneficiaries from marginalised people have had no access to housing and other services in both rural and urban areas (Mzolo, 2016). Beyond this increased number of housing beneficiaries, there has also been a fundamental restructuring of government institutions and legislative, policy and regulatory frameworks, which has in turn contributed to a change in systems of resource allocation, in order to tackle the dilemma faced in implementing government subsidised housing programmes in South Africa (Muthambi, 2015).

Despite the advances from Nelson Mandela's to Cyril Ramaphosa's administrations, there are still serious concerns about whether government subsidised housing developments provide suitable living conditions for the nation's poor. For example, despite a clear commitment to the Millennium Development Goals, the Sustainable Development Goals and the New Urban Agenda for sustainable human settlements, there is a continued growth of informal settlements in the urban centres of South Africa, which is exacerbated by a failure to fast track the upgrading of informal settlements in the urban outskirts and the lack of a comprehensive housing strategy on sustainable rural housing development. The democratic government's housing policies and practices are producing unintended results similar to those under the apartheid regime, namely poor-quality housing located far from opportunities and wealth. These are a clear reminder that the housing challenge has not been resolved despite the introduction of government subsidised housing. The African National Congress (ANC) acknowledged this reality in its 2019 Elections Manifesto by stating that, while the party has improved the lives of millions of South Africans through the provision of housing and associated basic services, the spatial patterns of apartheid have not been addressed (African National Congress, 2019).

Apartheid legacy is not only the intractable housing problem in post-apartheid South Africa. The post-apartheid period experiences conflicting rationalities and demands. There is a growing empathy to the post-apartheid rationality of rule that confronts apartheid legacy and has to balance many conflicting demands while also facing realities of the global economy. There is a reality and a growing concern that government subsidised households, often represented by low-income and elderly households, risk their right to property as they become involved in informal sales of their houses. This informality contributes to risk and legal consequences. One of the risks associated with the practice of informality is that it undermines title-deeds registration systems, and there is potential expansion of end-user finance in the secondary housing market; and in turn the ability of banks and lenders to operate at the lower end of the market is severely limited. The legal consequences are informal sales, which contribute to the discrepancy between occupants and owners; difficulty in title correction and confirming ownership; and unresolved estates. Most beneficiaries of government subsidised housing remain without title deeds due to delays in township establishment and proclamation. Overall, titling of government subsidised housing is not happening because of the time taken for conveyancing and delinking of subsidy from beneficiaries. In addition, this has damaged the prospects of selling government subsidised housing in an open market, while also restricting beneficiaries of government subsidised housing from using it as collateral.

To our knowledge, these diverse phenomena associated with government subsidised housing pose curious problems for social scientists. This is due to the growing gap between the rich and poor over time. There is no agreement among planners and policy-makers about whether government subsidised housing is beneficial for poor people, yet its recurrence in discussions over the past two decades is striking. Adding to this is the fact that policy decisions on housing are favourable towards ownership rather than renting. The diverse chapters in this volume examine a confluence of factors that affect the implementation of government subsidised housing from colonial times and apartheid to neoliberal reform of the public sector in post-apartheid South Africa. Contributions in the book interrogate the viability of subsidised housing in South Africa. The chapters examine various housing options in this context from both empirical and theoretical backgrounds. In addition, innovative models of housing provision are examined with the goal of establishing the extent to which they contribute to addressing the country's backlogs. To this end, this book covers the complexity of the steps different actors take to allocate government subsidised housing to low-income people. The other area of concern this book contributes to is the participation of beneficiaries in decisions regarding allocation of government subsidised housing.

The context of government subsidised housing in South Africa

The concept of government subsidised housing was made popular through housing policies in South Africa over the years. This was in response to South

Africa's political past, which was characterised by the spatial segregation as well as the uneven and unequal development of the apartheid era (Matlin and Mogaladi, 2013). Thus Nelson Mandela's administration promulgated a number of legislative and policy frameworks such as the Reconstruction and Development Programme of 1994, the White Paper on Housing of 1994, the Growth, Employment and Redistribution of 1996, the 1996 Constitution, the Housing Act of 1997, and the Prevention of Illegal Eviction Act of 1998. The subsequent Thabo Mbeki administration in 2004 promulgated the Breaking New Ground policy. Breaking New Ground, as a phrase, is used to refer to fully subsidised housing produced under the framework of the policy created as a replacement amendment policy of the Reconstruction and Development Programme (RDP). Under the RDP, government subsidised housing was built for people with a total income below the standard defined by the state, but its focus was on reconstructing the nation and addressing the imbalances caused by the apartheid regime.

The government subsidised housing programmes constitute an important segment of the government's redistributive policy stance and have seen some successes, for example as evident in the provision of approximately "2.5 million houses and another 1.2 million serviced sites" (Tomlinson, 2015: 16). Despite this progress, the provision of sustainable housing continues to be a moving target. A recent report notes an increase of housing backlogs "from 1.5 million to 2.1 million units, while the number of informal settlements has gone up from 300 to 2,225, an increase of 650%" (Tomlinson, 2015: 1). Over the years, the provision of government subsidised housing has been bedevilled by a plethora of challenges including political interference, the perpetuation of the geography of apartheid, exclusion, maladministration, poor services, lack of basic amenities, corruption and gender inequality in distribution. In recent years, the rising impacts of climate change on human settlements continue to worsen the already dire situation in the provision of sustainable housing. In the context of these challenges and the inability of the government to meet public demands in the delivery of sustainable housing options, there has been an upsurge of housing related protests (which are increasingly becoming violent) around South Africa. This is an indication that the housing question should be an important policy consideration for South Africa.

Unpacking the concept of government subsidised housing

In the housing literature, the concept of housing allocation to government subsidised housing remains crucial. According to Dugard and Tissington (2013), housing allocation is a process that entails distributing government subsidised housing opportunities to intended beneficiaries. These beneficiaries can be either eligible or non-eligible and this process includes their registration, selection and subsidy application. Haffner and Hoekstra (2006) define housing allocation as a process that entails registering people who need housing on a waiting list or database. They are then identified as housing candidates, applicants who are waiting to be assisted with their housing need. These housing candidates have to meet some eligibility criteria for them to be included in the database. The outcome of the housing allocation process is a house, through which a citizen may claim membership to an inclusive polity (Patel, 2015).

Housing allocation is the last process in any housing project that includes awarding someone ownership (tenure) of a newly built housing unit. For government subsidised housing, this is where the state (through devolving powers to municipalities) and its citizens interact closely (Patel, 2015). It must be noted that subsidised housing allocation also includes units built under the Upgrading of Informal Settlement Programme. These are re-planned settlements in which demolished shacks are replaced with government subsidised housing units with complete services (electricity and water) and some form of legal tenure (Patel, 2015). This book considers both definitions, as both identify housing allocation as a process undertaken to provide qualifying individuals with housing.

The other concept well considered in the housing literature is eligibility, which is linked to demand and supply of government subsidised housing. The word "eligible" refers to a state of having the right to do or obtain something through satisfying certain conditions. This "state" must fit into something, to be chosen, to be worthy or desirable. Eligibility also refers to meeting a stipulated requirement in order to qualify for something. According to the Department of Housing (1994), the term "eligibility" applies to all citizens of South Africa earning a monthly income (joint spouse) below R3,500, identified as suitable for state subsidy assistance in the foreseeable future. Tissington's (2011) definition is in line with this definition when she asserts that to be eligible means to be part of a group of people deemed suitable for housing assistance by the government. This book adopts the definitions provided above, according to which eligibility is as a standard or criteria used to measure or identify a group of people deemed suitable to obtain state assistance in terms of receiving government subsidised housing. Accordingly, to be eligible for government subsidised housing, your income must be below certain income limits set by the government. You must also meet other qualifications.

The significance of the collection

The post-apartheid ANC-led government committed to the delivery of government subsidised housing.. The ANC-led government sought to enlarge the housing programme(s), increase the number of subsidised families and discourage racialised housing provision. In a nutshell, there were serious efforts to fight against racial neoliberalism and to dismantle racial power structures at various levels. Indeed, one of the promises of the ANC-led government as evidenced in its policies was that of the provision of basic services (including housing, water, sanitation, education, health and electricity). Two decades after the politics of transition, South Africans in different geographical spaces and locations witnessed some of the most dramatic processes of collective resistance from South Africans against the failure of the supply of promised services (housing as the focus of this book) to keep pace with growing demands.

The mismatch between the demands and supply of housing in South Africa is contributing to a fidgety population that is becoming exasperated with the government and is beginning to express its dissatisfaction through protests (sometimes violent in nature). Consequently, the policies of the government of South Africa have been vehemently criticised by some social movement organisations and intellectuals who emerged to challenge the South African government's "neoliberal turn", which was viewed to have exacerbated both social and class divides and prioritised South Africa's standing in the global economy at the expense of the poorest citizens.

Contributions to this book show that government subsidised housing is complex and contested as it is shaped by state–society relations in post-apartheid South Africa. The book unpacks government housing policies in order to identify the failures and weaknesses of these policies and propose policy options to address the identified challenges. It is the view of this book that a poor understanding of government subsidised housing programmes and their consequences resulted in policies that are failing to attend to the triple challenges of poverty, unemployment and inequality. These practices redirect our thinking on the nature of the triple challenges in South Africa. Recognising these gaps in the production of knowledge and challenges in the implementation of in in South Africa, it was critical to put together a collection of chapters that unpacks the political economy of government subsidised housing in South Africa. This book aims to stimulate debates and knowledge sharing on government subsidised housing in South Africa with the aim of proffering solutions to address what has essentially become a "wicked problem" for the South African government.

The book confronts the following key questions: What are the historical legacies of past housing policies for housing delivery in democratic South Africa? What is the linkage between the sustainable development goals, the new urban agenda and housing delivery in the South African context? What is the nature of power exercised in housing delivery in post-apartheid South Africa? To what extent are gender issues mainstreamed into housing provision in South Africa? What are the implications of climate change for housing delivery for poor people in urban South Africa? Contributions to the book tackle the housing challenge from a theoretical and practical perspective. The book, therefore, in order to confront the challenges associated with housing development, locates the practice of government subsidised housing delivery within the contours of political rationalities and debates on integrative human settlements approaches that have developed over time to challenge historical societal fragmentation. What unites the collection of chapters or contributors is their willingness to challenge the intellectual hegemony and the application of "social constructionism that takes as its basic premise the social construction of reality through social interaction" (Clapham, 2009: 4).

The collection of chapters presents a variety of perspectives and positions in housing development in either rural or urban areas. Each chapter seeks to demonstrate concepts and themes drawn from what has now become a wide-ranging debate on subsidised housing delivery, often in combination with theories from various intellectual trajectories that offer new perspectives on the governing of poor people in public spaces by technocratic elites. Some of the chapters in this collection analyse contemporary rationalities and housing programmes allowing us to understand political rationalities of internationalism, imperialism and cosmopolitanism as well as an urban entrepreneurial approach, which is "useful to reflect on localised knowledge production processes and the actors and power embedded in them, which in turn result in urban development outcomes" (Martel and Sutherland, 2018: 397). They further argue that "within this broad urban entrepreneurial approach, it is useful to reflect on localised knowledge production processes and the actors and power embedded in them, which result in particular urban development outcomes in cities" (Martel and Sutherland, 2018: 97).

This book presents a collection of analyses of the delivery of government subsidised housing in South Africa and takes a multi-disciplinary approach, thus providing multiple perspectives on the South African housing conundrum. The book is relevant to students and academics from different disciplines including housing, urban and regional planning, political economy, environmental studies, development studies, human geography and community development. Students (both undergraduates and postgraduates), professionals/practitioners, researchers and the general public will find this book an invaluable information source on government subsidised housing delivery in South Africa.

Themes and structure of the book

Oliver Mtapuri and Sithembiso Myeni (Chapter 1) show how the contemporary debate about government subsidised housing, framed through the discourse of globalisation in the form of the sustainable development agenda and the New Urban Agenda, continues to be faced by complex difficulties in dismantling segregation and fragmentation of housing development. Although these international discourses are associated with new forms of connectivity, Mtapuri and Myeni show that urbanisation presents opportunities and challenges. Despite the concern with urbanisation as a powerful theme in contemporary global politics, Mtapuri and Myeni posit four types of spaces within the context of a theory of desperation: spaces of comfort (dignity) and discomfort (flooding and storms); spaces of oppression characterised by domination; spaces of restricted choices and constrained opportunities (noxious laws and regulations); and spaces of participatory exclusion undergirded by multi-layered governance systems which constrain initiative by creating fewer spaces in which poor people can cooperate and collaborate. They conclude that although the government has taken some strides in housing delivery to vulnerable groups, circumstances reproduce existing relations of exclusion, which in turn further marginalise the agency of poor people.

Andrew Okem, Sithembiso Myeni, Oliver Mtapuri and Sipho Nkambule (Chapter 2) present the historical context that informs subsequent chapters in this book. They draw from historical writings in mediating the divide between the contemporary discourse that demands the prioritisation of poor people in order to address the injustices of the past while focusing on the structures of oppression, particularly the land question, which continues to undermine housing delivery efforts. The authors examine the various housing policies of the past and explore how they contributed to racial and institutional segregation in contemporary South Africa. They introduce the land question and housing provision as the goal in an effort to address urban poverty. In striking a balance of the effect of the tradition of capitalism, Okem and others argue that the racial separation inherited from the past through land policies contributed to poverty, inequality and human settlement backlogs, particularly among the black population.

Sithembiso Myeni and Andrew Okem (Chapter 3) assess the performance of South Africa's National Development Plan (NDP) in the actualisation of government subsidised housing in South Africa. These contributors reviewed various pieces of legislation, programmes and projects that emerged out of the broad policy objective of the National Development Plan. Myeni and Okem highlight that while some progress has been made in actualising the ideals of the NDP, there is a real danger that the intended target will be missed. This is more so in the context of a shrinking fiscus, which is projected to continue on a declining path in the coming years. They appeal that to truly meet the NDP's objective of redressing the spatial geography of the apartheid era and providing sustainable housing for all, the government must become more proactive in engaging the private sector in addressing the country's housing conundrum.

Sipho Nkambule (Chapter 4) provides a contextually rich account of the relationship between apartheid housing and urban livelihoods in apartheid South Africa. Nkambule examines the historical development of housing and livelihoods during apartheid South Africa in the context of the broader political economy of the country, and with specific reference to black urban spaces. He speaks of the deeply racialised and repressive character of the white state's housing policies and programmes as well as the livelihood activities of black urban poor people living in townships. In his chapter, Nkambule takes some of the contemporary researchers to task for their bias in ignoring the effects of the past in studying the livelihoods of poor people in urban areas. Nkambule is insistent that it is of utmost importance to reflect on the past to understand how the injustices of the apartheid era continue to manifest in post-apartheid South Africa and in order for the democratic state to creatively engage in the restructuring of human settlement patterns in the post-apartheid era.

Judith Ojo-Aromokudu, Michael Samuel and Rubby Dhunpath (Chapter 5) present concerns on the effects of government subsidised housing, which is currently missing its target. They show how, over the years, government subsidy practice has created the unintended consequence of exaggerated demand for low-income housing. In their chapter, these contributors argue that the current subsidy criteria promote double-dipping into state resources and perpetuate dependency, instead of alleviating poverty. In their strong empirical account of government subsidised housing through a case study in northern KwaZulu-Natal, the contributors show the difficulties in achieving the housing target through the current housing subsidy selection criteria. While housing subsidy selection criteria remain a thorny issue in South Africa, the chapter engages the diverse practices of subsidy selection criteria. Ojo-Aromokudu and others conclude with the proposition that for the state's redress policy to serve its (original) intended outcomes, dependency on the state needs to be systematically reduced by shifting from a supply-driven subsidy to a demand-driven subsidy. They propose that this can be done by providing more leverage for poor people to address their housing needs.

Ndwakhulu Tshishonga (Chapter 6) assesses stakeholders' participation in the implementation of one of the mega-housing projects in eThekwini Municipality. Tshishonga focuses on one of the national pilot projects, the Cornubia Housing Project, implemented through the Breaking New Ground policy. The Cornubia development is perceived as an integrated human settlement and "a catalytic intervention undertaken jointly by eThekwini Municipality and Tongaat Hulett Developments" (Govender, 2016). The project presents opportunities and challenges regarding holistic planning and implementation. Tshishonga's chapter goes beyond presenting different role players in this mega-project, searching instead for a deeper framework with which to align sustainable human settlement. Tshishonga argues that stakeholders' participation is important not only in the rolling out of the Cornubia Housing Project, but is also fundamental in the maintenance and sustainability of such housing programmes. His work points to the many different and contested relationships between urban development and sustainability, and also to the ambiguous linkage between urban poverty and the broader goals of the Sustainable Development Goals.

Vincent Myeni and Phumelele Khumalo (Chapter 7) interrogate women's participation in state subsidised housing programmes. In their empirical account of women's participation in government subsidised housing through a case study of the Federation of Urban Poor in Durban, the contributors argue that women are often excluded from participating in the construction of their housing because of their limited involvement during the planning processes. These contributors present an important perspective on urban planning, namely the tricky issues of difference and identity. They show how hegemony is bringing difficulty in urban planning. Myeni and Khumalo maintain that social, economic and cultural challenges continue to perpetuate this phenomenon among African women. These contributors suggest that despite a renewed emphasis on "politics of presence" in post-apartheid South Africa, the formal planning system has given scant recognition to African women. In order to challenge this hegemony and insensitivity to diversity, the authors propose initiatives that encourage the participation of beneficiaries in the delivery of their own houses.

Sithembiso Myeni and Tafadzwa Chibvongodze (Chapter 8) tackle the question of citizenship, gender and the technologies of governance from Foucauldian and Lefebvrian perspectives with reference to a rural municipality – Jozini in KwaZulu-Natal. They show how the delivery of housing in South Africa has been utilised by the state in the (re)production of socio-democratic citizenship and how it has been instrumental in shaping the "politics of democratic participation". These contributors return to Foucault's discourse of power and Lefebvre's theory of production of space to demonstrate how the construction of gender, citizenship and the governance of the so-called "poor" in the new democratic dispensation has intersected with the actual production of government subsidised low-income houses. These contributors, through the lived experiences of poor people, take the government to task about government subsided housing and advance an argument that rather than increasing the agency of poor people in addressing their poverty conditions, state-directed development and service delivery programmes such as the rural housing subsidy have systematically transformed poor people into objects of knowledge, management and governance.

Lovemore Chipungu and Knowledge Zungu (Chapter 9) revisit land challenges in housing urban poor people in post-apartheid South Africa. These contributors focus on the neglected area of legislative and policy framework in relation to property rights, planning, urban space and housing. Chipungu and Zungu argue that, emerging out of a highly skewed apartheid system characterised by poverty and discrimination, most of South Africa's urban poor households are yet to witness improved service delivery; especially in the housing sector. In their chapter, these contributors engage neoliberal principles in a bid to explore the extent to which they explain the contemporary land–housing matrix and the resultant impact on housing urban poor people. Their findings show that there are prevailing land ownership patterns coupled with municipal land delivery systems; which are at variance with expectations of urban poor people, and are among the factors that are aggravating the housing problem. While not oblivious to the complexity of forces at play in expediting the release of land for housing urban poor people, the contributors recommend that meaningful change in urban land delivery systems require both political will and a positive attitude among all stakeholders.

Sithembiso Myeni and Oliver Mtapuri (Chapter 10) tackle the question of government subsidised housing drawing from Marxist, neo-Marxist and positivist views with reference to South Africa. In this chapter, they explore the power relations of subsidised housing inherent in its conceptualisation and practice. These contributors locate their contribution in contemporary trajectories and practices within unequal relations of power and the consequential differentiated experiences of beneficiaries pertaining to the theory of incompatibility. Myeni and Mtapuri's chapter contributes to the understanding of contemporary forms of housing production in emerging economies and indicates "how individuals pervade the circuits of market and survival, constructing their livelihoods on the basis of the economic and social resources from subsidised housing" (Lonardoni and Bolay, 2016). They conclude with a brief review of the direction of subsidised housing policies in post-apartheid South Africa and reflect on "where next?". They also note the importance of subsidised housing in the political and managerial sustainability of housing development, rural development and housing production as well as maintenance and management.

Claudine Hingston (Chapter 11) engages the theme of women's access to government subsidised housing in South Africa. She points to the optimism of April 1994, when progressive policy-makers promulgated the White Paper on Housing, which stipulates that all South Africans "should have access to a permanent residential structure with secure tenure" (Department of Housing, 1994). Hingston argues that despite numerous shifts in South Africa's housing policy, and taking cognisance of the South African Constitution, women in South Africa still experience many challenges in accessing housing. In this chapter, Hingston argues that these challenges stem from gender constructs that place women in marginalised positions. She draws on the intersectional feminist framework to highlight that a particular group of women experience the most challenges with regards to housing access. Hingston warns that factors such as violence, patriarchy, culture, religion and economic status impede women's access to housing in South Africa.

Andrew Emmanuel Okem, Mdoda Davidson Zondo, Siyabonga Ntombela, and Sarah Bracking (Chapter 12) focus on the neglected area of planning and housing provision in the context of climate change. The authors argue that the frequency of climate-change-related disasters and the vulnerability of resource-poor urban communities necessitate that the question of housing provision move beyond the provision of physical dwelling units to explore the extent to which these are resilient to a changing climate. The chapter concludes that the consideration of climate change in planning is important given South Africa's vulnerability to climate change and its poverty and inequality extremes.

References

Clapham, D. 2009. Introduction to the special issue – a theory of housing: problems and potential. *Housing, Theory and Society*, 26(1), pp. 1–9, doi:10.1080/14036090802704445.

Department of Housing, 1994. White Paper: a new housing policy and strategy for South Africa. www.dhs.gov.za/sites/default/files/legislation/Policies_Housing_White_Paper.pdf

Dugard, J. and Tissington, K. 2013. Civil Society and Protest in South Africa: a view from 2012. www.researchgate.net/profile/Kate_Tissington2/publication/303248941_Civil_Society_and_Protest_in_South_Africa_A_View_from_2012/links/5800986408aec7368bdc4dea/Civil-Society-and-Protest-in-South-Africa-A-View-from-2012.pdf?origin=publication_detail.

Govender, V. 2016. Analysis shows positive impact. News24, 7 April 2016. www.news24.com/SouthAfrica/Local/Coastal-Weekly/analysis-shows-positive-impact-20160406.

Haffner, M. and Hoekstra, J. 2006. Housing allocation and freedom of movement: a European Comparison. *Journal of Economic and Social Geography*, 97(4), pp. 443–451.

Lonardoni, F. and Bolay, J. 2016. Rental housing and the urban poor: understanding the growth and production of rental housing in Brazilian favelas. *International Journal of Urban Sustainable Development*, 8(1), pp. 49–67.

Martel, P. and Sutherland, C. 2018. Durban's Back of Port Project: a local spatial knowledge production process framed by urban entrepreneurialism. *Urban Forum*, 29(4), pp. 397–412.

Mitlin, D. and Mogaladi, J. 2013. Social movements and the struggle for shelter: a case study of eThekwini (Durban). *Progress in Planning*, 84, pp. 1–39. https://doi.org/10.1016/j.progress.2012.12.001.

Muthambi, X. 2015. *Inside the box: responsive design for diverse and changing households*. Master's thesis, Technology University of Tswane. https://repository.up.ac.za/handle/2263/46130.

Patel, L. 2015. *Social Welfare and Social Development in South Africa*, 2nd edition. Cape Town: Oxford University Press.

Tissington, K. 2011. *A Resource Guide to Housing in South Africa 1994–2010: legislation, policy, programmes and practice*. Socio-economic Rights Institute of South Africa. www.urbanlandmark.org.za/downloads/SERI_Housing_Resource_Guide_Feb11.pdf.

Tomlinson, M. 2015. *South Africa's Housing Conundrum*. Institute of Race Relations. https://irr.org.za/reports/atLiberty/files/liberty-2013-south-africas-housing-conundrum.

1 Sustainable Development Goals and the New Urban Agenda

A South African experience

Oliver Mtapuri and Sithembiso Lindelihle Myeni

Introduction

Urbanisation has been widely researched and written about with some associating it with industrialisation and socio-economic growth. Others regard it as the root cause of most of the challenges (including those considered to be wicked such as poverty and hunger) that haunt the world today. Urbanisation has also captured the interest of many stakeholders from various sectors such as governments, non-governmental organisations (NGOs), donors, local governments, academic/research institutions and independent researchers. Many policy documents have been tabled at local, national, regional and international levels as parties seek to better understand this phenomenon. It is not surprising that the call for sustainable development, which has links to urbanisation, has been dominating international conferences from various disciplinary angles. This chapter specifically focuses on the Sustainable Development Goals (SDGs) and the New Urban Agenda. It looks at how the two are interlinked and the challenges and opportunities that urbanisation presents in pursuit of realising sustainable urban development.

The New Urban Agenda and SDGs

The New Urban Agenda is an action-orientated plan that comprises a set of global principles, policies and standards necessary for the world to realise sustainable urban development. It is an agreement reached at the Habitat III conference of October 2016, in Quito, Ecuador. The agreement seeks to expand on a vision and commitments by national governments around sustainable urban housing and sustainable urban development (Habitat for Humanity, 2017). It prescribes a set of guidelines that are deemed important in transforming the ways in which cities are constructed, managed, operated and inhabited. The plan is meant to guide efforts, by a wide range of actors, such as national governments, city administrators, regional leaders, international development agencies, the private/business sector and civil society, to enhance urbanisation and make it a more positive phenomenon for the next 20 years (Charles, 2016).

According to the United Nations (2017), the New Urban Agenda embodies a common vision for an improved and sustainable future where all people have equal rights and access, and enjoy the benefits and opportunities that are often associated with urban environments. The New Urban Agenda, as a shared vision, also recognises the need for stakeholders to reconsider urban systems and the physical form of urban spaces as a prerequisite to achieving the desired levels of urban sustainability. It arose from the realisation that:

> there is a need to take advantage of the opportunities of urbanisation as an engine of sustained and inclusive economic growth, social and cultural development, and environmental protection, and of its potential contributions to the achievement of transformative and sustainable development.
>
> (United Nations, 2017)

The Agenda aims to transform existing challenges associated with urbanisation into opportunities by:

> leveraging the potential of urbanisation for structural transformation … through promoting proactive and responsive planning, innovation, industrialisation and sustained economic growth through high productivity, value added activities, resource efficiency and harnessing local economies and resources.
>
> (Ministry of Transport, Infrastructure, Housing and Urban Development, 2017: xii)

The premise is that by revisiting the "way cities and human settlements are planned, financed, developed and governed" (United Nations, 2017: 3), the New Urban Agenda can be a positive step towards ending poverty and hunger, lowering inequalities and promoting inclusive and sustainable socio-economic growth. It is also deemed instrumental in achieving gender equality, empowering women and improving human well-being and health while protecting the physical environment. Such interventions are believed to be instrumental in opening up more opportunities and employment for the increasing urban population and at the same time promoting intergenerational interactions and environmental integrity (Ministry of Transport, Infrastructure, Housing and Urban Development, 2017). Cities have become hubs of both the good and bad of urbanisation. In many countries of the world, cities have catalysed the form and content of progress occurring within nation states and have morphed to become engines of both growth and decay, hope and hopelessness, and homeliness and homelessness.

The New Urban Agenda also acknowledges culture and cultural diversity as important sources of enrichment for humankind, which play an important role in the sustainable development of urban centres, human settlements and citizens. It further recognises the need to consider culture in the promotion of sustainable production and consumption patterns as well as the controlled use of resources and addressing the negative effects of climate change (United Nations, 2017). It presents a paradigm shift in urban perspectives based on the science of cities, laying out the standards and principles for key areas like planning, construction, development, management and improvement of urban centres. The new paradigm is anchored on five main pillars of implementation, which are national urban policies, legislation and regulations, urban planning and design, the local economy, and municipal finance and local implementation. It is regarded as an asset for every level of government, the private sector, constituent groups and everyone who regards a town or city as his or her "home" (Charles, 2016; United Nations, 2017).

According to the United Nations (2017), the New Urban Agenda recognises that there is a new connection between good urban practices/urbanisation and development. It acknowledges that there is a positive relationship between urbanisation and employment creation, enhanced livelihood opportunities as well as improved life and living standards. This ushers in the nexus between the New Urban Agenda and the 2030 Agenda for Sustainable Development, with a special emphasis on SDG No. 11, which advocates for sustainable cities and communities (Cities Alliance, 2015). The SDGs are a set of development targets which are an extension of the Millennium Development Goals set by the United Nations in 2000 to deal with extreme poverty through the creation of a development framework for more inclusive and sustainable patterns of growth (UN-Habitat and UNECA, 2015). These goals are holistic in their attempt to address the socio-economic and environmental aspects of sustainable development and are also designed to be pursued as a combination and not one at a time (United Nations Development Programme (UNDP), 2016).

The New Urban Agenda embraces existing synergies created by a wide range of other global agreements such as the SDGs, the Paris Agreement, the Addis Ababa Action Agenda, Sendai Framework for Disaster Risk Reduction 2015–2030, the Vienna Program of Action for Landlocked Developing Countries, SAMOA and the Istanbul Program of Action for the Least Developed Countries to adopt a holistic transformation approach meant to address the multiple and complex challenges associated with contemporary urbanisation (Cities Alliance, 2015). This resonates with Aspiration 1 of the African Union's Agenda 2063, which states that the Union aspires to "a prosperous Africa based on inclusive growth and sustainable development" (African Union Commission, 2015: 2).

The following are the three guiding principles that provide a strategic direction to the New Urban Agenda for the successful transformation of towns and cities:

- Urban Policies: the New Urban Agenda is aimed at developing and implementing those urban policies that are deemed instrumental in promoting cooperation between local and national government and also encourage the building of multi-stakeholder partnerships that enhance their chances of achieving sustainable and integrated urban development;

- Urban Governance, Rules and Regulations to enhance municipal finance: the New Urban Agenda also operates on the premise that the quality of urban settlement is dependent upon the quality of the rules and regulations that are put in place for this purpose and their effective implementation. It thus advocates for the strengthening of urban governance and legislation meant to direct urban development projects/programmes and the necessary stimulus to municipal finance; and
- Urban Planning and Design: the New Urban Agenda also focuses on strengthening urban and regional planning to ensure the best utilisation of the spatial dimension of the urban form and for the benefit of towns and cities.

Fabre (2017) argues that although urban areas occupy just less than 3 per cent of the earth's crust, they are currently home to at least 50 per cent of the world's total population with latest estimates projecting that towns and cities will experience an inflow of 2.5 billion first-time urban entrants by 2050, more than the current combined population of India and China. So intense is the rate of urbanisation that by 2007 almost 50 per cent of the world's population was already living in towns and cities (Maxwell *et al*., 2008). This, in turn, points to the dire need to construct more settlement areas sufficient to meet the housing demands of the ever-increasing number of urban dwellers (Fabre, 2017). Planning and enactment of those plans for these sprouting settlements enable harnessing the energies, synergies, capabilities, talents, vitality and vibrancy that these people bring.

Commentators also forecast that, if left uncontrolled, urban population figures can expand to unsustainable levels and result in vast unsustainable urban sprawl, and the consequent creation of densely populated urban slums where living conditions and provision of basic sanitation and municipal services range from extremely poor to absent. Urban centres also generate an excess of more than 80 per cent of the world's gross domestic product, consuming up to 75 per cent of the world's natural resources and over 75 per cent of global energy supplies (UNDP, 2016; Fabre, 2017). They have resultantly earned themselves the qualification "engines of employment, social and economic growth and are thus thought to be accompanied by improved living standards" (Collier, 2014). We add that they have become the engines of inventions and innovation. Only their "pollutive propensities" are degenerative and devalue various environments and ecosystems – of the living and non-living, of the physical and chemical, and the human and non-human.

Scholars like Clos (2010: ii) argue that "urbanisation is jump-starting industrialisation". Urbanisation has thus been regarded as being synonymous with industrialisation and economic development (Scott and Storper, 2014). According to UN-Habitat (2015), the continuous shift of today's world from predominantly rural to urban (a phenomenon that Jones and Nelson (1999: 1) called a shift from a "global village to an urban globe") makes the process of urbanisation a very important global trend. This is a significant change that has been recorded over the past two decades and has provided a lot of insight to and significant recognition of the important role that urbanisation plays in development. Stimuli for urbanisation include better road infrastructure, housing, water and sanitation, educational facilities, availability of better municipal services, and jobs, as compared to the areas from where people come.

Of note, however, is the observation that a significant number of cities are located in less developed economies which lack the capacity and resources to grow within the confines and dictates of sustainable development. Most of them struggle to provide decent housing, clean water, sewer treatment, drainage; ideal infrastructure for industrial, transport, clean energy, and socio-economic growth; and adequate employment and livelihood opportunities for the people as they accumulate more than the population they can sustain. There has also been a massive transfer of poverty from rural areas to urban centres as people flee from conflict, poverty, disappearing agricultural land/land dispossessions, natural disasters and the effects of climate change in search of better living standards and employment opportunities in the city (UNDP, 2016). This has also taken a toll on the environment as the deprived populations resort to unconventional means to cope with the ever-increasing urban human needs resulting in what Morreira (2010) described as "living in disappearing modernities". The latter is exemplified by slums and shacks which are make-shift housing forms/settlements constructed using cheap rudimentary materials collected from rubbish dumps or bought but of low quality.

Some informal settlements have electricity while some do not. When they have electricity, it is usually illegally connected to the main grid. Housing structures in these settlements are unable to withstand storms and floods. They are prone to catching fire given the poor materials used, their proximity to each other and the reliance on unsafe energy sources for cooking, lighting and heating. The absence of planning in these settlements also makes fire control extremely difficult for the authorities. The three guiding principles of the New Urban Agenda, while well-meaning and idealistic, can only be effectuated if they accommodate and capture the histories and variegated contexts of cities and their countries. For South Africa, the legacy of apartheid is both persistent and chronic and could undermine the attainment of these three principles.

The New Urban Agenda and housing

Putting the above into consideration, the New Urban Agenda becomes a critically important measure that governments should implement in their effort to arrest negative developments associated with negative urbanisation. It also recognises that cities are the critical spaces for achieving the implementation of the SDGs, global climate agreement and New Urban Agenda.

The New Urban Agenda encourages national and city governments to create an enabling environment that allows for public–private cooperation and coming up with well-defined urban development/planning policies that are meant to promote multi-stakeholder collaboration, as well as urban management rules that provide a political pledge and protect long-term investments. The Agenda also calls on governments to have the political will to empower cities as a way of enabling them to build their capacity and resources, and raise revenue that will enhance sustainable urban development. Governments also pledged to ensure the security of land tenure for all, giving particular attention to disadvantaged groups such as women as a way of empowering them. Government is, thus, supposed to put in place "strong, inclusive management frameworks and accountable institutions that deal with land registration and governance" (Habitat for Humanity, 2017).

The New Urban Agenda commits governments to promoting participatory approaches which are age and gender-sensitive at all stages of the urban planning processes from conceptualisation to design, budgeting, implementation, evaluation and review in development projects (Housing for Humanity, 2017). The participation of city citizens in matters that affect them is critical for securing their buy-in and involvement in planning their cities in circumstances of community-led development. The needs of people in their life cycles are different. Children need to grow in proper housing. As they become youth and adult, their demand for accommodation grows in tandem with the growth of their families. At old age, places for retirement become necessary.

UN-Habitat (2015) argues that urban housing is a critical area that urbanisation has failed to address that the New Urban Agenda should consider. It notes that cities, especially in the developing world, are confronted by the incessant problem of poor provision of housing, noting that the challenge is not only limited to the enormous lack of adequate housing, but also to its quality as well as poor provision of housing-related/municipal services and housing affordability, which have exacerbated urban inequality (UNDP, 2015). UN-Habitat (2015) further argues that the manner in which housing has been and continues to be produced and consumed shapes urban growth, and has in many cases regretfully produced cities that are characterised by fragmentation and inequality, and are largely dysfunctional due to poor planning. This has, in turn, compromised the future of today's cities and left a lot to be desired with respect to sustainable urban development. UN-Habitat (2015) again notes that housing in most cities, especially in the developing world, has not been aptly incorporated into urban planning practice, the fact that residential areas occupy the majority of city land notwithstanding. This is evidenced by the various housing interventions that have been put in place, which only result in new challenges such as informal development, sprawl, spatial fragmentation and segregation, which in turn lead to further problems like social exclusion, inequalities and violation of human rights (Fabre, 2017). Housing inequalities manifest in plush and luxurious housing juxtaposed with informal settlements in the neighbourhood, which leads to societal dissonance as othering emerges in "us and them" dilemmas.

Habitat for Humanity (2017) notes that both formal and informal sector housing is seen as a factor that promotes urban stability and self-reliance and occupies the centre of key development problems that continue to haunt cities. The report further argues that the population of people residing in slums is on the increase and an estimated 1.6 billion people across the world do not have access to housing, which is a basic need. Although some positive progress has been realised, the ability of most of the world cities to adequately address the housing demand of the urban dwellers is lagging behind the rate of urbanisation. Consequently, this has made urban housing a central aspect of the New Urban Agenda for the twenty-first century. This is in line with SDG No. 11, which states that "cities and human settlements [should be made] inclusive, safe, resilient and sustainable and a target to ensure access to adequate, safe and affordable housing for all by 2030" (Habitat for Humanity, 2017: 2). This can be achieved by introducing innovative ways of decision-making and up-scaling like adopting decision support tools for human settlements. The housing question features prominently throughout the New Urban Agenda, in which governments agreed to "foster the progressive realization of the right to adequate housing" (Paragraph 31) and to come up with and put in place "sustainable urban development programs with housing and people's needs at the centre of the strategy" (Paragraph 112), as well as developing "appropriate and affordable housing finance products … to invest in affordable and incremental housing in all its forms" (Paragraph 140) (Habitat for Humanity, 2017). As a way of achieving the New Urban Agenda, the Habitat for Humanity (2017) and UNDP (2016) proposed the following recommendations.

Establish country-led commissions

According to Housing for Humanity (2017), national governments are encouraged to establish commissions and/or other bodies to spearhead plans, funding and initiatives that are related to the New Urban Agenda. Such commissions must then be tasked with addressing priority areas like surveying, strengthening urban laws/policies and coming up with financial plans. These bodies/commissions should be made up of diverse stakeholders who might include national and subnational policy-makers, donor funders, civil society, technical experts, local leaders and communities. We argue that communities are important because they have their own ways of doing things, of innovating in the face of adversity and finding ways to meet their basic needs such as housing, clothing and food and lead "normal" everyday lives.

Strengthen and enact urban laws and regulations

Governments are encouraged to strengthen laws and regulations that govern towns and cities, especially in areas of housing and land. They should also come up with urban policies that take into consideration demographic changes, availability, use of municipal land and provision of adequate and affordable housing while at the same time recognising and respecting the continuum that exists between urban areas and peri-urban and rural communities and understanding the economic relations, socio-cultural associations and environmental synergies that exist between them. It is important to note that both the SDGs (Target 11.a)

and the New Urban Agenda (Paragraph 49) (United Nations, 2017) acknowledge these connections and the complementary relationship that exists between sustainable cities and human settlements as well as rural development. Laws can be enablers as well as inhibitors of progress. This implies that laws and regulations need to be examined and evaluated in terms of how they further/inhibit human and sustainable development.

Develop financial plans

The implementation of the New Urban Agenda obliges governments to come up with a financial plan that serves as a framework for the complete understanding of governance structures and fiscal conditions. Financial plans should concentrate on the generation of revenue and building partnership opportunities to speed up the provision of housing, enhance affordability and promote access to land and related basic services. Government housing construction subsidies, housing microfinance programmes and rental subsidies also play a role in realising this. Traditional funding means such as mortgages are often unavailable or unaffordable to low-income populations who mostly lack collateral and rely on unconventional and unreliable sources of incomes. Under such circumstances, providing just land even with minimum services is not sufficient for poor people to build their own housing units and that way reclaim their humanity.

Collect and promote open, accessible and disaggregated data

The role of governments in promoting the New Urban Agenda also includes collecting disaggregating data at the neighbourhood/household level and making it readily accessible to all stakeholders. Without such data or access to it, governments, businesses and other concerned stakeholders are not able to weigh investments and budgets. Habitat for Humanity (2017) suggests that since the New Urban Agenda does not have specific indicators/measurements, SDGs can be considered as a good starting point. For example, housing which is regarded as a way of improving the quality of urban life can be one such indicator. Habitat for Humanity (2017) also notes that there are two important housing indicators in the SDGs which can be used as the starting point towards the realisation of this New Urban Agenda. Cities Alliance (2015) also suggests that the relationship between the two is intricate to the extent that the SDGs are an opportunity to strengthen the New Urban Agenda while the New Urban Agenda itself is also a positive step towards the attainment of the SDGs.

The first one speaks to the proportion of the total adult population that has secure land tenure rights and has legally recognised documentation. The second one relates to the proportion of urban populace that lives in slums and informal settlements or that lack access to adequate or proper housing. These indicators show that there are strong links between the New Urban Agenda and the SDGs and the two are complementary. The eradication of slums cannot happen on its own without concerted and deliberate effort by all stakeholders led by the state.

The state cannot shirk its duties to its citizens. The minimum that state could do is provide land for housing as well as promulgate laws and regulations that support various forms of affordable housing types in order to restore the dignity of its citizens and the enjoyment of the same rights as others in the same territorial jurisdiction without circumstantial prejudice. Prieur-Richard *et al.* (2018) are of the view that: first, cities will require financial and political empowerment; second, there is need for them to galvanise their efforts when addressing global agendas; and, third, their monitoring and evaluation initiatives should be able to help them to showcase the impacts of their actions.

Prospects

There are a number of opportunities that arise from urbanisation that cities/governments can take advantage of in their effort to realise the New Urban Agenda and related SDGs. This follows the realisation that, in as much as cities are regarded as being associated with challenges, there is a strong potential for transforming some of these challenges into opportunities (Ministry of Transport, Infrastructure, Housing and Urban Development, 2017). According to van Noorloos and Kloosterboer (2018: 1224), there is a myopic view that:

> while private-sector property investment and "new cities" are presented as a rational response to projections of high urban population growth and unsustainable patterns of urbanisation, clearly the pressing housing needs of Africa's urban poor are in no way met by these projects: almost all these investments seem directed at the "rapidly growing" middle and high classes of Africa's cities.

Freire *et al.* (2014: 24) argue that fast-growing cities can take advantage of this rapid growth as an opportunity to make effective decisions when it comes to both investment and the city form: "the most important policy tool would be forward-looking urban participatory planning, which could guide urban expansion and the associated infrastructure needs." In this regard, future planning would then be done with the population growth rate in mind. A lot of data/evidence from past researches have also shown how catastrophic urban expansion can be if it is done in an uncontrolled manner. This data can thus present an opportunity for current governments to learn from past mistakes and consider planning more seriously. As Freire *et al.* (2014) suggest, planning should ensure a reduction in urban sprawl, encourage densification and avoid development in environmentally unstable areas since the effects of these are already known. Data are important for forward planning and in order to avoid reacting to urban sprawl. This is particularly true given that, just like change, urbanisation is unavoidable – it will take place unabated as a form of a natural progression of the city as equally new forms of urbanism emerge. Relations between cultures and people are critical in shaping places as places shape cultures and people in all directions – vertically and horizontally.

Large and fast-growing cities in developing countries can also capitalise on increased economic activity. These cities have many universities producing engineers and planners who can play a role in sustainable urbanisation (Freire *et al.*, 2014). This chapter argues that large cities also bring many opportunities for growth and prosperity where basic infrastructure and policies are available. Those cities with adequate infrastructure have better chances of attracting investment. Where the economy runs normally, it is easier to frequently maintain existing infrastructure, preventing it from decaying, as well as constructing a new one. Investment will also ensure some constant revenue to the government, which can then be channelled towards public infrastructure and social amenities. It also leads to employment creation, which in turn is a positive step towards poverty reduction. Employed people can budget for their own houses or at least afford to rent in proper housing thus reducing the likelihood of opting to settle in informal settlements. The benefits to people are manifold including socio-economic and psychological benefits. People are happier in situations where they can get jobs, build houses, have good educational and health institutions for themselves and family and realise their individual and collective potential, which a community of people presents.

This chapter argues that countries in Africa should take advantage of their many resources and provide incentives to investors who provide for the welfare needs of their workers, especially housing provision or housing finance, as their work invariably will promote the New Urban Agenda and the SDGs. This will assist in resolving the housing shortage and can reduce the emergence of substandard and unplanned housing (Mthethwa, 2014). The provision of formal jobs can also save cities from the destructive informal economic activities which poor people usually resort to if they fail to gain employment. Such activities pose a threat to environmental sustainability in the city. Reasoning in the same way, the International Monetary Fund (2012) argues that the growth of Pan-African Banks can also be an opportunity that can be exploited towards the realisation of the New Urban Agenda and SDG No. 11. Such banks could increase economic integration in Africa more generally and increase competition to reduce the monopoly of multinational financial institutions. They also tend to have less stringent borrowing requirements, thus promoting financial inclusion, and hence low-income people can access housing loans. While finance is an important component of housing, this chapter argues that land is important as a place to stay, as a place to generate income and as a place to relax and regenerate and reproduce the human and humanity.

Charles (2016) argues that the private sector can be utilised in realising sustainable urban development. She argues that there is need to take advantage of the enterprising private sector and forge public–private cooperation which can then complement efforts by different urban stakeholders meant to realise immediate and long-term urban development plans and come up with sustainable human-centric solutions to the challenges that come with urbanisation. The presence of civil society and NGOs also gives an opportunity for governments to work with them to provide support in the form of funds, advice and expertise in areas around urbanisation. The problem of housing is not only a state problem – it is a societal problem.

Constraints

What has the potential to overcrowd the prospects are constraints. Therefore, despite the above opportunities/prospects, the New Urban Agenda faces a number of constraints. First, according to Partnership for Action on Green Economy (2016), the establishment of institutions, laws, policies and strategies that promote the Agenda provides a critical foundation for its implementation. It is important to realise that most of these institutions are still too weak to fully perform their intended functions effectively and thus still require a lot of support if they are to play a leading role in influencing development policy. It is argued that in many of the pilot nations of the Agenda, which include Ethiopia, Kenya and Kyrgyzstan among others, the development of these institutions has been a very slow process that is meant to pass through several stages before they can become fully functional. For example, lack of political will to implement agreed strategies and plans is a huge challenge.

Although there have been efforts to transform public administration systems, old-fashioned bureaucratic commands are still firmly in place. In the end, there is a huge disconnection between development plans/objectives and the administrative tools used by those in authority and this impacts negatively on overall development. Tissington (2011) blames poor inter- and intra-governmental relations, especially in areas such as provision of bulk services connections to housing settlements, which in turn result in delays and poor coordination and implementation of the programme. He also identified a shortage of technical skills to monitor progress and corruption as some of the limitations that hinder housing development, especially in developing countries. UNDP (2016) also concedes that, currently, most countries are facing funding challenges, to varying degrees, and this has contributed to a shortfall in the implementation of the New Urban Agenda as well as the SDGs. Thus, it is important in the case of South Africa for the three spheres of government – national, provincial and local – to work in unison in coordinating policy and marshalling resources and skills in order to attain the New Urban Agenda and the SDGs.

Poverty, unemployment, low incomes and lack of access to housing finance also increase the likelihood of shanty settlements as most urban dwellers cannot afford to build their own homes, especially if we are to consider that, despite governments' pledges to ensure secure tenure of land for all, it still remains difficult for poor people to legally acquire land in urban centres where the value is often inflated. Moreover, poor people's access to urban land and proper housing is also a result of the resistance that municipalities face from private landowners when they try to allocate well-located land to low-income earning groups and this resistance is largely from high-income groups (Lall *et al.*, 2007). This is worsened by the ever-escalating cost of housing (Gunter, 2014; Lall *et al.*, 2007). Governments also struggle to fund housing for poor people and tend to rely on private sector funding, yet at the same time they fail to come up with financing alternatives that result in a win-win situation for both the client and the financier (Tissington, 2011).

Political interference has also stalled the implementation of the New Urban Agenda. Chatiza (2013) noted that the populating of informal settlements where there is a total absence of municipal services in developing countries is often the brainchild of political parties, especially those in power. This is normally done to consolidate their support and gain more political power in urban centres where ruling parties tend to be very unpopular among the electorate. Chatiza (2013) argues that after orchestrating the birth of some of these settlements, politicians and political parties rarely go beyond mere settling of people; they make no or very little efforts to provide standard housing and basic services to these settlements. To these politicians, it is good for these settlements to remain neglected so that they can always canvas for their votes by continuously promising to attend to their challenges "once things are in order".

Manase and Fawcett (2010) argue that politicians are sometimes seen to be advocating for free service delivery for their constituencies just to gain political mileage, something that is beyond the capacity of many urban authorities. This also tends to discourage those residents who have the capacity to pay for services from boycotting paying and, in turn, paralysing service delivery. Such interference has seen the emergence of informal settlements which do not have health care centres as well as access to clean water, toilets, refuse collection, proper houses and roads and are often constructed in wetlands and flood-prone areas (Manase, 2009; Nhapi, 2009; Mukonoweshuro, 2014). Tissington (2011) also confirms this, arguing that the provision of urban housing and informal upgrading is normally impeded by the politicisation of the programmes. These, in turn, are against sustainable urban development and thus stand as constraining factors to the implementation and ultimate realisation of the New Urban Agenda and the SDGs at large. Wilkinson (2014) also notes that another major constraint that cities encounter as they try to realise sustainable urban housing is the lack of a strategy to unlock well-located land for development of human settlements. This, therefore, has seen little or no connection of bulk infrastructure to newly established settlements.

Discussion

The realisation of the New Urban Agenda and SDG No. 11 requires new ways of doing while leveraging on experience but avoiding mistakes of the past. The role of the state is key in driving many of these processes that deliver the Agenda as well as the SDGs. In articulating and unpacking the imperative to deliver on these basic rights, we find that poor people are at a disadvantage – what others have called a cumulative disadvantage. To this we postulate a theory.

We present a theory of desperation which postulates that poor people are forced, out of necessity, to construct their own dwellings using available materials, using their own life skills, with such dwellings being in any area irrespective of whether the area is ecologically and environmentally viable (vulnerable) and irrespective of the consequences on the ecology and environment. Desperation is distinct from resilience in that it goes beyond it. It is closely linked to destitution arising from placelessness, landlessness and homelessness. Reclaiming place (land) becomes an imperative, which manifests when people occupy spaces which are uninhabited and in other instances integrate themselves into spaces reserved for the lifestyle of the elites.

We posit that in their quotidian lives, people find themselves in four types of spaces. The first are spaces of both comfort and discomfort: comfort from the only place that gives them some semblance of "(in)dignity" – their dwellings; and discomfort such as floods and storms, where the ravages and vicissitudes of the weather wreak havoc on their dwellings and livelihoods. In this space, for them to be recognised, they need to exercise their agency, which is visible in mobilisation and protest. Second, there are spaces of oppression, which are characterised by domination and oppression. Domination is exercised by municipal authorities, property owners and shack lords as well as whoever has authority/power over the land on which poor people build their dwellings. Oppression relates to the trampling of their human rights and freedoms – as their rights to housing and privacy are threatened and contravened. They do not fully enjoy the same freedoms as their compatriots in the same country.

Third, there are spaces of restricted choices and constrained opportunities where poor people's choices are restricted by regulation and laws, property owners and authority – this includes choices related to the type of building material to use, the size of dwellings and where to build. Their opportunities are constrained and manifest as both positive and negative. Negative opportunities include opportunities of circumstance – the dwelling must be make-shift; it cannot be permanent because of placelessness characterised by lack of title deeds and temporality of tenure. The negative opportunities also include the inability to fully access municipal services (water, sanitation, refuse collection, transport, and so on) and the inability to network with those not of their "lot" (the affluent/rich). The positive opportunities are their solidarity, as shown in their own grassroots organisations (such as the Abahlali baseMjondolo in South Africa), their risk-taking appetite, and their spirit of self-reliance, adaptability, resourcefulness, imagination and inventiveness (innovation). The solutions applied by those in authority (municipalities, NGOs and others) seem not to be effective in addressing housing and human settlement matters, leading to the abrogation of poor people's human and socio-economic rights, as they are left literally waiting in a backyard shack.

Finally, there are spaces of participatory exclusion directed to those waiting to become beneficiaries of a house funded and built by the state in South Africa. The use of technologial channels by the government in opening spaces for poor people to apply for subsidised housing or to actively register on housing databases has been rendered meaningless, as they leave potential beneficiaries with little power to influence the processes that affect them. This is because these spaces are monopolised by political representatives in order to protect and advance their vested interests. The struggle for poor people to become beneficiaries is waged in multiple institutional sites during the process, to the extent that all spheres of government – national, provincial and local – have to play a role in framing who qualifies as a beneficiary in a house funded by the state. As a result, those in spaces of discomfort find themselves on waiting lists for an extended period. Moreover, there is a contradiction in hegemonic design where there is a multi-layered governance system in identifying beneficiaries for housing. There is a huge hazard in the system in that accountability cannot be sited institutionally, whereas participatory exclusion becomes more visible when there is a commitment renewed every electoral cycle. Accordingly, poor people constitute the majority of housing beneficiaries but they are excluded through the design of project steering committees, which in turn have a duty to transfer their deliberations through representative structures to relevant authorities. There are fewer spaces in which poor people can collaborate, owing to the fact that institutional rules are made in such a way that poor people would have to pay allegiance to their political representatives. Overall, the newly created structures connected with existing institutions have become significant in reproducing existing relations of exclusion for further marginalisation of the agency of poor people.

Conclusions

This chapter explored the relationship between the New Urban Agenda and the Sustainable Development Goals (No. 11 in particular) and how these can work together towards achieving sustainable urbanisation and urban development. It also examined the potential opportunities that the New Urban Agenda and the SDGs present for cities as they develop as well as the challenges or constraints that they encounter as they seek to meet the targets of the Agenda. It was also presented that the unavailability of disaggregated data is one of the major challenges. The chapter presented a theory of desperation, which is divided into four types of space: space of comfort and discomfort, spaces of oppression, spaces of restricted choices and constrained opportunities as well as spaces of participatory exclusion. Citizens – slum dwellers – should vote for people who deliver on their promises; that is, quality grassroots politicians arising from their own ranks and file who understand grassroots problems of placelessness, waterlessness and shelterlessness and other "lessnesses" linked to informal settlements and slums.

References

African Union Commission, 2015. *Agenda 2063*. www.un.org/en/africa/osaa/pdf/au/agenda2063.pdf [accessed 8 February 2019].

Charles, A. 2016. *Cities*. Geneva: World Economic Forum.

Chatiza, K. 2013. *Capacity Building for Local Government and Service Delivery in Zimbabwe*. Harare: Development Governance Institute.

Cities Alliance, 2015. *Sustainable Development Goals and Habitat III: opportunities for a successful New Urban Agenda*. Cities Alliance Discussion Paper No. 3.

Clos, J. 2010. Foreword to *The State of African Cities 2010: governance, inequality and urban land markets*. Nairobi: UN-Habitat.

Collier, P. 2014. Presentation for Round Table convened by Centre for Development and Enterprise on Cities of Hope, CDE Round Table 24 March 2014.

Fabre, E.A. 2017. *Local Implementation of The SDGs and The New Urban Agenda Towards A Swedish National Urban Policy*. Stockholm: Global Utmaning.

Freire, M.E., Lall, S. and Leipziger, D. 2014. *Africa's Urbanisation: challenges and opportunities*. Washington: The Growth Dialogue. www.dannyleipziger.com/documents/GD_WP7.pdf [accessed 25 January 2016].

Gunter, A. 2014. Renting shacks: landlords and tenants in the informal housing sector in Johannesburg South Africa. *Urbani izziv*, 25, pp. 96–107.

Habitat for Humanity, 2017. *Opportunities for Action Policy Priorities for Implementing the New Urban Agenda June 2017*, working draft. Washington, DC: Habitat for Humanity.

International Monetary Fund, 2012. The impact of global financial stress on Sub-Saharan African banking systems, in *Regional Economic Outlook: Sub-Saharan Africa*, April. Washington: IMF.

Jones, S. and Nelson, N. 1999. *Urban Poverty in Africa*. Southampton: Intermediate Technology Publications.

Lall, S.V., van den Brink, R., Leresche, K.M. and Dasgupta, B. 2007. *Subsidized Housing and Access to Land in South African Cities*. Pretoria: World Bank Publications.

Manase, G. 2009. *Cost Recovery for Sanitation Services: the case of poor urban areas in Zimbabwe*. Riga: VDM Verlag.

Manase, G. and Fawcett, B. 2010. *Cost Recovery for Sanitation Services: the case of poor urban areas*. Southampton: Council for Scientific and Industrial Research.

Maxwell, D., Webb, P., Coates, J. and Wirth, J. 2008. *Rethinking Food Security in Humanitarian Response*. Paper Presented to the Food Security Forum, 16–18 April, Rome.

Ministry of Transport, Infrastructure, Housing and Urban Development, 2017. *Kenya's Popular Version of the New Urban Agenda: towards inclusive, safe, resilient and sustainable cities and human settlements.* Nairobi: State Department for Housing and Urban Development.

Morreira, S. 2010. Living with uncertainty: disappearing modernities and polluted urbanity in post-2000 Harare, Zimbabwe. *Social Dynamics*, 36(2), pp. 352–365.

Mthethwa, Z. 2014. *Investigating the Viability of Rural Housing Finance as A Vehicle for the Creation of Sustainable Human Settlement in Moletlane Village – Lepelle Nkumpi Municipality*. Masters of Public Administration thesis, University of Stellenbosch. https://scholar.sun.ac.za/handle/10019.1/86571.

Mukonoweshuro, T.F. 2014. *Barriers to the Provision of Basic Sanitation in Two Selected Informal Settlements in Harare, Zimbabwe*. Master's thesis, Johannesburg, University of Wits.

Nhapi, I. 2009. *The Water Situation in Harare, Zimbabwe: a policy and management problem*. Butare: National University of Rwanda.

Partnership for Action on Green Economy, 2016. *Integrated Planning and Sustainable Development: challenges and opportunities*. www.un-page.org/files/public/undp_synthesis_report.pdf.

Prieur-Richard, A.-H. *et al.* (2018). Global Research and Action Agenda on Cities and Climate Change Science (2018). https://citiesipcc.org/wp-content/uploads/2018/09/Research-Agenda-Aug-10_Final_Long-version.pdf [accessed 8 February 2019].

Scott, A. and Storper, M. 2014. The nature of cities: the scope and limits of urban theory. *International Journal of Urban and Regional Research*, 39, pp. 1–15.

Tissington, K. 2011. *A Resource Guide to Housing in South Africa 1994–2010: legislation, policy, programmes and practice*. Johannesburg: SERI.

UN-Habitat, 2015. *Housing at the Centre of the New Urban Agenda*. United Nations Human Settlements Programme.

UN-Habitat and UNECA, 2015. *Towards an Africa Urban Agenda*. Nairobi: United Nations.

United Nations, 2017. Habitat III. http://habitat3.org/wp-content/uploads/NUA-English.pdf.

United Nations Development Programme, 2016. Policy in focus. *The International Policy Centre for Inclusive Growth*, 13(3). UNDP.

van Noorloos, F. and Kloosterboer, M. 2018. Africa's new cities: the contested future of urbanisation. *Urban Studies*, 55(6), pp. 1223–1241.

Wilkinson, K. 2014. *Factsheet: the housing situation in South Africa*. https://africacheck.org/factsheets/factsheet-the-housing-situation-in-south-africa/ [accessed 16 June 2018].

2 A historicity of housing policies in apartheid South Africa[1]

Andrew Emmanuel Okem, Sithembiso Lindelihle Myeni, Oliver Mtapuri and Sipho Nkambule

Introduction

Apartheid South Africa was characterised by the segregation of the country's population into different racial groups. The aggressive implementation of various segregationist laws by the apartheid regime led by the National Party facilitated the emergence of a human settlement pattern characterised by the settlement of different race groups in different locations. In this chapter, we examine the various housing policies of the past and explore how they have contributed to racial and institutional segregation in contemporary South Africa. The chapter provides the historical context that informs subsequent chapters in this book. The chapter is divided into two main sections. In section one, we examine housing and land policies from 1910 to 1947. Section two examines housing and land policies from 1948 to 1993 marking the end of the apartheid era and a transition to a multi-party democratic system.

Housing and land dispossession policies: 1910–1947

Land dispossession in South Africa goes back to the arrival of Europeans and the ensuing conquests (Walker, 2017). As the European settlers moved gradually inland to form new settlements, they took possession of the new expanse of land on which they settled. The Natives Land Act (Act 27 of 1913) was a major setback in local people's quest for land ownership. The act marked the first formal process of systematic dispossession of black people of their land. Because of this Act, black people in certain parts of South Africa lost their land and other land-based livelihoods thus rendering most of them poor (Beavon, 2005). This law also paved the way for race-based spatial segregation and at the same time introduced a set of stringent property ownership requirements that made it impossible for blacks to own or acquire land (Thomas, 2010). After losing their land, homes and assets through dispossession and being deprived of their livelihoods, the main livelihood opportunity for black South Africans was to offer their labour in white-owned mines and farms, often tantamount to slave labour. The labour of black people was often poorly remunerated. In addition, black labourers lived in appalling working conditions and housed in overcrowded filthy mining compounds. As farm labourers or mine labourers, black workers did not have any rights to express grievances and were not entitled to strike or protest against poor housing, working and wage conditions (Mabin, 2005). Land dispossession during the colonial and apartheid periods is at the root of the poverty, inequality, vulnerability and precarity of black South Africans to this day, which manifests in many dimensions including housing.

According to Kloppers and Pienaar (2014: 680), "the Act introduced ethnic differentiation based on the mistaken belief that differentiation between dissimilar races was fundamentally desirable." The Act legalised and formalised the systematic dispossession of black people of their land, an act that further pushed them into impoverishment and marginalisation.

The first housing legislation in the Union of South Africa was the Housing Act of 1920. While the legislative framework lacked a clear statement of the intended beneficiaries, these turned out to be poor whites and side-lined all other races living in urban squatter camps and housing complexes known as "locations". These "locations" were known for being unhygienic, overcrowded and disease infested (Ramashamole, 2011). In 1923, the government passed the Native Urban Areas Act, which was meant to remove "excess" blacks from urban areas (Wolpe, 1972: 445–447). The temporality of sojourns by blacks in cities was meant to remove the sense of territoriality and belonging among blacks, as travellers ordinarily do not belong to places they traverse. These removals would serve to embed a sense of isolation and deprivation among blacks and a latent source of requite in pursuit of equity and social justice.

In 1936, the Native Trust and Land Act authorised the government to establish the South African Native Trust tasked with the administration of land and human settlements in native areas. It prohibited Africans from purchasing, owning, leasing or using land, except in the so-called "reserves" meant for Africans (Mabin, 2005). All land previously owned by black people was transferred to the custody of the South African Development Trust. The Trust was tasked with the purchase and administration of land earmarked for black settlement (Mabin, 2005; Kloppers and Pienaar, 2014). However, the Trust could only acquire land in areas that were reserved for the blacks. Effectively, the Native Trust and Land Act of 1936 resulted in the reservation of only 13 per cent of the country's land for 80 per cent of the population (Kloppers and Pienaar, 2014: 683). The densification to heightened levels of black South Africans had implications with wide and variegated impacts on their livelihoods, health, production and reproduction. Sources of livelihoods were disrupted, living conditions became congested and unhygienic, spaces to work or do business became constrained and limited through laws and regulation, and families were fragmented and dismembered thereby affecting family reproduction.

Housing and land dispossession policies: 1948–1993

In apartheid South Africa, housing policies, particularly those related to land, were a continuation of the policy trajectory from the onset of colonialism. In fact, the apartheid land and housing policies of the National Party's government from 1948 onwards was premised on the systematic exclusion of the black population from urban centres. Similarly, Kloppers and Pienaar (2014: 679) argue that "the then National Party government's strategy of territorial segregation, population resettlement and political exclusion was founded on a history of conquest and dispossession enforced through oppressive land laws". Walker (2017: 1) summarised the stance of the apartheid government noting that:

> Beginning in the 1950s, the apartheid government attempted to maintain white hegemony, drive an urban–industrial economy, and deflect political resistance by turning these reserves into the ethnic "homelands" of African people. This involved increasingly repressive policies of urban influx control, population relocation, and the tribalization of local administration in the reserves.

More interesting was the apartheid government's need to control the urban population by eliminating surplus "natives" to the reserves or Bantustans (Department of Native Affairs, 1951: II, cited in Wilkinson, 1998: 219*)*. This targeted several "black spots" on the perimeters of some of the larger centres, which had their origins in irregular sales of land to blacks. This, in essence, relegated the issue of land, tenure and housing for blacks to the homelands. The setting up of homelands led to another widespread wave of forced relocation of the black population forcing them to abandon their homes in the process. The homelands were nominal regimes and had neither the capacity nor the resources to respond adequately to the overwhelming demand for housing (Lemon, 1991: 24–25, cited in Lombard, 1996). Smith (1992) and Lombard (1996) added that in fast-growing townships like Soweto, homeownership rights were restricted to a 30-year leasehold tenure – thus effectively abolishing the existing system of 99-year leaseholds. At the time, restricted tenancy had the effect of constraining improvements which one could make on the property as well as alienating citizens in their own country.

To ensure that its policies were enforced, the colonial government resorted to preventing African people from accessing housing in towns and cities while simultaneously ensuring "tight control over increases in housing stock" for Africans residing in cities (Thomas, 2010: 192). According to Thomas (2010), the apartheid government housed African labourers in compound settlements and its segregation policies were meant to curb black people's access to urban housing. Wolpe (1972, in Thomas, 2010) noted that this type of housing denied the Africans permanent urban residence and facilitated the strengthening of a cheap labour system. The assumption was that access to land in the homelands and not in the city would render them temporary residents in the city, as they remained connected to the homelands, which would also supplement their meagre earnings in the white-controlled city. blacks were, therefore, viewed as temporary travellers in urban areas. The apartheid government used the reinforcing of the stay by black South Africans in cities as impermanent as a tool to buttress, from a human rights perspective, their disenfranchisement.

The Group Areas Act (Act 41 of 1950) further reinforced race-based residential segregation. As Kloppers and Pienaar (2014: 684) argue, the primary goal of the Act was to:

> provide for the establishment of group areas and for the control of the acquisition of immovable property and the occupation of land and premises. The Act established three groups of people – a white group, a native group and a coloured group.

Through this Act, hordes of blacks were dispossessed of land and homes near or around urban centres, which they had owned for generations (Soni, 2001). Examples of such places include Sophiatown in Johannesburg and District Six in Cape Town, which was set aside as part of "white" South Africa. Maylam (1995) argued that at least three million black South Africans were forcibly removed from their land under a number of apartheid mechanisms, which included the Group Areas Act, the "Black Spot Removals" and the eviction of labour tenants by their employers – farmers. Land dispossession was carried out with brute force such that the de-housing of black people included dispossession of land upon which those houses were built and land upon which they farmed for subsistence and surplus. Table 2.1 presents a summary of forced population removal from 1960 to 1983 indicating that more than 3.5 million people were forcefully relocated within a space of just over two decades.

In the early years of apartheid, specifically in 1950 and 1951, a survey by the National Building Research Institute examined the capacity of urban African households to pay for housing. The results from the survey revealed that 40 per cent of African families could afford to pay unsubsidised rentals or build houses for themselves, 13 per cent could pay for subsidised rent only, and 47 per cent

Table 2.1 Forced population removals under apartheid, 1960–1983

Category of relocation	*Number*
RURAL	
Eviction of farm workers and labour tenants from white commercial farms.	1,129,000
Removal of landowners and tenants from expropriated African- or mission-owned farms ("black spots") and the relocation of "badly situated" "native reserves" to consolidate the Bantustans.	614,400
Relocation for strategic and infrastructural projects, e.g. for military purposes or forestry and conservation projects.	103,500
URBAN	
Removals in terms of the *Group Areas Act.*	860,400
Relocation of African townships from "white" areas into the Bantustans.	730,000
Eradication of informal settlements in urban centers (incomplete data).	112,000
TOTAL	**3,548,900**

Source: Walker (2017: 12).

were not in a position to make any significant contribution to housing costs. Clearly, even by government estimates, the majority of urban households were in desperate need of subsidised public housing. It was projected at the time that – over the next ten years – approximately 350,000 houses were required for Africans, at a value of 100 million pounds. Against this backdrop, the Native Services Levy was introduced in 1952. This levy meant that, in cities where there were over 20,000 African workers, employers had to contribute to the cost of roads, sewerage, lights and water in African townships (South African Institute of Race Relations, 1999; Khanya College, 2001).

The Native Building Workers Act was also enacted in 1951. According to this Act, Africans were to be trained en masse (including on-the-job training) to build township housing under white building inspectors. By the end of 1953, 456 plasterers, 359 painters, 1,065 bricklayers and 432 carpenters had applied for these jobs (Morris, 1981; Robbins, 1997; South African Institute of Race Relations, 1999; Khanya College, 2001).

The Prevention of Illegal Squatting Act was passed in 1951. According to Muller (2013: 382):

> parliament enacted the Prevention of Illegal Squatting Act 52 of 1951 with the aim of making good on the Party's promise to "take vigorous and effective steps to care for the safety of … as well as property and the peaceful lives" of white people.

The Act criminalised illegal "occupation of both public and private land as well as buildings including land in native locations" (Thomas, 2010: 199). It also authorised the eviction of people who occupied such places and the demolition of such structures. It was obvious that the policy was directed at Africans since they constituted the majority of people who resided in such areas. The Act was also aimed at ensuring that blacks were prevented from becoming permanent urban residents. However, the attempt to push all Africans to homelands remained a partial success as many people chose to settle in townships and informal settlements located on the periphery of cities and towns. These settlements accorded access to places of work but were devoid of basic municipal services – proper housing, clean water, sanitation, refuse collection and electricity – and thus manifested appalling living conditions (Muller, 2013). The effects of the laws used by the apartheid regime had multiple impacts on black South Africans, namely citizenship effects (the regime alienated blacks by devaluing their citizenship); residency effects (residency for blacks was precarious and peripheral); identity effects (blacks could not establish an identity with the land of their birth, which was liable for distortion by apartheid laws); ownership effects (ownership of housing was at the whim of the apartheid regime); and socio-economic effects (access to health, education and economic opportunities for blacks were at the mercy of the apartheid regime).

Although ownership of a township housing unit was possible, the land itself (on which the unit stood) was not purchasable because – particularly under the apartheid regime – land ownership for Africans was confined to the reserves-cum-Bantustans. Under apartheid, purchase of a publicly built housing unit could be pursued (for example, on a sort of hire-purchase basis) but, alternatively, the unit could simply be rented. In seeking to resolve the housing challenges, some local municipalities received loans from the national government and bought building materials in large bulk. Qualifying Africans could purchase building materials to the value of up to 150 pounds to build their own houses and repay the loan in instalments. By the end of January 1956, the Native Services Levy had been implemented in 37 towns and, by this time, the money collected under the programme was over seven million pounds. Local municipalities also continued to raise funds from the sale of liquor in the townships to finance infrastructure (Parnell, 1988; South African Institute of Race Relations, 1999).

In 1957, the Housing Act was passed to repeal the housing and financing legislations that were passed earlier between 1920 and 1948. In effect, it broadly entailed a continuation of the previous housing legislation. In line with apartheid ideology, a Housing Commission (previously known as the Housing Board) was set up in 1957 in which provision was made for a Bantu Housing Board to administer housing specifically for Africans. Perhaps unsurprisingly, the Bantu Housing Board had no African representatives. The Commission was given the power to expropriate land, buy building materials and hire contractors for the purposes of building houses on expropriated land. According to Thomas (2010: 199), the "law tightened controls on accessing housing loans from the National Housing Fund and private sector building societies". It was the same strict National Housing Fund that was given the authority to administer loans for black people for urban housing making it difficult for them to own their own houses.

At times, the nearest local municipality was required to offer basic social services for the housing scheme built. Any incurred financial burdens were shared with the state (Morris, 1981; Lester *et al.*, 2009). Furthermore, if a local municipality was reluctant or incapable of carrying out housing schemes, the Commission itself could undertake the scheme and recover the costs from the local municipality. Perhaps unsurprisingly, the Bantu Housing Board had no African representatives. Additionally, the Commission identified a number of housing options with regard to financing. Under certain conditions, loans could be provided by the Commission to local municipalities for up to 50 years for low-income housing (Calderwood, 1953; Khanya College, 2001), but individuals could also receive loans directly. The offering of loans to build houses was fostered through a means-test.

According to the Housing Act, the local and central government remained responsible for housing for lower-income groups. While local municipalities constructed housing in black townships, the central government provided loans to fund the projects. In general, the state encouraged homeownership, and the goal was to ensure certain minimum standards at minimum costs.

In as much as the apartheid government was against the settlement of black populations in towns and cities, the rapid expansion of manufacturing industries increased demand for labour in the cities; a demand that could only be obtained from Africans. Wolpe (1972, in Thomas, 2010: 201) argues that this new reality increased the population of blacks with permanent urban residence status such that "by 1970, many urban African industrial workers had lost their links to the reserves". Thomas (2010: 15) also argues that:

> what needs to be understood of apartheid is that the urban status of Blacks, whether permanent or not, impacted the extent of housing stock provided for Blacks by the authorities of the white-controlled state and that the demand for housing was an issue that impacted the political organisation of Blacks in urban areas.

As black urban influx continued owing to increased labour demand, overcrowding also persisted. Marx (1992: 62) noted that:

> the African population in the ten largest urban centres doubled from 1971 to 1975, but the housing stock grew by only 15 per cent in the same period. By 1975, each house in Soweto had an average of seventeen inhabitants, and the vast majority of these houses had no toilet, running water, or attached buildings. Those who could find no room in their houses built their own adjacent shacks.

Responding to this increasing workforce, a number of houses were constructed for blacks and new townships were established. Thomas (2010: 202) argues that it is critical to note "the predominant role of white policymakers in determining all material factors concerning black housing". It was the whites who determined which blacks could own residences in terms of quality and quantity and where they could live. Thomas (2010) quotes Mr Prinsloo – a Pretoria municipality officer who was responsible for black housing – in 1950 arguing that housing provided to blacks was not supposed to "Europeanise" but was supposed to resemble their village settlement. He argued that housing was supposed to "use the same types of building material" that were used by their ancestors (Thomas, 2010: 202) and was supposed to avoid costly products, which could have seen white taxpayer money being subsequently used to subsidise funding of such housing projects. The housing was also supposed to be on a self-help basis, which did not require expensive white labour but cheap black labour. The housing woes were worsened by the tendency by urban employers to favour newly arrived non-unionised black employees as opposed to those who had settled in urban centres (Language, 1950, in Thomas, 2010). Housing loans provided to build houses for blacks were acquired at very uneconomic and high rates and this hindered black people from acquiring housing despite the increased demand.

Assisted by the Native Affairs Department, the National Building Research Institute published a booklet in 1952 titled *Build Your Own House*. Contained in the booklet were plans for different types of houses in black townships and the kinds of construction materials required. The Central Council of the Institute of

Architects held a competition on the best design for houses with two to three bedrooms for urban Africans. The idea was to encourage people to construct their own houses by making designs available free of charge (South African Institute of Race Relations, 1999; Khanya College, 2001). At the same time, and in part because of pressure from urban manufacturing companies, the government increasingly promoted homeownership for urban blacks, preferably though through the market rather than public housing. In promoting the privatisation of housing, the government sold off old housing that was previously being rented. Rentals were in fact increased to compel people to purchase their own houses. The apartheid state also promoted and pursued self-help site-serviced housing schemes. In this context, the then Minister of Co-operation and Development indicated that individuals must bear the responsibility of building their own houses (Khanya College, 2001).

Apartheid also segmented urban housing provision for the black urban population into two: (1) the "insiders", people whose housing needs were overseen by the state and the private sector, and (2) the "outsiders", who settled in informal settlements (Lupton and Murphy, 1995). The white administration made it clear that recognition of the urban permanence of black people did not translate into a commitment to provide housing to all blacks. Lupton and Murphy (1995) note that in places where freehold rights for blacks had existed before 1955, they were revoked by 1968 through the prohibition of the sale of land to blacks and their independent construction of houses on such land. Consequently, shacks, squatter camps and informal settlements emerged as an outgrowth of policies prior to 1994. It should thus become clear that housing was a big problem for the black population in South Africa under the apartheid system. Housing that was set aside for the blacks was not only in critical shortage but was also constructed out of substandard material and was ultimately of poor quality with no access to municipal services such as clean water, toilets/sewer system, electricity and drainage.

From 1976, countrywide protests against the apartheid regime led to significant destruction of property in black townships and local administration was severely disrupted. People vandalised property especially structures owned and operated by local government including clinics, administration board offices and beer halls. Because of all this, and the effect on government operations, limited housing delivery took place particularly between 1976 and 1980. During this period, there was also a shocking increase in the number of informal settlements on the urban periphery and along homeland borders (Morris, 1981; Robbins, 1997; Lester *et al.*, 2009). From 1978, though, the government took a more liberal approach to segregation policies. This was mirrored in the approval of the permanence of urban Africans, the extension of property rights, the abolition of the Group Areas legislation and efforts to consult with township communities about local development. This was also in response to an increasing acknowledgement by both the government and the corporate sector that the living conditions in townships were appalling and needed to be improved.

In 1978, the Minister of Plural Relations and Development launched a 99-year leasehold scheme for black townships. The (business-funded) Urban Foundation, in collaboration with the Association of Building Societies, played a vital role in bringing about this leasehold scheme. The leasehold arrangement was important as it involved a firmer guarantee of tenure security, which made private sector housing finance accessible to Africans and gave them an opportunity to develop a capital base. New township rules administering the conditions of residence in townships were introduced and these eradicated the arbitrary powers of township administrators to evict residents.

In 1979, the Housing Amendment Act was introduced. Under the terms of this Act, the separate Bantu Housing Board was dismantled and all applications for loans for Africans and other race groups were to be processed by the Department of Community Development through the National Housing Commission. From 1978, the amount of finance provided by the government for African housing increased significantly compared to earlier years. At the end of the 1980 financial year, the government sourced funding of R150 million from overseas countries for the development of township infrastructure (Robbins, 1997; Morris, 1981; Bonner and Segal, 1998; Reeves, 1998; Lester *et al.*, 2009).

Despite these programmes, the unevenness in housing expenditure across racial lines was evident during the apartheid era. For instance, in 1967, approximately R14.4 million was spent by the national government on housing for whites, and only R5 million on Africans. By 1975, the housing budget for whites had increased to R67 million while, for blacks, it was a mere R7.8 million (Morris, 1981; Robbins, 1997; South African Institute of Race Relations, 1999; Khanya College, 2001).

In April 1979, housing loans were offered to Africans at rates and criteria similar to those for other race groups. The new arrangement also permitted Africans to apply for home loans from building societies. This shift led to the construction of more expensive suburban-type houses in the townships by commercial developers throughout the 1980s. In 1983, the government withdrew its direct and formal status as property owner of township housing and offered all tenants in townships the opportunity to purchase their houses. The initial response to this proposal by township residents was not particularly positive, and it only improved after the costs of the houses had been considerably reduced and the inhabitants were required to make the purchase (Bonner and Segal, 1998; Bonner and Nieftagodien, 2008; Lester *et al.*, 2009).

The late 1980s and early 1990s saw the further disbandment of some of the country's race-based land and housing policies. This was in response to the sustained local and international pressures on the apartheid government to end its segregationist and oppressive policies. In 1986, the apartheid government repealed the influx control laws marking the beginning of support for self-help housing. Furthermore, council houses were sold to homeowners and some to women (Todes and Walker, 1993). This led to a mass influx of people to the cities, which also led to an increase in informal settlements. The Abolition of

Racially Based Land Measures Act (Act 108 of 1991) ushered in a new era in the land and housing policies of the country.

Conclusion

This chapter has explored key land and housing policies implemented in South Africa before the advent of the democratic regime. It notes that the disposition of land through various pieces of legislation resulted in massive poverty among the black population and made them dependent on wage labour as the only source of livelihood. However, the laws, which barred blacks from settling in or owning properties outside of the Bantustans, ensured that, for many, informal settlements on the fringes of urban centres were the only places they could reside. Where the apartheid government provided housing for the blacks, these were not only in critical shortage but were also constructed out of substandard material and of poor quality with no access to municipal services such as clean water, toilets/sewer system, electricity and drainage. While the race-based policies of the apartheid era have been abolished, their legacies continue to be evident in contemporary South Africa as seen in the emergence of shacks, squatter camps and informal settlements as an outgrowth of policies prior to 1994.

Note

1 Part of this chapter is based on the doctoral thesis of Sipho Nkambule (2016).

References

Beavon, K.S.O. 2005. Post-apartheid city: hopes, possibilities, and harsh realities. In D.M. Smith (Ed.), *The Apartheid City and Beyond Urbanization and Social Change in South Africa*. London and New York: Routledge.

Bonner, P. and Nieftagodien, N. 2008. *Alexandra: a history*. Johannesburg: Wits University Press.

Bonner, P. and Segal, L. 1998. *Soweto: a history*. Pinetown: Maskew Miller Longman (Pty) Ltd.

Calderwood, D.M. 1953. *Native Housing in South Africa*. Unpublished PhD thesis, Department of History, University of the Witwatersrand, Johannesburg 2001, South Africa.

Khanya College, 2001. *GEAR and Housing in South Africa*. Booklet No. 3. Johannesburg.

Kloppers, H.J. and Pienaar, G.J. 2014. The historical context of land reform in South Africa and early policies. *Potchefstroom Electronic Law Journal*, 17(2), pp. 666–706, www.ajol.info/index.php/pelj/article/view/107144/97034.

Lester, N., Menguele, F., Karuri-Sebina, G. and Kruger, M. 2009. *Township Transformation Timeline*. The Department of Co-operative Governance and Traditional Affairs, and the European Commission. http://sacitiesnetwork.co.za/wp-content/uploads/2014/07/township_transformation_timeline.pdf.

Lombard, J.J.G. 1996. *Housing Strategies and the Urban Poor in South Africa: a brief critical evaluation*. Working Paper No. 80. www.ucl.ac.uk/bartlett/development/sites/bartlett/files/migrated-files/WP80_0.pdf.

Lupton, M. and Murphy, S. 1995. Housing and urban reconstruction in South Africa. In A. Lemon (Ed.), *The Geography of Change in South Africa*. New York: John Wiley.

Mabin, A. 2005. Dispossession, exploitation and struggle: an historical overview of South African urbanization. In D.M. Smith (Ed.), *The Apartheid City and Beyond Urbanization and Social Change in South Africa*. London and New York: Routledge.

Marx, A.W. 1992. *Lessons of Struggle. South African Internal Opposition, 1960–1990*. Cape Town: Oxford University Press.

Maylam, P. 1995. Explaining the apartheid city: 20 years of South African urban historiography. *Journal of Southern African Studies*, 21(1), pp. 19–38.

Morris, P. 1981. *A History of Black Housing in South Africa*. Johannesburg: South Africa Foundation.

Muller, G. 2013. The legal-historical context of urban forced evictions in South Africa. *Fundamina*, 19(2).

Nkambule, S. 2016. *A Critical Analysis of the Housing Provision, Livelihood Activities and Social Production in Urban Communities in South Africa: the case of Ezamokuhle, Mpumalanga*. PhD thesis, University of Rhodes.

Parnell, S. 1988. Shaping a racially divided society: state housing policy in South Africa, 1920–50. *Environment and Planning C: Government and Policy*, 7, pp. 261–272.

Ramashamole, B. 2011. *Sustainable Housing Development in Post-Apartheid South Africa*. Master's thesis, Johannesburg, University of The Witwatersrand.

Reeves, O.J. 1998. *The Effects of Apartheid on South African Cities*. Dissertation submitted to the Faculty of Architecture, University of Witwatersrand.

Robbins, D. 1997. *Learning the Hard Way: lessons from the urban foundation experience, 1976–1994*. The Urban Foundation and H.F. Oppenheimer.

Smith, C. 1992. *Preaching as Weeping: confession and resistance*. Kentucky: John Knox Press.

Soni, D. 2001. The apartheid state and Black housing struggles. In D. Smith (Ed.), *The Apartheid City and Beyond. Urbanization and social change in South Africa*. Johannesburg: Witwatersrand University Press, pp. 41–53.

South African Institute of Race Relations, 1999. *South Africa Survey 1999/2000*. Johannesburg.

Thomas, C.G. 2010. *The Discourses on the Right to Housing in Gauteng Province, 1994–2008*. PhD thesis, Johannesburg, University of the Witwatersrand.

Todes, A. and Walker, N. 1993. Women and housing policy in South Africa: a discussion of Durban case studies. In H.C. Dandekar (Ed.), *Shelter, Women and Development*. Michigan: George Wahr, pp. 4–53.

Walker, C. 2017. *The Land Question in South Africa: 1913 and Beyond*. African History: Oxford Research Encyclopedias. http://oxfordre.com/africanhistory/view/10.1093/acrefore/9780190277734.001.0001/acrefore-9780190277734-e-79. doi: 10.1093/acrefore/9780190277734.013.79.

Wilkinson, A. 1998. *Empowerment: theory and practice*. IEBM Handbook of Human Resource Management. Connecticut: International Thomson Publishing

Wolpe, H. 1972. Capitalism and cheap labour-power in South Africa: from segregation to apartheid. *Economy and Society*, 1(4), pp. 425–456.

3 An assessment of the National Development Plan in the actualisation of government subsidised housing in South Africa

Sithembiso Lindelihle Myeni and Andrew Emmanuel Okem

Introduction

Since the demise of apartheid and the beginning of the democratic rule, South Africa has undergone various changes. A key priority of the post-apartheid government was to remedy past socio-economic injustices. To achieve this, the state formulated new socio-economic policies that would tackle these imbalances. Post-apartheid South Africa is, therefore, characterised by a hybrid of various policies that have been implemented in the past 25 years. Over the years, there has been a serious critique of the post-apartheid policies in terms of implementation failures. Against this backdrop, this chapter examines the commitment of the ruling party, the African National Congress (ANC) to the National Development Plan (NDP) in relation to housing delivery.

Overview of national development polices in post-apartheid South Africa

There are at least five national policies which have been introduced in the policy environment since 1994: Reconstruction and Development Programme (RDP); Growth Employment and Redistribution; the Accelerated and Shared Growth Initiative for South Africa; the New Growth Path (NGP); and the recent NDP. Although all of the five national policies are products of the ANC and its alliance partners, some alliance partners have criticised some of the national development plans that have been adopted by the ANC and subsequently the national government.

The RDP was the first post-apartheid policy adopted by the ANC and became the national development policy that would guide the socio-economic transformation agenda. The RDP was "an integrated programme, based on the people; that provides peace and security for all and builds the nation, links reconstruction and development and deepens democracy" (ANC, 1994: 7). According to the National Planning Commission (NPC) (2012: 260), it was aimed at "breaking down apartheid geography through land reform, more compact cities, decent public transport and the development of industries and services that use local resources and/or meet local needs".

The framework of the NGP was formulated by the Department of Economic Development (DED) and was meant "to implement a set of macro-economic and micro-economic interventions with clear and concrete stakeholder commitments to move South Africa to faster, more inclusive and sustainable growth" (DED, 2010; Hendriks, 2013: 6).

Background and context of the NDP

Despite realising some commendable progress in terms of social and economic development, it is also important to realise that 18 years after attaining independence (counting up to 2012 when the NDP came into being), South Africa remained a highly unequal society in which the majority endured poverty. The NPC, in a 2011 diagnostic report, noted that policy implementation failures and the failure to engage stakeholders undermine the country's socio-economic progress. It identifies nine challenges that the country and its people continue to face even after realising political independence:

1 Too few people work
2 The quality of school education for black people is poor
3 Infrastructure is poorly located, inadequate and under-maintained
4 Spatial divides hobble inclusive development
5 The economy is unsustainably resource intensive
6 The public health system cannot meet demand or sustain quality
7 Public services are uneven and often of poor quality
8 Corruption levels are high
9 South Africa remains a divided society.

To speed up progress, deepen democracy and establish a more inclusive South Africa, the NPC (2012: 24) observes that there is a need to "translate political emancipation into economic wellbeing for all". The NDP was born in response to these challenges and the need to find lasting and sustainable solutions to these challenges.

The NDP, by definition, is a long-term socio-economic development blueprint adopted in 2013 following the Mangaung Conference of 2012 (COSATU, 2013). The policy was developed by the NPC under the headship of the then Minister of Economic Development, Ebrahim Patel, and the administration of former president Jacob Zuma. It was a product of the realisation by the then cabinet that it was difficult or rather impossible for the country to realise social cohesion and sustained economic development without the involvement, active participation and working together of all concerned stakeholders (NPC, 2012). It was also based on South Africa's achievements and shortcomings in as far as realising socio-economic development is concerned in the post-apartheid era (NPC, 2012).

The NDP aims at eliminating poverty and reducing inequality by 2030. It seeks to achieve these goals by bringing together the different energies from its people, developing an inclusive economy, building capabilities, improving the capacity of the state, and promoting leadership and partnerships throughout society (NPC, 2012). The NDP is aimed at ensuring that every South African manages decent living standards and thus strives towards poverty elimination/reduction as well as reduction of social and economic inequalities (Hendriks, 2013). The NPC (2012: 40) identified the following as some of the fundamentals of decent living standards:

- Housing, water, electricity and sanitation
- Safe and reliable public transport
- Quality education and skills development
- Safety and security
- Quality health care
- Social protection
- Employment
- Recreation and leisure
- Clean environment
- Adequate nutrition.

By aiming to achieve decent living standards, the NDP "seeks to reduce poverty, unemployment and inequality" (Hendricks, 2013: 6), and at the same time create more jobs. The NDP is also heavily inclined towards a strong developmental state orientation (Consultancy Africa Intelligence, 2012). It is based on development and changes "through state intervention, investment and transformation of society" (Hendricks, 2013: 6).

The NDP is premised on the fact that, although South Africa's past is marred by colonial and apartheid oppression, injustices, dispossessions and inequalities along racial lines, it is imperative to look beyond this history, heal the pains of the past and remedy the inequities caused by centuries of racial marginalisation. It envisions a country in which each and every one of its citizens feels unrestricted yet confined to others; where everyone realises his or her maximum potential, and a nation where opportunities are determined by ability, level of education, skill and hard work as opposed to one's skin colour (NPC, 2012). In this regard, the NDP is deeply rooted in the national constitution, which "enshrines a rights-based approach and envisions a prosperous, non-racial, non-sexist democracy that belongs to all its people" (NPC, 2012: 24). When it comes to housing, the NDP is also in line with the constitutional provisions given by the Bill of Rights, which speaks to the right of everyone to "a healthy environment; access to adequate housing; and access to basic services" (Sections 24, 26 and 27) (Republic of South Africa, 1996).

The NDP also recognises that to realise a just and equal society, the economy must be transformed and all efforts must be directed towards building the country's capabilities. Thus, to achieve a speedy elimination of poverty and reduction of inequality, the economy needs to grow at a faster rate and in ways that will allow all South Africans to benefit from it. Table 3.1 provides a summary of the NDP.

Table 3.1 A summary of the NDP

The National Development Plan	
Aim	All South Africans attain a decent standard of living through the elimination of poverty and reduction of inequality.
Priorities	Jobs and education.
Targets	Eliminate poverty by 2030.
Challenges identified	The diagnostic report on which the NDP is based identified nine main challenges (NPC, 2011): • Too few people work. • The standard of education of most black learners is of poor quality. • Infrastructure is poorly located, under-maintained and insufficient for growth. • Special patterns exclude the poor from the benefits of development. • The economy is too unsustainably resource intensive. • The failing public health system compounds a widespread disease burden. • Public services are uneven and often of poor quality. • Corruption is widespread. • South Africa remains a divided society.
Policy elements	The effective implementation of the Plan depends on the following principles: • Broad ownership. • Continuous capacity building. • Policy consistency. • Prioritisation and sequencing of elements. • Clarity of responsibility and accountability. • Continuous learning and improvement. • Coordinated action (PMG, 2013).
Measurable indicators	By 2030, the number of households living below R418 per person per month (in 2009 Rand) should fall from 39 per cent to zero. The level of inequality as measured by the Gini coefficient should fall from 0.7 in 2009 to 0.6 in 2030.

Source: adapted from Hendriks (2013: 8–9).

Policy statements of NDP on human settlement in South Africa

The NDP has been receiving a lot of attention from many stakeholders across the country. The ruling ANC's 2014 election manifesto was hugely informed by the NDP. The manifesto advocated for what the party called the "second phase of democratic transition", which was aimed at addressing the "triple threat" of poverty, unemployment and inequality, and deeply articulated the Vision 2030 as contained in the NDP. The ANC once again demonstrated its trust in the NDP as the solution to the country's development challenges in its 2016 local government election manifesto, in which it pledged its commitment to deal with unemployment, poverty, inequality and other challenges that continue to bedevil the country (ANC, 2016). As was the case with all its other previous policies, the manifesto pledged to continuously work towards improvement of critical areas like the need to scale up service delivery, infrastructure and local economic development as well as pledging to create safer communities, ensure social cohesion, fight corruption and support local governments in rolling out National Health Insurance.

The NDP has received a lot of attention from across the country's various departments and it has been instrumental in guiding departmental plans (National Treasury, 2013). The 2014 budget emphasised the need for accelerated public infrastructure investment, new spatial plans for cities and improved public transport and upgrading informal settlements (National Treasury, 2013). Similarly, the 2015 budget presented by the then new Minister of Finance, Nhlanhla Nene, acknowledged the commitment to the NDP, adding that it was imperative to accelerate economic growth, creating jobs and broadening economic participation, for the NDP goals to be realised. The minister also made reference to NDP in terms of urban housing and development: "As the NDP emphasises, realising the economic dividends of urban growth requires a new approach to providing infrastructure, housing and public transport services, while overcoming the spatial divisions of apartheid" (National Treasury, 2015: 14).

In the 2017 annual budget, the government committed over R29.8 billion to housing (*Fin24*, 2017). The then Finance Minister, Pravin Gordhan, noted that it was important "to have intergovernmental cooperation between the different spheres to improve delivery of services such as housing, water and sanitation and public transport, among others", noting that such a collaboration was pivotal in "reversing the spatial legacy of apartheid" emphasising that "spatial transformation is a massive challenge involving land acquisition and development, infrastructure and transport services, housing and industrial and enterprise support" (*Fin24*, 2017). Muller (2017) reported in the *Financial Mail* also reported that the Department of Human Settlements (DoHS) was involved in 25 housing projects running between 2017 and 2019 and noted that it aims to deliver 55,171 social rental housing units by 2019. The report also noted that the DoHS was focusing on the provision of title deeds to the beneficiaries of subsidised housing through the title deeds restoration programme (Urban Landmark, 2011). These policy pronouncements point to the NDP and how it is gradually shaping housing provision in South Africa.

A survey of projects/programmes emerging from the NDP

Several housing projects/programmes have been initiated based on the NDP. Some of these are discussed under this section.

National Upgrading Support Programme (NUSP)

The NUSP is one of the new housing initiatives by the government which is influenced by the NDP. The programme is aimed at *in situ* informal settlement upgrading. The policy supports the National Department of Human Settlements in the implementation of its Upgrading of Informal Settlements Programme (Ziblim *et al.*, 2013). The objective of the programme is to eventually upgrade all informal settlements in South Africa and to build capacity in municipalities across the country for them to be able to deal with the challenges of slow delivery of subsidised houses through incremental upgrading of informal settlements (PEP, 2016). As is recommended by the NDP, the DoHS works with other partners whose contribution includes providing socio-technical assistance to boost the capacity of municipalities to develop robust informal settlement upgrading plans. Karam and Huchzermeyer (2015) argue that informal settlement housing upgrading had become an important component of the national DoHS as it seeks to address the housing shortage constraints.

An example of a project that was born out of the NUSP is the Cape Town Slum Upgrading project, rolled out from 2013 to 2014. The project brought organisations like the Development Action Group, People's Environment Planning (PEP), the DoHS and the City of Cape Town to work together in mapping a way forward on how to plan, implement and roll out upgrading of 25 selected informal settlements around Cape Town and build bridges between informal settlement communities and the city. The project achieved various outcomes including improving the working relationship with the city and informal settlement residents; establishing and strengthening relevant committees (e.g. infrastructure, disaster, waste management, security, education, etc.) to support the development of informal settlement; improving social facilities; and facilitating regular maintenance of communal infrastructure, drainage, roads and collection of waste material, among others (PEP, 2016).

Individual subsidy housing

Subsidy housing is a state-driven housing development initiative that is meant to provide decent housing for urban poor people in South Africa. Under this scheme, a grant is given to deserving/qualifying beneficiaries by the government for housing purposes. According to van Niekerk (2013), the housing subsidies are not paid directly to the beneficiaries. Instead, they are passed to housing agents who then facilitate the housing process, either through selling completed houses or constructing new houses that conform to the minimum norms and standards as required by the DoHS, after which ownership of the houses is conferred to the qualifying beneficiaries. The Department of Co-operative Governance, Human Settlement and Traditional Affairs (2013) emphasised that in both cases, the housing properties belong to the beneficiaries and are registered under their name. Subsidies are constituted by a one-off grant paid by the government, and the amount is adjusted annually and accordingly (Scheepers, 2014). While housing subsidy started as far back as 1994, it is important to note that the NDP was a positive step towards the enhancement of the programme.

Scheepers (2014: 41) notes that subsidy funds are used to "finance the planning, acquisition and servicing of land as well as to build the houses, adding that it also guarantees secure tenure and provision of basic housing services".

Management of subsidised housing projects is entrusted to Provincial Departments of Human Settlements or accredited local governments. Although the subsidy programme initially was regarded as a method of meeting basic needs, it has of late been seen as a way of alleviating poverty through homeownership. The logic here is that "the beneficiaries can improve their own socio-economic conditions by investing in this property then later sell it to someone with a low income as entry-level accommodation" (Scheepers, 2014: 41). The profits realised from selling the property are then channelled towards procuring a better house (Scheepers, 2014). Charlton (2010) notes that this method also plays a role in the housing supply chain.

The Social and Rental Housing Programme (SRHP)

Although this SRHP started well before the institution of the NDP, it is important to note that the coming of the NDP amplified it. The SRHP is meant to provide government subsidies to develop medium-density rental housing in well-located parts of selected urban centres and it is primarily meant to provide decent, affordable and well-managed rental housing to households whose income lies between R1,500 and R7,500. The policy is also geared towards achieving racial and economic integration of population groups in urban centres. The responsibility of implementing social housing is entrusted to accredited Social Housing Institutions under the Social Housing Act of 2008 (No. 16 of 2008) to provide rental or cooperative housing and manage these houses on a long-term basis (Scholtz, 2014). While all implementing agents were initially non-profit making, private institutions are now allowed to apply for subsidy funding that is meant for social housing provision.

Sikota (2015) notes that with the increasing demand for housing, the challenge of housing seems to be here to stay. As such, the government has invented ways of lessening the problem. Housing opportunities do not necessarily translate to one owning "a house of their own but may come in the form of getting a housing subsidy, incremental housing with or without tenure, rental housing and social housing for low-income households" (Wilkinson *et al.*, 2014, quoted in Sikota, 2015: 4). Scholtz (2014) argues that, although in the past housing policy favoured homeownership, the importance of rental housing is increasingly receiving acknowledgement since it enables groups which may choose not to or may not have the financial capacity to acquire their own properties to access affordable, well-located accommodation in the city. It also suits those who are employed in basic jobs which are less secure.

Because of the unmet demand for affordable housing in the country's major urban centres, Scholtz (2014) notes that new social housing projects in cities such as Durban, East London, Johannesburg and Port Elizabeth are characteristically over-subscribed by a factor of ten or more. It is also important to note that the objectives of this programme and those of the NDP share some commonalities since both seek to minimise housing challenges and enhance the living standards of every citizen. Scholtz (2014) also argues that rental stock provided by both the social housing and private sectors play a significant role in the socio-economic and spatial restructuring of South Africa's urban centres.

Gap Housing Market Vision 2030 of the NDP on human settlements speaks to the need to provide housing for urban poor people based on the new concept of "gap housing". Gap housing is a term invented to describe the shortfall or gap between residential housing units supplied by the government and those delivered by the private sector. The gap housing market is made up of households or individuals whose monthly income is between R3,500 and R15,000 per month, making them ineligible for government funded housing, but who do not earn enough to guarantee them home loans. Those who fall into this category include nurses, firefighters, teachers and uniformed forces. Housing projects under this policy are funded by the National Housing Finance Corporation via an intervention known as the Finance Linked Individual Subsidy Programme (DoHS, 2015).

Financial programmes/provision of social and economic facilities

According to Scheepers (2014: 42), financial programmes are those "facilitating immediate access to housing goods and services creating enabling environments and providing implementation support". Housing products under this category include Individual Housing Subsidies, the Enhanced Extended Discount Benefit Scheme, Social and Economic Facilities, Accreditation of Municipalities, Operational Capital Budget and Housing Chapters of Integrated Development Plans as well as Rectification of Pre-1994 Housing Stock. It is important to note that responsible authorities in most of the new settlements have not been able to provide basic social and economic facilities: schools, clinics, community halls, recreational facilities and trading facilities (Department of Human Settlements, 2010). This scheme is thus meant to provide these facilities – a development that is meant to establish quality sustainable human settlements. Subsidies under this programme are provided to all municipalities that lack sufficient financial resources to construct these facilities. Players in this programme include municipalities, Provincial Departments and the National Department, where municipalities will play the part of the developer.

Housing assistance in emergency circumstances

This programme is meant to provide temporary accommodation during times of emergencies. It should be understood that during the process of informal settlements upgrading, there might arise cases which call for temporary relocation such that re-housing of affected households would become imperative as upgrading services are being put in place. This also applies to cases where formal housing units are constructed on sites previously occupied by informal settlement structures. The programme also extends to households that may have been affected by natural disasters or those caused by people, such as fires, storms, floods, etc., as victims are provided with relief housing as their houses are repaired. Funding under this programme is provided to municipalities as grants. Municipalities work with Provincial Departments and communities under this programme (DoHS, 2015).

Community Residential Units programme (CRU)

The CRU is meant for the provision of more secure, stable rental tenure to poor and low-income households or individuals. It provides a comprehensive framework on how to deal with the many different types of already existing public sector residential accommodation. The programme was a result of the realisation that the increasing demand for affordable rental housing has seen many people and households renting substandard and overcrowded accommodation in backyards and informal settlements. It was also necessitated by the realisation that social housing tends to exclude very poor people, who are mostly employed in the informal sector because of the relatively high costs of multi-level units and the slightly high rental charges, which poor people cannot afford. The programme thus supports the upgrading of public or government-owned communal rental accommodation. Municipalities which identify such housing that needs to be upgraded/renovated apply for a grant to the Provincial Department and, once approved, the funds are released (DoHS, 2014).

Rural housing subsidy

The rural housing subsidy is one of the programmes that can easily be linked to the NDP. As the name suggests, this programme was put in place to improve housing in rural settlements or communities. Since the rest of the housing initiatives were channelled towards housing in towns and cities, there was a need to balance the equation and come up with similar initiatives meant to benefit rural communities. Programmes targeting rural communities are also important considering the fact that the majority of the rural population are without jobs or reliable sources of income such that poverty is a common phenomenon. It is also important to note that rural areas had, for a long time, been neglected as the previous apartheid government prioritised urban infrastructural development. Although the programme started before the NDP, it is important to consider the fact that the NDP encouraged speedy implementation of the programme.

The rural housing subsidies are set to benefit people in those communal areas where tenure rights can be confirmed through some processes prescribed by the Department of Rural Development and Land Reform. The target population for housing are people who are settled on land that belongs to the state, i.e. those communal lands that are registered under the state's name or land that is owned by community members in respect of the rules or customs of that community. Housing in rural settlements which does not fit in these two categories of land ownership do not qualify. Subsidies under this programme are normally project based. The programme is in line with the "objective of the Comprehensive Plan for the Creation of Sustainable Human Settlements for a needs-orientated rural development programme that provides for traditional technologies, addressing issues of tenure security and livelihoods" (Department of Human Settlements, 2010: 17). The objectives of the programme are consistent with the housing objectives of the NDP.

Achieving NDP Vision 2030: opportunities and constraints

Achieving NDP Vision 2030, just like any policy/programme, is bound to come with its own opportunities and constraints. This section takes a look at these.

Opportunities

While the lack of land has been seen as a primary constraint of the NDP, an opportunity may arise from the ongoing land reform programme where the government seeks to expropriate land from colonial beneficiaries without compensation. This is an opportunity for government to regain control of land in and around urban settlements then share it equitably to the landless or develop housing settlements which are then extended to the beneficiaries. With land being available for free, the government/individuals will start off with developing expenses as opposed to footing the bill for acquiring the land. Land reform will also unlock prime land owned by very few landowners around cities and allow poor people to move away from not-so-well-located areas which are difficult to develop, where most informal settlements are located.

Freire *et al.* (2014: 24) urge cities to take advantage of rapid growth and use it as an opportunity to make effective decisions in terms of both investment and the city form, arguing that "the most important policy tool would be forward-looking urban participatory planning, which could guide urban expansion and the associated infrastructure needs". This, in turn, calls for future planning to consider future population growth since the challenges that government and municipalities are facing in their attempt to meet the 2030 housing objective of the NDP have taught them that haphazard and uncontrolled urban expansion can result in complex and catastrophic consequences. The lessons learned from this process could be implemented in future planning.

Constraints

An assessment of the housing subsidy programmes in the Western Cape by the PEP (2018) found that housing subsidy programmes are likely to be affected by a number of constraints including:

1 Questionable political will – the study doubts if there is enough political will to eradicate the housing challenge. This is in line with the realisation that the government has lowered its spending on housing over the recent years. This is evidenced in the 2018 national budget speech where the then Finance Minister, Malusi Gigaba, announced that "a considerable reduction

would be made in estimated public sector infrastructure spending from the values projected in 2017" (*Engineering News*, 2018).

2 Funding/grant instruments constraints – with the increasing demand for urban housing against an economy that is not performing at its best, it is difficult for the government to provide adequate housing funding for everyone. Joffe (2006) also notes that about 86 per cent of South African households do not earn enough to afford decent housing and this means the government has a lot of people to assist and might not be able to accommodate everyone.
3 Land unavailability – most of the urban land is privately owned and it is not easy for the government to acquire it. Successful housing is dependent upon land ownership.
4 Rapid urbanisation pressures – too many people are flocking into cities and the housing challenge is ever-unfolding such that totally eradicating it will be a tall order. The South African Institute of Race Relations (2015) noted that in 1993 there were 300 informal settlements across the country, but because of rapid urbanisation, the number had shot to at least 2,225 by 2015.

Gunter (2014: 96) also argues that "factors like high and rising costs of ownership, inability to apply for subsidised housing, irregular and low income have limited access to formal housing by the urban poor". Increasing poverty is another constraint that the NDP faces in terms of housing delivery. As Lall *et al.* (2007: 5, cited in Sikota, 2015: 15–16) noted, it is difficult for poor people to enter formal housing as "it is difficult for them to access land". It is also important to note that the housing programmes in some cities face resistance from municipalities, which are reluctant to allocate prime land for low-income housing. This resistance is also propped up by some high-income groups who believe that having low-income housing settlements near them will devalue their property (Lall *et al.*, 2007).

Conclusions and recommendations

This chapter examined the critical role of the NDP in relation to the provision of human settlements in South Africa. We noted that the NDP informed many policies and, in terms of its housing objectives, has seen a number of housing policies and programmes meant to alleviate the shortage of urban and rural accommodation and the poverties associated with not owning a home or a decent place to stay. Such programmes include the rural housing subsidy, informal settlements upgrading, upgrading communal infrastructure and public hostels among others. The chapter also noted the opportunities that are available or may arise from pursuing the NDP housing agenda. It ends by giving the following set of recommendations for the actualising of the objectives of sustainable housing:

1 There is a need for the government to rethink its role as the sole/main financier of the housing subsidies and consider pursuing diverse funding streams as well as the involvement of other stakeholders.

2 It is imperative for cities to control the development of informal settlements. This will prevent the establishing of settlements on areas that are not so well located since they are difficult to develop in future should there arise a chance for upgrading.
3 Decentralisation of economic activities to smaller urban centres and prioritising growth in these towns will help to decongest major cities where the cost of land and cost of living are very high and unaffordable for many.
4 There is also a need to incentivise companies/employers into assisting their employees in acquiring housing at affordable costs and on fair terms. This can also speed up housing delivery.

References

ANC, 1994. *The Reconstruction and Development Programme: a policy framework.* Johannesburg: Umanyano Publications.

ANC, 2016. *2016 Local Government Manifesto: together advancing people's power in every community*. www.anc.org.za/sites/default/files/docs/lge-manifestou.pdf.

Charlton, S. 2010. Inclusion through housing: limitations and alternatives in Johannesburg. *Urban Forum*, 21(1), pp. 1–19.

Consultancy Africa Intelligence, 2012. *Can South Africa be Considered a Developmental State? The New Growth Path and National Development Plan in perspective*. www.polity.org.za/article/can-south-africa-be-considered-a-developmental-state-the-new-growth-path-and-national-developmental-plan-in-perspective-2012-03-09.

COSATU, 2013. *Mangaung and the Second Phase of the Transition: discussion document for the COSATU CEC*, 25–27 February 2013. www.cosatu.org.za/docs/discussion/2013/analysis.pdf.

DED (Department for Economic Development), 2010. The New Growth Path: the framework. www.info.gov.za/view/DownloadFileAction?id=135748.

Department of Co-operative Governance, Human Settlement and Traditional Affairs, 2013. *Subsidy Basics*. Pretoria.

Department of Human Settlements, 2010. *National Housing Policy and Subsidy Programmes*. http://policyresearch.limpopo.gov.za/bitstream/handle/123456789/1084/National%2520Housing%2520Policy%2520and%2520Subsidy%2520Programmes.pdf?sequence=1.

Department of Human Settlements, 2015. *Pocket Guide to South Africa 2016/17*. www.gcis.gov.za/sites/default/files/docs/resourcecentre/yearbook/Pocket%20Guide%202016-17%20Full%20File.pdf.

Engineering News, 2018. Decrease in government spend could harm the infrastructure sector. www.engineeringnews.co.za/article/decrease-in-government-spend-could-harm-the-infrastructure-sector-2018-03-05.

Fin24, 2017. Budget makes room for more housing opportunities. www.fin24.com/Budget/Budget-and-Economy/budget-makes-room-for-more-housing-opportunities-20170222.

Freire, M.E., Lall, S. and Leipziger, D. 2014. *Africa's Urbanisation: challenges and opportunities*. Washington: The Growth Dialogue. www.dannyleipziger.com/documents/GD_WP7.pdf [accessed 25 January 2016].

Gunter, A. 2014. Renting shacks: landlords and tenants in the informal housing sector in Johannesburg South Africa. *Urban Forum*, 25, pp. 96–107.

Hendriks, S. 2013. South Africa's National Development Plan and New Growth Path: reflections on policy contradictions and implications for food security. *Agrekon*, 52(3), pp. 1–17.

Joffe, H. 2006. Reporting on Wits University School of Public Development and Management forum. *Business Day*, 6 June. www.wits.ac.za/media/wits-university/footer/about-wits/governance/documents/WitsAnnualReport2012FINALwebPart1.pdf.

Karam, A. and Huchzermeyer, M. 2015 *Informal Settlements. Changing Space, Changing City: Johannesburg after Apartheid*. Open Access Selection, WITS University Press, Johannesburg, pp. 154–175.

Lall, S.V., van den Brink, R., Leresche, K.M. and Dasgupta, B. 2007. *Subsidized Housing and Access to Land in South African Cities*. Pretoria: World Bank Publications.

Muller, J. 2017. Budget 2017 human settlements: housing scores big. *Financial Mail*, 24 February 2017. www.businesslive.co.za/fm/features/2017-02-24-human-settlements-housing-scores-big/.

National Treasury, 2013. *Strategic Plan 2013/2017*. National Treasury of the Republic of South Africa. www.treasury.gov.za/publications/strategic%20plan/Strat%20Plan%20 2013-2017.pdf.

National Treasury, 2015. *Annual Report 2015/16*. National Treasury of the Republic of South Africa. www.treasury.gov.za/publications/annual%20reports/national%20treasury/nt%20annual%20report%202015-16.pdf.

NPC (National Planning Commission), 2011. *Diagnostic Overview*. Pretoria: National Planning Commission, Office of the Presidency.

NPC (National Planning Commission), 2012. *National Development Plan*. Pretoria: National Planning Commission, Office of the Presidency.

PEP (People's Environment Planning), 2016. *National Upgrading Support Programme (NUSP)*. http://pep.org.za/programmes/national-upgrading-support-programme-nusp/.

PMG (Parliamentary Monitoring Group), 2013. *Post SoNA Briefing by Ministers Trevor Manuel and Collins Chabane on Implementation of National Development Plan*. https://pmg.org.za/briefing/19000/.

Republic of South Africa, 1996. *Constitution of South Africa* (No. 108 of 1996). Pretoria: Government Printer.

Scheepers, E.Y. 2014. *Sustainable Subsidy Housing Provision: a planning approach*. Master's thesis, North-West University, South Africa.

Scholtz, L. 2014. *Why Is There Not Enough Affordable Rental or Social Housing for the Poor in South Africa's Cities?* The South African Civil Society Information Service. http://sacsis.org.za/site/article/1996.

Sikota, Z. 2015. *No Meaningful Participation Without Effective Representation: the case of the Niall Mellon Housing Project in Imizamo Yethu, Hout Bay*. Master's thesis, Cape Town, University of the Western Cape.

South African Institute of Race Relations, 2015. South Africa's housing conundrum. *@Liberty, The policy bulletin of the IRR*, No. 4, 2015/6 October 2015/Issue 20.

Urban Landmark, 2011. *Investigation into the Delays in Issuing Title Deeds to Beneficiaries of Housing Projects Funded by the Capital Subsidy*. www.urbanlandmark.org.za/downloads/title_deed_delays_report_2011.pdf.

van Niekerk, L. 2013. Housing. www.info.gov.za/aboutsa/housing.htm.

Ziblim, A., Sumeghy, M.G. and Cartwright, A., 2013. The dynamics of informal settlements upgrading in South Africa. *Habitat International*, 37, pp. 316–334.

4 Apartheid housing and urban livelihoods in apartheid South Africa[1]

Sipho Jonathan Nkambule

Introduction

Remedying the inherited disparities of apartheid has created a complicated and challenging environment for providing housing in post-apartheid South Africa. This chapter examines the historical development of housing and livelihoods during apartheid South Africa in the context of the broader political economy of the country, and with specific reference to black urban spaces. It highlights the deeply racialised and repressive character of the white state's housing policies and programmes as well as the livelihood activities of black urban poor people living in townships. The main argument made in this chapter is that it is of utmost importance to reflect on the past to understand how the injustices of the apartheid era continue to manifest in post-apartheid South Africa and to see the need for restructuring human settlement patterns in the post-apartheid era by the democratic state.

Theoretical background

In this chapter, the Sustainable Livelihoods Framework (SLF) is used to understand and analyse the agency of black households during the apartheid era, without implying that their livelihood outcomes are marked by sustainability. Also, household-based agency takes place within prevailing structures, which often inhibit agency but also may facilitate it. The SLF is not used for merely programmatic purposes but is first and foremost an analytical framework or investigative instrument for understanding and explaining household-based livelihoods (Carswell and Jones, 2004).

The framework is grounded in the idea that assets, sometimes called resources or capitals, are vital to the pursuance of livelihood strategies. Assets are utilised by households to build livelihoods and offer them the capability to be and act (Bebbington, 1999). Housing, whether provided by the state or arising through self-provision, is a key asset. Overall, the SLF identifies a range of resources including social, physical, political, human and natural capital. But the pursuance of livelihood activities based on existing or acquired assets occurs, in the case of poor households, in a context marked by vulnerability (Moser, 1998).

This vulnerability context, marked by uncertainty in terms of sustainability, is systemic or embedded in the lives of poor households. It also involves specific threats from the external environment in the form of seasonal cycles or sudden shocks such as the death of a breadwinner (Oblack, 2008). The different assets or capitals which regularly appear in livelihood literature are financial capital, natural capital, physical capital, human capital and social capital.

Financial capital is mainly made of income from the sale of labour, or from income generated from self-employment including within the informal sector. Kollmair and Juli (2002) note that financial capital can be derived from two main sources: first, from accessible stocks including bank deposits, cash or liquid assets such as furniture for which there are no liabilities; and, second, from fixed inflows of money including social grants from the state, remittances and (as indicated) labour and self-employment income.

Human capital consists of education, knowledge, skills, expertise, health and the ability to work (Carney, 1998). There is a strong association between human capital and financial capital. For example, access to employment opportunities as a financial capital element is in large part dependent upon suitable human capital (Rakodi, 2000). Investments in the education of children in households are often seen as a future gateway out of poverty, while poor health, particularly of an adult household member engaged in full-time formal employment, may undermine financial capital sources. At the same time, employment itself may lead to health problems, which is regularly the case for those working in unsafe conditions in for example underground mining.

Natural capital concerns the natural resource base from which households draw to sustain themselves. It involves water, forests, erosion prevention, air quality, land, the degree of biodiversity, forests and land (Kollmair and Juli, 2002). Natural capital is normally divided into two categories, namely renewable and non-renewable resources. The appropriate use of any accessible natural resource, renewable and non-renewable, contributes to the possibility of viable social reproduction. Renewable resources replace themselves over a certain period of time, such as trees used for firewood and fishery stock; while "non-renewable resources exist in limited supply and cannot be replaced once they have been extracted and used, including oils and metals" (Ellis, 2000: 32).

Physical capital is directly related to the question of human settlements, as it refers to housing, basic services and infrastructure required to support housing, sufficient water supply and sanitation, affordable transport and clean, affordable energy. Though many of these resources are considered as public goods and are thus provided from the national fiscus, in urban areas some of them are commodified to various degrees, for example water through policies such as privatisation and user fees (Ellis, 2000). In urban areas, people depend heavily on physical capital to exist and make a living (Sapir, 1996). According to Chambers (1997), many household goods also may be categorised as physical assets or transferable physical assets at least, as they store value and may be sold in times of financial crisis to accrue income. Housing, in particular, is critical for poor urban people as a site for even minimal social reproduction but it is also used at times as a source of income generation, for example through rentals or house-based informal economic activities (Moser, 1998). Urban households with very limited financial capital, insufficient even to rent a room in an existing house, may decide to reside in informal settlements where they likely live in fear of officials demolishing their shacks. In this regard, housing location is a very important component of physical capital. Houses which are nearer to places of employment or economic opportunities are often an advantage if only because this reduces transport costs to and from work, and this often is a reason for households residing in informal settlements which may be closer to town than government-sanctioned urban settlements (Farrington *et al.*, 2002). It is also sometimes the reason for households in informal settlements resisting relocation by the state, even with a promise of better housing elsewhere. In urban areas, access to affordable transport is in fact very important to allow people to move from one place to another in order to carry out various livelihood strategies.

Central to the SLF and its focus on assets is social capital, which entails, in the pursuit of livelihoods, "negotiating social relationships within the household and managing social networks and institutions within communities and the city" (Beall and Kanji, 1999: 1). It is also important to the question of housing in particular because the notions of human settlement and social reproduction bring to the fore the socially framed character of livelihood activities. Despite the fact that human settlements need material resources such as forms of financial, natural and physical capital, the very existence and well-being of human settlements are not reducible to such capitals, as social capital involving social relationships and networks along with trust and collaboration is critical.

Besides assets and vulnerabilities, the SLF highlights the importance of policies, institutions and processes (PIPs), which involve a number of economic, environmental, political and social factors that facilitate or constrain livelihoods, such as legislation, institutions, organisations and policies. In a sense, the PIPs, at least institutions and policies, set the structural context within which livelihoods are constructed and pursued, and they affect assets and vulnerabilities in either a negative or positive way. For example, in apartheid South Africa, there were a number of national state institutions involved in the delivery of low-cost housing, notably the local municipalities, as well as the prevailing ruling political party in the form of the National Congress. Relevant state institutions also existed at the national level, namely the Department of Plural Relations and Development. More distant international groups such as multinational financial institutions, for instance the World Bank, are relevant by way of influencing and establishing policies and programmes at the nation-state level.

Livelihood activities

The apartheid government viewed the informal economic sector as a threat to the system as it had the potential to provide black people with economic freedom. Research in Durban by Maasdorp and Pillay (1983) de Smidt (1988) revealed that the majority of the respondents who were black started their own businesses due to economic motivation. They were not forced into informal businesses due to retrenchment or absence of formal employment, but they wanted to be financially independent. Overall, though, apartheid economic and social planning involved a regime of strict regulations governing street trading and the formation of built markets for blacks in "white" cities; similar regulations existed with reference to informal economic activities more generally. The Group Areas Act of 1950 contributed to these problems as the legislation restricted the right of entry for blacks to urban areas by controlling black movement, economic mobility and residential options. The migration of blacks into these cities was thereby controlled by reinforcing the existing pass laws in 1952, forcing blacks including black women to carry identity documents in order to control their urban entry. Only employed blacks were permitted in the cities, making it unlawful for blacks to enter a city for any business other than to sell their labour to whites. At the same time, the Bantu Investment Corporation Act of 1959 was enacted to restrict black economic activities to the newly formed homelands (Karumbidza, 2011).

By the 1970s, it had become clear that control of black economic activity in cities in "white South Africa" was difficult to completely achieve. The Licensing and Business Hours Ordinance 11 of 1973 (later the Licensing and Business Hours Act 11 of 1984) was endorsed to regulate and administer the increasing street vending activities in some areas of cities. This law provided for permits and levying of a fee to work as an urban street vendor. Through this piece of legislation, however, it was also possible to regulate the volume of people who could enter a city for the purpose of street vending, thus serving as an influx control mechanism (Karumbidza, 2011). Besides national-level legislation, city councils also had the authority to pass regulations that would restrict informal economic activities in city centres. Despite all this, throughout South African "white" cities and towns, there were large numbers of street vendors who sold flowers, vegetables, fruits and other food stuffs (Tabe, 2014; Nduma, 1992).

One example of city council regulations for street vendors is the case of Cape Town. New rules were launched in 1948 which minimised trading hours and required street vendors to have stockrooms for their goods and products. It was claimed that street vendors stored fruits and vegetables under unhygienic conditions, and their new stockrooms had to be approved by the Medical Officer of Health (Rogerson, 1988; Green, 1989). Vendors also needed to now provide their photograph and signature on their business registration certificate. The requirements for storage had a negative impact on their livelihoods as storage entailed an extra cost for the vendors. The shortening of trading hours from 1948 also took place in other cities. Before 1948, street vending hours in South Africa were between 6 am and 11 pm, but the new closing hour was 6 pm in places like Johannesburg and Durban (Tabe, 2014). However, considerable illegal trading activity took place, as "structural economic factors such as unemployment and poverty actually forced individuals to defy the law despite the severe threat it posed" (Nesvag, 2000: 41).

In Cape Town, between September 1957 and August 1958, there were 1,247 arrests made with some street vendors being prosecuted a number of times. After these incidences, a joint committee of Traffic Control, Markets and Licenses (1958) recommended the introduction of a designated police force with powers to arrest street vendors in prohibited areas, and the granting of further powers to the municipality to confiscate the goods of street traders. The committee also recommended the termination of a street trader's licence after three convictions. However, the large numbers of street vendors in the so-called forbidden area of the city centre made it almost impossible for a single police officer to successfully make an arrest because in most instances he was overpowered by the many hawkers. Street traders, in fact, started using different strategies of trading which sometimes involved relying on children to operate their business for them. This worked in the street traders' favour as even the apartheid judiciary system was not willing to impose heavy penalties on children (Nesvag, 2000; Tabe, 2014).

In 1991, the government introduced the Businesses Act, which marked a radical shift in policy aimed at regulating informal economic activities including street trading throughout South Africa. It did so first because it wanted to substitute the four provincial licensing regulations of Natal, the Orange Free State, the Transvaal and the Cape with a national framework. The second reason was to stimulate economic growth by doing away with increasingly pointless limitations on entry into the economy (Knight and Rogerson, 1986; Nattrass, 1987; Tabe, 2014). The Act indicated the kinds of businesses which needed licences, and it relieved traders from applying for licences, except those who sold food. It also instituted a heavy penalty of a fine of R1,000 or a three months' sentence for street traders who violated the new regulations (Tabe, 2014).

The powers to control the operation of traders were transferred from local governments to the provincial administrations. However, some municipal authorities in South Africa opposed the Business Act since it took away their powers. The Cape Town and Cape Province city councils cooperated with the provincial administration to implement the Act (Green, 1989; Nduma, 1992; Tabe, 2014). In the Transvaal, and in Johannesburg specifically, the Act was not implemented. The rejection by the Johannesburg municipality meant that, for some time, there was no control over the activities of hawkers. Without any control, the situation in the city became very disordered as hawkers operated everywhere and streets were littered with fruit and vegetable remains, plastics and boxes (Beavon and Rogerson, 1986; Rogerson, 1988; Nesvag, 2000).

Access to natural resources, especially land, was an important marker for black women of the patriarchy's prevalence. Even in the reserve or homeland areas, which were supposed to be key sites for social reproduction for black households, the state's land tenure system excluded women in large part from direct access to land (Smith, 1992). Based on a skewed customary law, assisted by Bantu Commissioners and magistrates, "it was not customary for women to manage or inherit land" (Pheko, 2014: 4). Women were often deprived of any right to security of rural tenure except through a male adult, and this sometimes compelled them to join the multitudes of cheap labourers on farms owned by whites, or in factories or as domestic workers in "white" urban areas (Smith, 1992; Pheko, 2014). Under apartheid, dispossession of citizenship through the erosion of property rights and constraints on access to particular places and spaces was enabled by denial of rights to land and housing, but this was particularly so for black women.

During apartheid, legislation was enacted which limited the movement of "African women into urban areas, the type of work available to them, where they lived and with whom they interacted" (Walker, 1982: 186). In the end, they were "obliged to perform the tasks of production and reproduction to support the male urban workforce" (Lallo, 1998: 37). Although they played a positive role in the reproduction of male labour for the apartheid regime, the challenges for black women compared to black men were particularly deep and pervasive. The apartheid social order in South Africa was clearly not only a racist social order but also a sexist one, with patriarchal discourses and traditions excluding women from certain work including within the mining industry. At times, though, women's entry into the informal economic sector involved degrading activities such as prostitution.

In summary, the lives and livelihoods of black people with informal businesses during apartheid South Africa were exposed to regular, often extreme, shocks and their daily existence was marked by major challenges and absolute hardships. But they showed significant endurance and perseverance in building and maintaining livelihoods centred on their households.

Conclusion

Significant forms of racial oppression and discrimination existed, with blacks in effect being considered as temporary sojourners in urban white South Africa; the quantity and quality of housing delivery took place accordingly. Such oppressive legislation and institutional discrimination, in conjunction with a whole slew of other discriminatory practices, led to a constant and daily struggle for social reproduction by urban blacks including in relation to livelihood activities. Housing served to reproduce the conditions of urban black poverty along with social, economic and spatial exclusion. Though in the later years of apartheid, there were attempts to reform the social order and to deracialise it, it is clear that the new post-apartheid state inherited systemic social reproduction challenges with reference to the urban black population. As was the case during apartheid South Africa in large part, the South African democratic government has failed to introduce programmes and initiatives that focus on improving the everyday lives and livelihoods of black households.

Note

1 Part of this chapter is based on the doctoral thesis of Sipho Nkambule (2016).

References

Beall, J. and Kanji, N. 1999. *Households, Livelihoods and Urban Poverty*. Conference Paper on Urban Governance Partnership and Poverty. University of Birmingham, UK.

Beavon, K.S.D. and Rogerson, C. 1986. *The Geography of South Africa: contemporary changes and new directions*. Cham: Springer

Bebbington, A. 1999. Capitals and capabilities: a framework for analysing peasant viability, rural livelihoods and poverty. *World Development*, 27(12), pp. 2021–2044.

Carney, D. 1998. *Implementing the Sustainable Rural Livelihoods Approach*. Paper presented to the DfID Natural Resource Advisors' Conference. London: Department for International Development.

Carswell, G. and Jones, S. 2004. *The Earthscan Reader in Environment Development and Rural Livelihoods*. CRC Press, Taylor & Francis Group.

Chambers, R. 1997. Responsible well-being: a personal agenda for development. *World Development*, 25(11), pp. 1743–1754.

De Smidt, M.B.P. 1988. *The Informal Sector in Theory and Practice: a case study*. Unpublished research, University of Cape Town.

Ellis, F. 2000. The determinants of rural livelihood diversification in developing countries. *Journal of Agricultural Economics*, 51(2), pp. 289–302.

Farrington, D.P. Loeber, R., Yin, Y. and Anderson, J. 2002. *Are Within-Individual Causes of Delinquency the Same as Between-Individual Causes?* Institute of Criminology, Cambridge University.

Green, C. 1989. *Patterns and Requirements of Home and Street-Based Economic Activity in Low Income Areas in Cape Town*. Technical Report DPVT 48. Cape Town: Council for Scientific and Industrial Research.

Karumbidza, B. 2011. *Criminalising the Livelihoods of the Poor: the impact of formalising informal trading on female ad migrant traders in Durban*. SERI Research Report, The Socio-Economic Rights Institute of South Africa.

Kollmair, M. and Juli, G. 2002. *The Sustainable Livelihoods Approach*. Input paper for the Integrated Training Course of NCCR North-South Aeschiried, Switzerland.

Maasdorp, G. and Pillay, N. 1983. *Informal Settlements: socio-economic profiles*. University of Natal, Economic Research Unit.

Moser, D.N. 1998. The asset vulnerability framework: reassessing urban poverty reduction strategies. *World Development*, 26(1), pp. 1–19.

Nattrass, N. 1987. *Street Trading in Transkei: a struggle against poverty, persecution and prosecution*. Carnegie Conference Paper No. 237, University of Natal.

Nduma, J.H. 1992. *Street Trading in Transkei's Major Urban Areas*. Unpublished M.A. thesis, University of the Witwatersrand, Johannesburg.

Nkambule, S. 2016. *A Critical Analysis of the Housing Provision, Livelihood Activities and Social Production in Urban Communities in South Africa: the case of Ezamokuhle, Mpumalanga*. PhD thesis, University of Rhodes.

Nesvag, S.I. 2000. Street trading from apartheid to post-apartheid: more birds in the cornfield? *International Journal of Sociology and Social Policy*, 20(3), pp. 34–63.

Pheko, L.L. 2014. *Women, Land and Livelihoods in South Africa's Land Reform Programme*. Policy Brief, Policy and Analysis Programme, Number 1, July 2014. www.ijr.org.za/portfolio-items/policy-brief-no-16-women-land-and-livelihoods-in-south-africas-land-reform-programme/

Rakodi, C. 2000. *Urban Livelihoods: a people centred approach to reducing poverty*. UK: Earthscan Publications Ltd.

Rogerson, C.M. 1988. The underdevelopment of the informal sector: street hawking in Johannesburg, South Africa. *Urban Geography*, 9(6), pp. 549–567.

Sapir, D. 1996. Health and nutrition of the urban poor: the case of the Calcutta slums. In M. Dasgupta, L. Chen and T.N. Krishnan (Eds.), *Health, Poverty and Development in India*. Delhi: Oxford University Press.

Tabe, F.E. 2014. *Street Trading in The Central Business District of Cape Town 1864 to 2012: a study of state policies*. PhD thesis, Philosophy in History in the Faculty of Arts, University of the Western Cape.

5 A demand-driven subsidised housing policy for South Africa

Judith Ojo-Aromokudu, Michael Samuel and Rubby Dhunpath

Introduction

In an attempt to deal with social and economic inequalities inherited from the apartheid era, the democratically elected South African government opted for a developmentalist, welfarist policy approach to redressing housing provision. This meant coupling the agenda of social reconstruction by providing indigent communities with housing through state subsidised investment.

The supply of housing in South Africa has been an ongoing issue since the apartheid years. With the dawn of democracy, South Africa had to confront many challenges created by the iniquitous policies inherited from the apartheid era. These included poverty, social inequalities, a dysfunctional housing market and slow economic growth. The state had an urgent need to grow the economy and to address social conditions essential for the continued relevance of the welfarist state. Housing was elevated to the sector that would simultaneously stimulate economic growth, create jobs and meet the increasing demand for housing (Department of Housing, 2004; Tissington, 2010). The role of the state in orchestrating these policy moves was ideologically sanctioned to pacify the demands of the broader electorate.

The origins of the South African subsidy system can be traced back to the 1940s when it was instituted as a mode of financial assistance to local authorities. The local municipalities acted as agents of the Central Housing Board, to deal with the challenges of the housing conditions of African people moving into "white" urban areas (Wilkinson, 1998). Wilkinson (1998) notes that prior to this period, and stemming from the 1923 Stallard principles that prohibited the right to permanent residence and freehold tenure, it was expected that the African would temporarily stay in the city for the purpose of offering services to white people, and then would return to the reserves when s/he ceased offering services. Subsequent housing policies were reported to be half-hearted initiatives by the state, in response to "plague spots" created by the substandard living conditions of Africans who stayed in the city (Wilkinson, 1998). Exacerbated by the First and Second World Wars, the slow pace of housing delivery and economic downturn placed a burden on the state and marked the start of the housing backlog. Towards the end of the apartheid era, the housing policy was supported by three main processes; the National Housing forum from 1992 to 1994, the rights commitment enshrined in the new Constitution and the economic strategy of the Reconstruction and Development Program (RDP).

The shortage of housing to meet the needs of poor people prompted the supply-driven housing policy, which sought to increase the dwindling supply of housing to deal with increasing demand. With a neoliberal point of departure, there were obvious tensions in the policy directions and the way state resources should be prioritised, whether to focus on economic liberalisation or to address basic needs. The low-income homeownership market in South Africa is dominated by the government's subsidised delivery instruments. The state views direct property ownership as a cornerstone not only to promote prestige, security and comfort but to alleviate poverty and create household wealth. The government recognises that property ownership is one of the leading wealth-building vehicles and that introducing policy and legislative reforms with deepening impact is the overarching principle of servicing the underserved markets (Moss, 2018).

The individual subsidy system is aimed at assisting those who cannot participate in the free market, as the very nature of free markets in functional economies is known to undermine the aspirations of poor people. This is because functional markets are expected to work towards a market equilibrium wherein a healthy demand is met with a corresponding supply. The South African housing market can be described as dysfunctional, as the demand side is incongruous with the supply side. While demand is unrelenting, it cannot be effectively met as households do not have the financial means to participate freely in the private housing market. On the other hand, investors who were uninterested in supplying a product in response to an unproductive demand (Rust, 2002) are encouraged to participate in this market through policy interventions to meet affordability constraints, which may be seen as advancing private capital agendas rather than contributing to redress. It can, therefore, be argued that with the current subsidy system, some benefits of housing are being lost to the suppliers of housing and could be described as advancing a disguised capitalist agenda, which benefits the rich over the poor unhoused citizenry.

This chapter reflects on the present supply-driven subsidy, presenting the intended and enacted outcomes, and then poses an alternative theoretical framing of a demand-driven housing subsidy approach. The findings of the case study are presented through the lenses of the enacted and experienced policy: the lived practices of implementing policy and the shared first-hand reflections of the intended beneficiaries of the housing subsidy project.

We argue that the current subsidy criteria paradoxically promote a revolving-door phenomenon, which incapacitates the government's social redress attempts, and simultaneously perpetuates a continued over-reliance on the welfarist developmental state – rather than alleviating poverty. Who the likely beneficiaries of this sustained dependence are is the critical question posed in this chapter. Furthermore, what unintended non-developmental consequences does this policy presently perpetuate? The authors demonstrate, using empirical data from a case study of the Slovas[1] informal settlement in the Mfolozi Municipality of KwaZulu-Natal, that the housing subsidy criteria allowed the demand for housing to increase exponentially, and how the policy objective of redressing poverty is subverted by the subsidy programme. The chapter concludes with the proposition that for the state's redress policy to serve its (original) intended outcomes, dependency on the state needs to be systematically reduced by shifting from a supply-driven subsidy to a demand-driven subsidy, so providing more leverage to poor people in addressing their housing needs.

Background

In democratic South Africa, the ruling ANC was under no illusion of the need to address social inequalities and macro-economic development in order to keep pace with global development (ANC Congress 1996, cited in Khan, 2003). Efforts were made to assist poor people who were not able to engage in the housing market. The existing housing backlog and the delivery of new housing were noted as key challenges and signalled a policy shift to the RDP that was geared towards addressing the challenge of slow economic development (Tomlinson, 2007). The iniquitous distribution of land and adequate shelter, and the expectant households waiting to be housed by the state became a driver of the government's focus to address these challenges at the micro- and macro-economic levels. At the macro-economic level, housing was (and still is) perceived as a component of macro-economic policy, which has influenced macro-economic development (Khan and Ambert, 2003).

The Department of Human Settlements (2018) reports having delivered 2.8 million government subsidised houses, benefiting an estimated 4.3 million households since 1994. This equates to R500 billion worth of disbursements for top housing units, bulk services, and social and economic amenities. While this record presents an active attempt at redress by the new government, it also indicates an alarming increase of those who are dependent on the state to provide housing. Ten years on from 1994, a policy shift in 2004 saw the introduction of the Breaking New Ground policy (henceforth BNG). The BNG highlighted the unintended outcomes of previous housing policies, which included perpetuation of "the increasing housing backlog, slowdown in delivery, poor-quality products, lack of community participation, corruption and maladministration, and the continued spread of informal settlements" (Ojo-Aromokudu, 2013: 2). However, the BNG did not directly address these shortcomings, but rather focused on the delivery of more-comprehensive human settlements, encouraging the development of a wider range of housing typologies and densities, which in turn allowed for a wider range of tenure options, housing credit and delivery routes (Mistro and Hensher, 2009). This is opposed to the RDP, which focused on the delivery of single dwellings often void of, inter alia, access to social services and infrastructure such as schools, recreational facilities and clinics. As opposed to the delivery of housing units, the supply-driven housing subsidy model embraced an expanded conception of housing, which provided more opportunities for economically inclusive settlements.

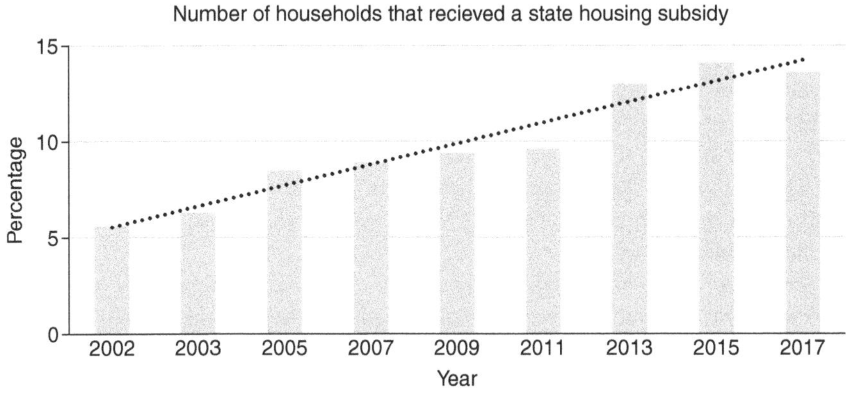

Figure 5.1 Increase in the number of households living in subsidised housing in South Africa.

Source: adapted from Statistics South Africa (2017) *General Household Survey*.

We believe that interventionist policies, particularly those with welfarist orientations, should have obsolescence as a core principle. In other words, strategy and resources should be directed at progressively eroding the need for the intervention, so that within reasonable time frames resources may be redirected to other areas of social need. In South Africa, efforts to reduce the demand for subsidised housing from the state have not been supported by a policy that renders the supply of housing "fiscally, financially and socially sustainable" (Khan and Thurman, 2001). Contrary to the spirit of the Housing Act (1997) that aims to facilitate the effective functioning of the housing market, the current policy promotes the continuing demand for state subsidised housing.

This prompts questions about the espoused policy, particularly housing subsidy criteria and its efficiency in addressing poverty and reducing the dependency of the low-income housing market on the state as the supplier of housing. For example, what accounts for the unremitting rise in demand for subsidised housing year on year, despite claims of accelerated delivery? Are policy intentions to promote redress and development too distant from the enacted policy? Can these policy ideals be realised in practice? Is the backlog for poor people indeed being addressed? Is there "a revolving door" where the increasing demand for housing subsidies persists, while the provisioning of subsidy investment is increasing to the economic benefit of the "suppliers" of housing? What explains the revolving-door syndrome? Will redress be an endemic feature of post-apartheid society? The following literature review will examine the welfarist policy and its developmental agenda in addressing housing of poor people and provides a theoretical framework for the discussions.

Welfarist policy frameworks and approaches to development

Development seeks to improve lifestyle and promises to improve the general well-being of both human beings and environment. Lang (2013) argues that development is linked to a promise of well-being, happiness and a better quality of life. The members of the Lang working group, however, believe that development inevitably ties us to a certain way of thinking – one that is Western, capitalist and colonial. This is because it seeks to get the excluded to follow a path marked out in advance by the Global North, in order to achieve their inclusion in the hegemonic way of life.

Since the early industrialisation and the subsequent technology era, four development approaches may be discerned: modernisation, global reform, dependency and underdevelopment, and self-reliance (Bragg, 1984). The modernisation approach pursues the goal of increasing production and economic growth, which is considered a strategy to improve living standards. It assumes there is a need for nation-to-nation aid and that there is a need to modernise traditional societies to achieve better productivity that eventually trickles down to benefit the neediest, thereby fostering development (Bragg, 1984). For example, foreign aid programmes in Kenya, as far back as the 1960s, activated a rural development fund supported by the Scandinavian government (Cohen, 1995) that was aimed at broader societal development by advancing better living standards and better productivity for poor people. Similar to the modernisation approach is the global reformism development approach. It stems from the modernisation theory and calls for equity, but with political and economic undertones that are noted to ignore the ecological implications of quick technological fixes and the potential perpetuation of selective development at the expense of poor people (Bragg, 1984: 155).

The dependency and underdevelopment approach has grown out of the continued and increasing disparity between rich and poor nations or disparate sectors within one society. It assumes that economic development is the most important outcome and that internal dependency is inevitable (Bragg, 1984). It therefore positions one entity as "the provider" and the other as the "recipient" of welfare assistance. This results in top-down dictates, with strong state controls, evident in the distribution of funding by the state to developers in the construction sector, under the premise of boosting the construction industry. Here, ostensibly, benefits accrue to the consumer and the developers, and these trigger broader macro-economic development. Lifestyle improvement occurs because of the abundant state expenditure. Even though the approach has welfarist intentions, the interests of poor people are secondary to the broader macro-economic benefits that accrue to the collective. This is similar to the South African post-apartheid subsidy scheme, which was targeted at poor people, but which encouraged private sector involvement. The supply-driven approach provides funding to the private sector for the supply of housing stock to qualifying low-income households. While the supply of housing stock is stimulated, low-income households depend on the private sector to deliver housing. As a result, it could be argued that, in practice, the South African subsidy scheme discourages households from improving their income levels, as this effectively disqualifies them from accessing state-assisted housing, thus entrenching dependency. While espousing autonomy, the policy as practised paradoxically fosters dependency.

Generally, these three approaches rely on external assistance and, even though they offer a welfarist agenda, the direct benefit to poor people and poverty alleviation becomes a secondary agenda. The fourth development approach provides a direct impact on poverty alleviation, in that it is targeted at poor households.

The self-help approach seeks development through the creation of self-reliance opportunities through structured policy mechanisms. According to Bragg (1984), the self-reliance approach to development is a more direct developmental approach, which does not rely on external constraints or dependency relationships. It is a bottom-up approach that is aimed at the redress of the inequitable distribution of economic and political power. The self-help policies in housing can be traced back to the Turner school of thought, which argued for pro-poor policies – suggesting that poor people had the self-knowledge needed to solve their housing problems and should be given the freedom to do so (Turner and Fitcher, 1972). Self-reliance requires a free market in which institutions encourage creativity that allows for innovative ideas that lead to growth (Schumpeter, 1912).

International evidence demonstrates that the developmental self-help approach is progressive, participatory and can be supported by the state. For example, in the Chilean context, the state shifted from supply-driven housing programmes in 1977 to a more market-based approach. It applied a demand-driven approach where households were given the subsidy and were encouraged to engage with the housing market once they demonstrated an ability to save. The pro-poor policy was aimed at improving the quality of housing by encouraging people to help themselves and invariably encourage the private sector to provide housing for low-income groups (Gilbert, 2012).

A supply-driven housing subsidy policy

Post-apartheid housing policies took on a welfarist approach, amid the need for economic development, aside from the much-needed social redress (Charlton, 2009). From a welfarist perspective, housing as a social service is made available through state subsidies to subsidise production or are made available directly to households to subsidise consumption (Malpass and Murie, 1982). This approach has been used in developing countries in Latin America which have had similar challenges to South Africa. However, this model has not deterred the sporadic growth of informal settlements and growing political protests over service delivery, as was the case in Chile, Lima (Peru), Mexico and Rio de Janeiro (Brazil) (Gilbert, 2012). This developmental, welfarist approach encourages state expenditure and boosts aggregate demand in the economy through public investment, particularly in the construction sector (Hassen, 2003). In this way, it addresses the immediate demand for housing and stimulates macro-economic growth through the construction sector. While the welfarist approach has the ingredients of a social justice agenda, it may be argued that the de facto motivation is linked to political expediency in terms of appeasing dissatisfied electorates who were promised a house in return for their votes (Ross, 2000).

In the supply-driven approach, the state makes subsidies available to the private sector through relevant state structures to deliver housing. It therefore puts the onus on the developers and the local authority who are in close contact with poor people (Sutherland *et al.*, 2016) to identify land and deliver the finished housing product to the beneficiaries respectively – often with limited input from the end-users. While the supply-driven approach places much responsibility on the state to deliver on housing promises, it provides a convenient marketing yardstick for measuring the achievement of delivery by the government in power. The delivery is usually measured as a quantum of electioneering promises and is often at the expense of quality for the low-income groups.

A demand-driven policy imperative

Unlike the supply-driven approach, the demand-driven approach fuels housing consumption by making subsidies directly available to households, in order to expedite access to housing in the free market. It accords agency and responsibility to individual households to participate in state-assisted self-help housing initiatives. This allows households to make decisions about their housing needs, as has been the case, for instance, with the Chilean experience. Here, the demand-driven subsidy was made available on a sliding scale to disadvantaged households who were evidently needy, but who could demonstrate attempts at saving for their housing requirements. The approach is lauded as being progressive and transparent, but is criticised for omitting the poorest of poor people who cannot save (Rojas and Greene, 1995), nor form part of a household. It raises the question of what constitutes a "household", as by the very definition of the term, it points to a group supposedly sharing a shelter which does not exist. The definition of household is better described as in the South African context, as a group of people sharing a common "pot", i.e. eating from a common income source. With this definition, the benefits of the subsidy trickle down to the poorest of poor people.

Whatever the approach, it is argued that the State Department plays a leading role in social spending (Tomlinson, 2007) and that it was a lead sector in economic growth and development, not only stimulating government spending, but also bringing about development outcomes like eliminating poverty, reducing inequality and redistributing resources. The housing sector also advances economic outcomes by improving the gross domestic product and creates employment opportunities. However, others have argued that underlying policy intentions remain focused on economic liberalisation dealing with political redress and legitimisation, offering leverage to private sector investment, and normalising the environment (Khan and Thurman, 2001) – much to the detriment of urban poor people (Huchzermeyer, 2003).

Policy as intention vs policy as enactment

Policy is that which happens in a particular situated context, sometimes which is not codified or not written down, but which has come to emerge as a set of rituals, habits or routines unique to a specific context … policy is that which is practised; "that which occurs" (Samuel, 2016: 5).

Policy may be contextualised as a set of practices (Samuel, 2016), with distinctions between official policy, espoused policy, enacted policy and experienced policy. Official policy is subject to interpretation by both street-level bureaucrats and the public, who experience policy and who often re-interpret policy to advance private agendas. This will be demonstrated later when examining the case of Slovas. Samuel (2016) further argues that policy, as an enabling steering tool, should be viewed in relation to contextual conditions, how it articulates with its environment and how it discharges its mandates in relation to its intended targeted audience. The enacted policy, that is "policies in practice", is frequently re-appropriated to service the constituencies, which then adapt it for their own purposes. This suggests that policy may even be implemented in contradiction to its officially declared textual claims or intentions. For example, in the British experience, the sale of council houses in Birmingham had both implicit and explicit aims. The Conservative government in 1966 adopted a policy to sell council houses to sitting tenants. While it was announced that the state owned far too many people's homes – proclaimed to be a dangerous situation – the implicit objective was to meet the wider political and economic goals of reducing state expenditure, rather than responding to housing needs (Malpass and Murie, 1982).

Others have argued that policy is not constant, but should continuously evolve to cope with existing dysfunctional situations (Malpass and Murie, 1982). The process of policy-making and implementation is not necessarily a linear one. Rather, it is a circular process entailing continuous feedback and responses to the ongoing interests and pressures, which require a complex set of interactions and contingencies with no clear start and finish points and overlaps between one transition stage and another (Malpass and Murie, 1982: 105).

There are, however, significant differences between policy formulations and government practices and intentions (Sutherland *et al.*, 2016). Policy is multi-scalar, as it is constructed and enacted at various governmental levels. However, Dhunpath and Paterson (2004) argue that while the making and implementation of policy involve multiple stakeholders, participants typically do not engage meaningfully in policy dialogue during the policy-making process. For instance, the initial public declaration in 2009 by the then Housing Minister, Tokyo Sexwale, that the housing subsidy scheme "cannot go on forever" (Engineering News Online, 2010) was met with criticism for the ANC. It can be argued this has added to the increased unrest regarding housing delivery in South Africa in recent years (*Mail and Guardian*, 2016). This well-intentioned policy position was dismissed as dereliction of statutory responsibility. Such a reception might have been averted through a concerted process of advocacy, dissemination and consensus building (Dhunpath and Paterson, 2004). In this context, failure to interrupt dependency on state hand-outs had the effect of entrenching dependence, so serving the interests of the sitting government, which had used housing as a mechanism of compensatory legitimation.[2]

Methodology

As outlined below, empirical data from a case study of the Slovas informal settlement in the Mfolozi Municipality in Northern KwaZulu-Natal demonstrate how the net effect of implementing the housing policy has caused the demand for housing to increase exponentially, while the policy objective of redressing poverty remains unaffected by the subsidy programme. This is evidenced in the Slovas settlement (selected for this study because of its position in a growing municipality) where the adequate allocation of housing using the subsidy criteria is proving to be an ongoing challenge. What then explains this recurrent challenge?

An open community meeting was convened by the Housing Manager, who briefed residents on the proposed outcomes of the research. During this meeting, preliminary questions were raised for discussion. Twenty-two residents were then randomly selected from the three settlement types. The scope of the study was limited to analysing expectations of households regarding their housing needs. Interviews were also conducted with housing practitioners in the local municipality. They were asked about the housing policy and practices, and how households are being helped to access state subsidised housing. The data were supplemented by a literature review of strategic policy objectives, alongside a review of other associated housing documents.

Case study

The case study is located in the Mfolozi Municipality, which is part of the uThungulu District Municipality, in northern KwaZulu-Natal. The Municipal Human Settlements report (Mfolozi Local Municipality, 2011) notes that 19,652 households in Mfolozi are eligible for low-cost housing subsidies. The population is projected to grow at a rate of 1.39 per cent (see Figure 5.2), and this growth rate is attributed to natural growth and migration into the area.

The Slovas settlement comprises three distinct dwelling types: RDP dwellings, transit camps and informal settlements. It has the advantage of being strategically located close to job opportunities in the agriculture sector, in which 25 per cent of the total population is employed (see Figure 5.3). It is also located close to a national road, so allowing easy access to broader district, provincial, national and international terrain. For this reason, the location of the settlement presents an attractive option for individuals from within the province and beyond.

At a strategic planning level, the low population size of the municipality was noted as a limitation to the pace of development. For instance, the municipal

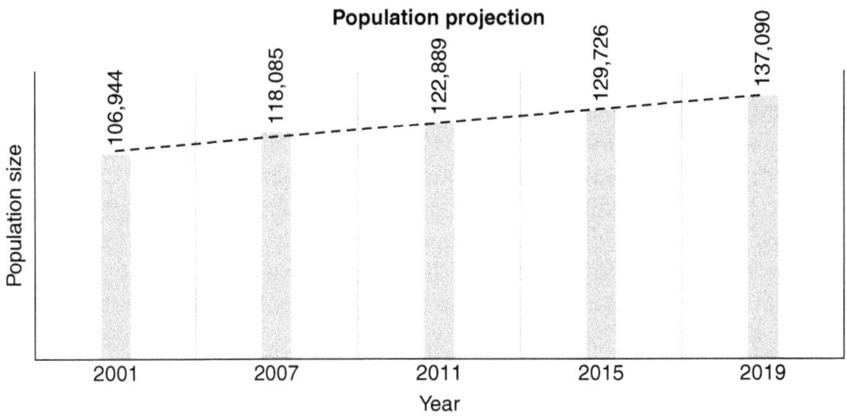

Figure 5.2 Population projection for Mfolozi Municipality.

Source: 2011 Census, adapted from Mfolozi Local Municipality Human Settlement Development Plan (Mfolozi Local Municipality, 2011).

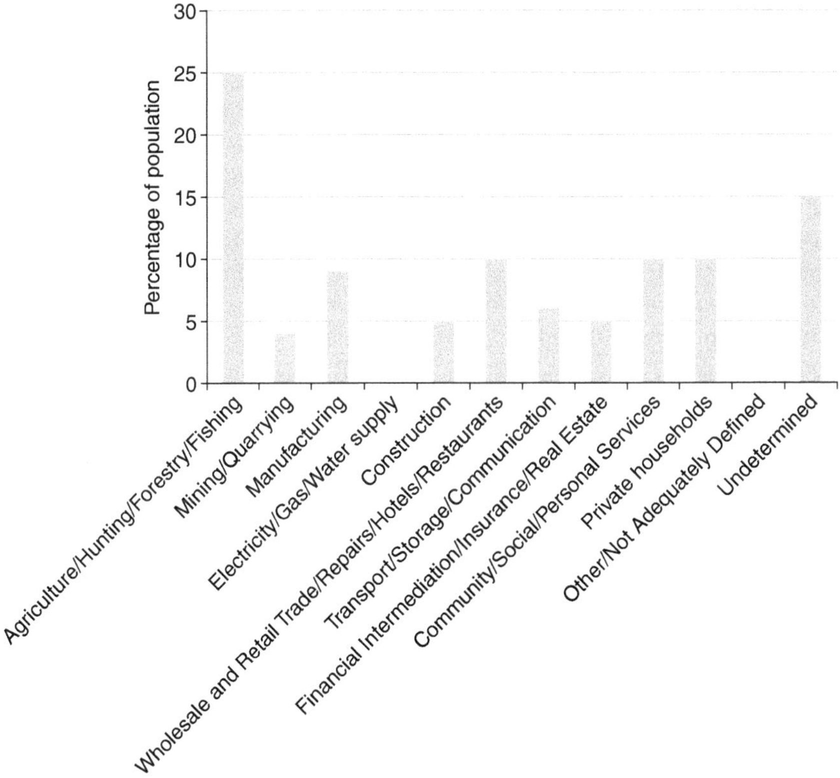

Figure 5.3 Job opportunities in Mfolozi Municipality.

Source: *Review of Spatial Development Plan* (Mfolozi Local Municipality, 2011).

manager notes that there are no large commercial activities such as shopping malls or banks. Increased housing provisioning was identified as a way to increase the population and consequently to contribute to development. In line with this objective, informal settlement dwellers were allowed to build their shacks, so giving the municipality grounds to apply for RDP housing from the national government, and thereby creating housing opportunities.

Like many other informal settlements, fire outbreak is bound to occur. A fire rendered 216 households homeless, creating an urgent need for the local municipality to respond: 167 emergency housing units were delivered and other informal dwellers were allowed to rebuild their shacks. In total, at the time of the survey, there were 507 RDP houses, 167 emergency (temporary) units and 326 households in the informal settlement.

This strategic plan created a means for accessing housing, increasing the population in the outlying municipality, thereby positioning it to attract capital investment from both the public and private sectors. However, it also created what can be termed a revolving door to state subsidised housing, whereby access through the informal settlement and transit camps was not easily shut down, as it was difficult to demolish the temporary dwellings. Measures to guard against the continuous expansion of the informal settlement were necessary, by carrying out formal enumeration and by using a security company to keep watch in case expansion took place. The situation was also compounded by the state subsidy criteria, which give the individual access to the state subsidy.

Interviews with residents from the Slovas settlement revealed the high expectations for housing – not only from those in the transit and informal settlements but also from beneficiaries of the state subsidised RDP houses. Respondents in RDP houses reported that the allocation was problematic. The reasons given flowed from expectations that adult children in RDP houses were entitled to access housing from the state. However, those in the informal dwellings and the transit camp were still waiting to receive houses. Due to the slow pace of housing delivery, there was a demand for RDP houses from three quarters, i.e. those living in the emergency shelters and the informal settlements, and also adult children of those in RDP houses. This placed unrealistic demands on the local municipality.

Enactment of the subsidy criteria in the case study

The housing subsidy criteria in South Africa appear to be targeted at poor people. However, expenditure is routed through private developers and actually aimed at a broader macro-economic agenda, which relies on the continuous demand for housing. To qualify for the subsidy, applicants needed to meet the criteria set out in the National Housing Code of 2009. First, applicants needed to be legally resident in South Africa, to be competent to contract, to not have benefited from the state previously and they should never have owned property. This selective welfarist approach, which targets the previously disadvantaged poor, creates room for political patronage where housing becomes a means of securing legitimacy for the government in power. As such, its continuous existence ensures continued loyalty to the ruling political party.

It is noted that the criteria have continuously been revised to address the injustices of the past. For instance, while intended as a one-off subsidy, the criteria allowed an individual who had benefited from living in a state subsidised house (as a child), to demand subsidised housing once they came of legal age. Furthermore, the beneficiating criterion offers room for those who may have previously benefited (by marriage but having lost out due to divorce) to "qualify for the purchase of a vacant serviced site" (National Department of Human Settlements, 2010: 15, Part B). This allows access for the individual to meet their housing needs, ostensibly through self-help efforts, but this, in fact, increases the burden on the state. The case study below further highlights these paradoxical challenges when enacting a pro-poor housing policy in practice.

Other eligibility criteria require that the applicant should be able to prove that their level of income is below the approved poverty line. Residents reported themselves as unemployed, but the data shows that the cumulative household income puts them above the poverty line. Apart from income from paid employment the data shows that households are substantially supported by various state welfare packages such as child support grant and pension funds. This approach of targeting poor households does not take into consideration other sources of income and does not encourage savings as in the Chilean experience discussed earlier. It therefore entrenches a dependency culture among low-income households. Eligibility is also extended to vulnerable groups, which include military veterans, old people and disabled people – in line with the welfarist approach. The subsidy criteria are discussed below.

Residency status

The selection criteria of the housing code target those legally resident in South Africa and include citizens and permanent residents. In practice, this is monitored by requiring the production of documented evidence of legal status in South Africa. It is expected that the applicant would occupy a state subsidised house, as the policy is based on the premise that applicants have no option other than to depend on the state's assistance. The evidence suggests that recipients sold their homes at prices below the state's cost of production. In response to these unintended outcomes, a sale restriction of eight years after state subsidy allocation was imposed to deter residents from selling their property, simply to offset the short-term needs of establishing cash flow to survive a depressed economy, and possibly lack of employment income. Others rented out their dwellings and returned to the inadequate shelters in the informal settlements. Moreover, research (Charlton, 2013) reveals that the housing delivered was not responsive to the immediate needs of access to food, job opportunities and social networks.

It emerged during the interviews that some RDP dwellings were not inhabited by the original applicants, but by close relatives, and sometimes by tenants.

Where the occupants were close relatives, the interviews revealed that they were also hopeful of accessing RDP houses by using their relative's house as a stepping stone. In this way the intended goal of supporting the welfare of poor people was, in practice, being sustained, in line with its original ideals of providing access to housing. The renting out of the houses has been met with mixed feelings by the municipality. During the interview, the municipal manager argued that residents are not expected to accept the houses and live in them. The practice displayed newer forms of entrepreneurship and survival strategies. It drove the activation of practices that subvert declared policy intentions of targeting the neediest.

Competency

Applicants are expected to be able to understand the implications of homeownership with respect to risks and responsibilities. These include, for instance, developing competence in maintaining homes, activating the opportunities in using housing as an asset to serve as collateral to access finance from formal financial institutions, or to generate additional financial resources from places of work. Residents bemoan the tendency of the state to absolve itself of the responsibility for developing competencies (beyond subsidy provisioning). Having offered a subsidised contract, the state simply uses this statistic to help it to state that it has met its target obligations in providing the right to adequate housing.

The "competency" criteria also present several loopholes, particularly in the way they are enacted in terms of age. For example, an individual who is not yet 18 years old cannot directly apply for the individual housing subsidy, but benefits from being listed as a dependent of the parent or guardian while underage. The interviewees revealed that once the child reaches legal age, s/he has a right to demand state subsidised housing, which they then actively pursue. At the Slovas RDP housing scheme, some residents indicated that they believed their children have a right to demand a house as they are competent to contract and need their own houses as they have outgrown prevailing housing arrangements. The pressing need for additional space and spatial constraints for the extension of the units (Adebayo, 2011) implies that young adults need to search for alternative housing solutions. The non-availability of self-help initiatives in the South African landscape, by default, activates a dependency on the state to provide. The current policy is silent on this expensive slippage, which allows demand to grow exponentially.

Beneficiating status

The concept of beneficiation suggests the right to receive an advantage and to profit from the acquisition of an asset. It can be argued that the benefit derived from an RDP house does not only accrue to the owner or the primary applicant, but to all who dwell within it, and even to the broader neighbourhood. For instance, in Lima, Peru (a comparator developing-world context), to benefit from state services, households are required to group themselves in community clusters as the state does not respond to individual service requests (Sutherland *et al.*, 2016). This implies that even though a neighbour is not living in the applicant's house, the neighbour benefits from being within the geographic space as part of the collective environment. This fosters collective dialogue about what common good can be achieved in attracting state responses to individual needs.

Social support systems were created particularly with sleeping arrangements for the adolescent male and female children who could no longer be allowed to sleep in the same room (see also Sutherland *et al.*, 2016). All male children slept together in one home, while females slept in another home. In this way, physical space constraints were resolved. Taking this into consideration, it can be argued that benefits accrue not only to the applicant (and spouse) by ownership but also to broader social development through integrating households and neighbourhoods. While the first-time owner criterion in the South African policy framework "attempts to guard against repeated application by those who have previously benefited" (Ojo-Aromokudu, 2013: 5), in practice this proves to be inadequate for dealing with repeat beneficiation. The practice indirectly reinforces the revolving-door syndrome – amounting to double-dipping into state resources, first as a dependent child and then as a dependent adult. The accrual of benefits seems to be directed towards individual beneficiaries, in contrast to the Lima or Chile legislation that aims to activate broader interconnected community and neighbourhood development.[3]

Financial status

South African legislation directs the housing subsidy towards those in financial need and who have limited access to the open housing market. However, the big challenge is how to establish the household financial status categorically and uncontestably – to ensure eligibility for subsidy application. The subsidy is based predominantly on the authenticated threshold income of the household, and it offers a sliding income-related subsidy (Charlton and Kihato, 2006). However, determination of poverty by an income threshold may be misleading (Zainal *et al.*, 2012). At higher income levels, salaried income is easily determined by formal bank records or salary slips. However, at lower levels, income is less easy to establish, as householders may be engaged in informal income-generating activities, for which there are no formal records. For instance, in the Slovas settlement, households report various sources of income, which include informal employment, informal trading and income from state grants. In one instance, the collective household recorded an average monthly income of over R5,000 per month, which exceeds a predetermined minimum income level of R3,500 per month in order to be eligible for a housing subsidy. Some demonstrated affluence, as evidenced in elaborate additions to the original dwellings. This therefore raises questions about what exactly constitutes the net worth of a household. Interview data suggest that the determination of household income is verified by political or traditional leaders in the community, such as the ward councillor or the "*nkosi*".[4] This requires the applicant to be known to the community leader, prior to being considered for the subsidy. This form of declaration of income, however, provides room for misappropriation of the housing policy to serve political agendas and also advances patronage. As practice suggests, the very policy criteria, which at face value appear incontestable and supportive of addressing social injustice, equity and development, may be leading to the subversion of intended goals. This is offered as one interpretation of the continued evidence of a demand-driven welfarist dependency on the state – to rescue or elevate from current circumstances. Dependence, rather than the development of the community, is therefore likely to persist.

Vulnerability

The vulnerability criteria to establish eligibility for housing subsidy allocation seek to cater to those who are perceived as susceptible to harm (Adger, 2006). The beneficiaries who are likely to access subsidised housing based on vulnerability are elaborated in the legislation to be inclusive, which further increases the demand for housing units to be supplied. For instance, it includes the military veterans if they have no financial dependants, even though veterans can access benefits through other state channels. Persons who may have received assistance are eligible for further assistance, if they become disabled, provided they still satisfy other qualification criteria. This is, however, at the discretion of the concerned Member of the Executive Committee (National Department of Human Settlements, 2010: 6, Part B).

The legislation accommodates variation to normative subsidy allocation, particularly as it relates to disabled people. It may be interpreted that the housing subsidy in this section aims to take into consideration the changing circumstances of the individual and household – thus allowing double-dipping into state resources. However, another interpretation might be that the state is conscious of the constitutional right of all citizens to be afforded specific rights, especially in the context where previous policies were exclusionary of people with disabilities. Whether the state can afford these rights for both individual households and additional subsidy in cases of changing circumstances (i.e. where a beneficiary becomes disabled) is a matter for further debate. However, the legislation brings into question the nature of a single household benefiting only once from the allocation of a housing subsidy

Synthesising the case study

Despite the policy intention of meeting adequate housing needs for all, enactors of the policy have strategically designed access to subsidised housing to be as inclusive as possible in an ever-extending and expanding spiral. This is a consequence of a policy that is constructed on a supply-driven approach, and which has the embedded intention of stimulating macro-economic benefits of the state over the socio-economic development of households. The entire edifice of the policy rationale will crumble if there is no demand for housing, that is, if households are enabled to independently meet their housing needs. In other words, the scheme focuses on the achievement of the state and enriches the developer at the expense of poor people, who are left unskilled and dependent on the state. The supply-driven approach benefits the state by first allowing for easy measurement of state efficiency and delivery by simple arithmetic and, second, at the macro level it provides uniformly "standardised" housing solutions that can be globally compared and accessed. The approach, however, places a heavy burden on the state to continually supply housing. Paradoxically, the case study reveals that rather than reduce poverty and produce self-growth and development, it generates new forms of habituated dependency on the political powers at local and national levels. Such dependency produces patronage, rather than the agency of individuals to lead their own growth trajectory out of poverty.

On the other hand, a demand-driven approach subsidises the consumption of housing. Households, as in the case of the variation of subsidy, are given access to funds to address their internal, individualised housing needs. This counteracts the claim that the housing subsidy product is a uniform and egalitarian form of provisioning as in the supply-driven approach.

There seems to be a mismatch between the enacted housing policy and its social reform objectives when considering South Africa as a developmental state. From the above discussion, policy prioritises short- and medium-term benefits of housing delivery. It can be argued that not enough thought has been given to the long-term progressive developmental and self-reliance ideals of the citizenry. The housing policy has consistently failed to directly address the recurring housing demand and consumption. The question must be asked whether the design of the policy (and its 20 years of democratic attempts to tackle redress) promotes a myth of the realisation of a developmental capacity-building economic rationality.

The findings show that policy intentions get subverted, and that policy tends to be reactive, rather than proactive. It also has created a dependency rather than a developmental culture – due to the entrenchment of the revolving-door syndrome. It is therefore highly unlikely that the housing backlog will ever be eradicated with the current supply-driven policy approach.

Concluding comments

If policy is that which is practised, it may be argued that the current South African housing policy – despite its professed welfarist agenda – contradicts its espoused intention of a sustainable approach to housing provision. This chapter has argued that in the enactment of the post-apartheid housing policy, the state has raised expectations, especially of its indigent population, thereby generating dependency rather than agency. This is an unintended consequence of the supply-driven subsidy on indigent people, residing among communities that are in transition towards development. The strategic action of the participants in this study should not be interpreted as maleficent; instead, it suggests how all policies are open to interpretation, re-interpretation and re-appropriation, which may even subvert original policy goals. Producing dependency on the state serves purposes other than development, such as courting political patronage. It remains a moot question whether the post-apartheid state will be willing to generate alternative policies that establish the values upon which the housing policy is being constructed.

A notable feature of the redress agenda is that the continued demand for subsidised housing indicates an abuse of state reforms, and/or a cultivated over-reliance on welfarist tendencies in a developmental state that is not producing adequate employment opportunities that will promote self-reliance in its citizenry. It further questions whether the policy criteria for allocation of subsidies are sufficiently refined to ensure that the agenda is directed at intended goals.

We contend that it is possible to redefine policy goals to move towards reducing dependency on the state in the supply of housing, thereby developing a more independent housing market and a more sustainable economic development path by encouraging self-help initiatives. To regulate alternative policy enactments, usually by street-level bureaucrats with dubious agendas, the power to determine who has benefited and who should benefit from housing subsidies, alongside more objective eligibility criteria, should be entrusted to multilateral agencies comprising the government, NGOs and civil society organisations. A sliding scale may provide a way of determining the level of individual benefit and the type of assistance that can be afforded in each circumstance. The determination of a poverty threshold, a mechanism for determining net worth rather than income, would also provide a means of effectively targeting the poorest of poor people.

The above pragmatic interventions to refine policy regulation, however, should not be misunderstood as resolving developmental rather than dependency relations. Revised policies may open spaces for alternative models, but constituencies with powerful agendas to selfishly pursue narrow interests are likely to be a continued feature of the housing landscape. This includes both manipulations by the providers of the policy service and the intended beneficiaries who will appropriate the policy spaces to service their own interests. As readers of the housing policy terrain, we must remain vigilant and critical of professed and hidden agendas. Without such vigilance, the current policy approach will continue to disguise capitalist agendas, which will benefit the rich suppliers of housing at the expense of the poor unhoused citizenry.

Acknowledgements

Come Write With Me organised by the University of KwaZulu-Natal Teaching and Learning Office in collaboration with the University of KwaZulu-Natal Extended Learning Office.

Disclosure statement

Funding

The financial assistance of the National Research Foundation towards finalising this chapter is hereby acknowledged. Opinions expressed and conclusions arrived at are the authors' and are not necessarily to be attributed to the National Research Foundation.

Notes

1 A pseudonym was chosen to ensure anonymity with respect to the case study.
2 Hans Weiler (1981) uses the construct of compensatory legitimation to explain the behaviour of de-legitimised governments that attempt to retrieve some legitimacy through what appear to be participatory forms of government.
3 It should be recognised, however, that the Lima legislation is not without its own challenges (Gilbert, 2012; Sutherland *et al.*, 2016).
4 Local traditional chief.

References

Adebayo, P. 2011. Post-apartheid housing policy and a somewhat altered state role: does incremental housing still have a place in South Africa? *The Built and Human Environment Review*, Volume 4.

Adger, N. 2006. Vulnerability. *Global Environmental Change*, 16(3), pp. 268–281.

Bragg, W.G. 1984. Beyond development to transformation. *International Review of Mission*, 73(290), pp. 153–165.

Charlton, S. 2009. Housing the nation, the city and household: competing rationalities as a constraint to reform?. *Development Southern Africa*, 26(2), pp. 301–315.

Charlton, S. 2013. *State Ambitions and Peoples' Practices: an expoloration of RDP housing in Johannesburg*. PhD thesis, University of Sheffield.

Charlton, S. and Kihato, C. 2006. Reaching the poor? An analysis of the influences on thr evolution of South Africa's housing programme. In: *Democracy and Delivery: urban policy in South Africa.* Pretoria: HSRC, pp. 251–282.

Cohen, J.M. 1995. *Ethnicity, Foreign Aid, and Economic Growth in Sub-Saharan Africa: the case of Kenya.* Papers 520 ed. Harvard University: Havard Institue for Development.

Department of Housing, 2004. *Breaking New Ground*. Pretoria: Department of Housing.

Department of Human Settlements, 2018. *Annual Report 2017–2018*, Pretoria: Department of Human Settlements.

Dhunpath, R. and Paterson, A. 2004. The interface between research and policy dialogue: substantive or symbolic? *Journal of Education*, Vol. 33, pp. 1–23.

Engineering News Online, 2010. *Urbanlandmark.org.za.* http://webcache.googleusercontent.com [accessed 12 August 2016].

Gilbert, A. 2012. What might South Africa have learnt about housing subsidies from Chile. *South African Geographical Journal*, 82(1), pp. 21–29.

Hassen, E.-K. 2003. When more means less: low-income housing and macroeconomic policy in South Africa. In: F. Khan and P. Thring (Eds.), *Housing Policy and Practice in Post-Apartheid South Africa.* Pretoria: Heinemann, pp. 115–160.

Huchzermeyer, M. 2003. A legacy of control? The capital subsidy for housing, and informal settlement intervention in South Africa. *International Journal of Urban and Regional Research*, 27(3), pp. 591–612.

Khan, F. 2003. Housing, poverty and the macroeconomy. In: F. Khan and P. Thring (Eds.), *Housing Policy and Practice in Post-apartheid South Africa.* Pretoria: Heinemann, pp. 77–85.

Khan, F. and Ambert, C. 2003. Preface. In: F. Khan and P. Thring (Eds.), *Housing Policy and Practice in Post-apartheid South Africa.* Sandown: Heinemann, pp. iv–xx.

Khan, F. and Thurman, S. 2001. *Setting the Stage: current housing policy and debate in South Africa.* s.l.: Isandla Institute.

Lang, M. 2013. Crisis of civiliastion and challenges for the left. In: M. Lang and D. Mokrani (Eds.), *Beyond Development: alternative visons from Latin America.* Amsterdam: Transnational Institute, pp. 5–14.

Lombard, J.J.G. 1996. *Housing Strategies and the Urban Poor in South Africa: a brief critical evaluation.* Working Paper No. 80. www.ucl.ac.uk/bartlett/development/sites/bartlett/files/migrated-files/WP80_0.pdf.

Mail and Guardian, 2016. New stats show that nine out of 11 protests a day are peaceful. Pretoria.

Malpass, P. and Murie, A. 1982. *Housing Policy and Practice.* London: The Macmillan Press Ltd.

Mfolozi Local Municipality, 2011. *Review of Spatial Development Plan*, s.l.: Mfolozi Municipality.

Mistro, R.D. and Hensher, D.A. 2009. Upgrading informal settlements in South Africa: policy, rhetoric and what residents really value. *Housing Studies*, 24(3), pp. 333–354.

Moss, V. 2018. Defaulting tenants and mortage debtors in South Africa should not be sheltered under the PIE Act1 principles. *Housing Finace International Journal*, Issue 2, pp. 57–63.

National Department of Human Settlements, 2010. *National Housing Policy and Subsidy Programmes.* Pretoria: Chief Directorate Policy Developement.

Ojo-Aromokudu, J.T. 2013. *Housing Subsidy Criteria and the Housing Backlog in South Africa.* The Southern African Housing Foundation International Conference, Exhibition and Housing Awards, 18–19 September 2013, Cape Town, South Africa. www.sahf.org.za/Images/2013%20Proceedings/Papers/OJO-AROMOKUDU,%20JUDITH.pdf.

Rojas, E. and Greene, M. 1995. Reaching the poor: lessons from the Chilean housing experience. *Environment and Urbanisation*, 7(2), pp. 31–50.

Ross, F. 2000. Beyond left and right: the new partisan politics of welfare. *Governance: An International Journal of Policy and Administration*, 13(2), pp. 155–183.

Rust, K. 2002. *Housing Policy and Programme Review. Policy Evaluation. Department of Housing, Gauteng Provincial Government.* South Africa: Human Science Research Council.

Rust, K. 2006. *Analysis of South Africa's Housing*. Johannesburg: FinMark Trust.

Samuel, M.A. 2016. Understanding policy analysis: South African policies shaping teachers as professionals. In: L. Ramrathan, L. Le Grange and P. Higgs (Eds.), *Education Studies for Initial Teacher Development.* Cape Town: Juta Publishers, pp. 3–29.

Schumpeter, J.A. 1912. *The Theory of Economic Development.* New York: Oxford University Press.

Statistics South Africa, 2017. General household survey 2017. www.statssa.gov.za/publications/P0318/P03182017.pdf

Sutherland, C., Braathen, E., Dupont, V. and Jordhus-Lier, D. 2016. Policies towards sub-standard settlements. In: V. Dupont, D. Jordhus-Lier, C. Sutherland and E. Braathen (Eds.), *The Policitcs of Slums in the Global South: Urban Informality in Brazil, India, South Africa and Peru.* New York: CRC Press, pp. 49–78.

Tissington, K. 2010. *A Review of Housing Policy and Development in South Africa since 1994*. Pretoria: Studies in Poverty and Inequality Institute (SPII).

Tomlinson, M. 2007. The development of a low-income housing finance sector in South Africa: have we finally found a way forward? *Habitat International*, Vol. 31, pp. 77–86.

Turner, J. and Fitcher, R. 1972. *Freedom to Build: dweller control of the housing process.* New York: Macmillan.

Weiler, H.N. 1981. *Compensatory Legitimisation in Educational Policy: legalization, expertise and participation in comparative perspectives.* West Germany: Institute of Research on Educational Finance and Governance.

Wilkinson, P. 1998. Housing policy in South Africa. *Habitat Intenaltional*, 22(3), pp. 215–229.

Zainal, N.R., Kaur, G., Ahmad, N. and Khalili, J.M., 2012. Housing conditions and quality of life of the urban poor in Malaysia. *Procedia Social Behaviour Sciences*, Vol. 50, pp. 827–838.

6 Assessment of stakeholders' participation in the implementation of Cornubia Housing Project in eThekwini Municipality

Ndwakhulu Tshishonga

Introduction

Current housing standards and procedures in many developing counties are inappropriate in the context of rapid urban development and decreasing resources (Schiderman and Lowe, 2002: 222). The inappropriateness of housing delivery is aggravated by its non-affordability to poor individual households. In most cases, housing standards are either imported or imposed on local conditions, culture and building traditions (Schiderman, 1992). This has made housing one of the most challenging sectors, especially housing as a "human right" (African National Congress (ANC), 1994: 23) and what Macedo (2009: 247) calls "the life of a community". In particular, the rapid growth of towns and cities especially in Africa has put tremendous pressure on housing and service provision. Residents of rapidly urbanising cities tend to move to city centres to be closer to job opportunities (Binns *et al.*, 2012: 177). Binns *et al.* (2012) argue that improving housing is not only desirable in its own right but can have a significant effect on economic and social development including the health of poor people in urban areas. Consequently, people are compelled to live in cramped and unhealthy conditions in many African cities. In this regard, poor people who are unable to afford formal houses and employment find themselves in housing projects such as the Cornubia project. To address this problem, the ANC (1994) proposed a variety of housing be provided to cater for different socio-economic groups comprising government-subsidised, private–public partnerships and housing assistance programmes. In this regard, Phillips (2015: 311) concedes that housing plays a dominant role in creating a sense of place and providing for basic needs to sustain well-being.

It is against this background that this chapter grounds the stakeholders' participation in the implementation of the Cornubia Housing Project as a national pilot of the Breaking New Ground (BNG) policy (South Africa, 2004). The chapter interrogates opportunities and challenges, regarding the holistic planning and implementation of this project.

The state of housing in South Africa and eThekwini Municipality

In the case of South Africa, housing challenges have been inherited from the apartheid era. Due to the majority disenfranchised by apartheid, Network (2011:

37) highlighted that the South African government remains under pressure to advance programmes and incentives aimed at driving the maintenance, upgrading and construction of housing infrastructure. The lack of adequate housing and basic services resulted from the absence of a coherent national housing policy (ANC, 1994: 22). Even in post-apartheid dispensation, housing delivery remains a challenge, hence the housing sector in South Africa is considered as "one of the greatest challenges facing the Government of National Unity" (Republic of South Africa, 1994). According to the White Paper on housing, "the extent of the challenge derives not only from the enormous size of the housing backlog and the desperation and impatience of the homeless, but stems also from the extremely complicated bureaucratic, administrative, financial and institutional framework" (Department of Housing, 1994) inherited from the previous government. However, despite various policies promulgated since 1994 aimed at addressing the housing backlog and improving the living conditions of all South Africans, the housing sector remains central in social actions and demonstrations (Johnson and Jacobs 2012). Making land available for housing infrastructure not only provides shelter as a constitutional right, but could also be instrumental in addressing the remaining backlog of two million housing units (World Bank Group, 2018: 80). Subsidising and providing housing microfinance could end informal settlements and further upgrade Community Residential Units (eThekwini Municipality, 2017: 9).

Section 26 of the South African Constitution (Republic of South Africa, 1996) guarantees the right of access to housing and, as a result, requires the state to take measures to fulfil this right. The Reconstruction and Development Programme (RDP) (Parliament of the Republic of South Africa, 1994) stated that although housing may be provided by a range of parties, it is the democratic government that has the ultimate responsibility for ensuring that housing is provided to all. Despite the delivery of 2.8 million subsidised housing opportunities created since 1994, the Department of Human Settlements reported that 2.3 million households remained inadequately housed in 2009 (Montiea, 2011: 16). To effect this obligation, the government has experimented with housing policies, models and programmes such as the Housing Act (Act 107 of 1997), the Breaking New Ground policy (2004–2009), the Emergency Housing Programme, the Upgrading of Informal Settlements Programme, the Social Housing Policy, the Community Residential Units Programme and the Integrated Residential Development Programme (Community Law Centre and Socio-economic Rights Institute of South Africa, 2013: 13).

The challenge facing housing in South Africa is to develop a strategy in the short term to direct scarce and insufficient state housing and other resources together with private, non-state resources, to ensure that all those in need (and particularly the poorest people in society) are housed. The housing backlog, lack or poor quality of housing, as well as informal settlements, co-exist alongside the problems of poverty, unemployment and inequalities (Johnson and Jacobs, 2012; eThekwini Municipality, 2017). It is therefore not surprising that fundamental to setting up these housing development schemes was the alleviation of poverty and the reduction of overcrowding, including addressing the housing backlog from the apartheid regime (Cross, 2006; Swartz, 2009). The failure by government to provide people with adequate housing, and community dissatisfaction with existing houses led to South Africans mobilising and protesting against their poor living conditions, lack of housing as well as corruption and irregularities in allocation of houses nationwide.

The apartheid regime left scars on human settlements in South Africa. As such, housing programmes have been criticised for their failure to contribute towards a spatial and economic transformation of cities and towns (Joseph and Karuri-Sebina, 2015: 5). Since the dawn of democracy in 1994, local governments have been positioned to play a crucial role in integrating the spatial landscape in their respective municipalities. Although housing is the mandate of the national government, municipalities are strategically positioned to provide a safe and healthy living environment where sustainable delivery of housing could be realised.

Although eThekwini has made considerable strides in redressing injustices left by apartheid planning, there are still a variety of challenges faced by the Municipality. First and foremost, gross disparities exist in the level and quality of service delivery across the Municipality. According to the eThekwini Municipality (2017: 6) *Integrated Development Plan*, eThekwini has 3.6 million people who face socio-economic, environmental and governance changes, including inadequate access to basic infrastructural services. Service delivery and good quality of housing are no longer privileges enjoyed by the minority white population but are legitimate rights of all citizens. Nonetheless, the urban areas, especially the suburbs, are the picture of wealth and prosperity; contrastingly, rural communities and townships are still battling to access adequate housing and better services with many living without proper sanitation. Another great challenge is the staggering rise of informal settlements. The mushrooming of informal settlements, squatter settlements or shantytowns in the context of South Africa is linked to land scarcity especially among black people. This situation is aggravated by the legacy of apartheid's separate development policy (Ngcukaitobi, 2018) – the Group Areas Act – and the decades of land dispossession since the arrival of Europeans. Return of the land is critical for the consolidation of democracy and the country's stability (Gibson, 2010: 31). As observed, land injustice (Atuahene, 2014) has a negative impact on housing infrastructure. According to the World Bank (2018: 80), human settlement programmes often focus on delivering housing units and have unintentionally perpetuated apartheid spatial patterns – leaving poor people on the periphery of urban areas with fewer economic opportunities.

The eThekwini Municipality (2016) asserts that urban sprawl makes it an arduous task to implement its development vision. There are approximately 3.8 million people residing in informal settlements in the municipality (eThekwini Municipality, 2016). There is a plethora of issues associated with informal settlements such as lack of access to adequate sanitation, clean and safe energy and roads. Some of the challenges, according to Johnson and Jacobs (2012: 94), include rapid population growth, slow economic growth, housing backlogs, an increasing number of informal settlements, increasing poverty, huge unemployment rates and an inadequate supply of basic services to the majority of the population. The shortage of funds available at the Municipality's disposal to implement plans is also a daunting challenge. According to eThekwini Municipality's IDP (2017), an estimated R55 billion is required to address the public housing backlog, which will still not be eradicated by 2050. Institutional arrangements need to be addressed if the municipality is to have any success in spatial transformation. Although local governments have been granted autonomy and responsibilities since the onset of democracy, municipalities still have difficulties in implementing their development vision as they still abide by national planning policy. Moreover, a lack of political coherence has been identified among government spheres as a constraint to housing delivery (Harrison *et al.*, 2003).

eThekwini Municipality has launched a number of projects in its efforts to address housing backlogs, which stood at 370,000 as at the end of December 2016 (eThekwini Municipality, 2017). First, the Social Facilities Accessibility Model has been developed, which entails designing nodes with facilities to have multiple uses. The demand for facilities is based on population numbers, income and age profiles (eThekwini Municipality, 2016). The second programme launched by the municipality is the Rental Housing Strategy to cater for low-income residents. The Rental Housing Strategy essentially pertains to creating a cooperative housing option, provided by the Municipality, which requires institutional management. Lastly, the Infrastructure Asset Management is another endeavour that eThekwini Municipality has adopted. The Asset Management initiative promotes proactive management and maintenance of infrastructure, which entails constant monitoring and addressing new issues immediately as they arise. This is opposed to reactive management, which often leads to insufficient funding.

Theorising stakeholder participation in housing delivery

Stakeholders and stakeholder management are the backbones of any successful developmental project (Burke, 2006). Stakeholders can be categorised broadly or more narrowly. Freedman (cited in Venter and Bricknell, 2012: 253) defines a stakeholder broadly as any group or individual who can affect or is affected by achievement of the organisation's objectives. Burke (2006: 44) describes "project stakeholders as people and organisations (both internal and external) who are either actively involved in the project or whose interests may be affected by the project being implemented". A more narrow approach seeks to define stakeholders based on the specific relevance they have for the organisation, and has the potential to exclude other stakeholders; hence, a hybrid approach is often preferred. This, according to Venter and Bricknell (2012: 253), includes any group who might influence and in turn be influenced by a particular project's outcome and on whom the project management ultimately depends for the success of the project.

According to Venter and Bricknell (2012: 254), stakeholder management entails the identification, analysis and development of stakeholder strategy, followed by engagement and communication. The identification of stakeholders is often done at the initial stage of the project. Fox (2007: 36) argues that getting a project started requires intelligent thinking and tough decision-making. It entails identifying various stakeholders to play a definite role in the success of the project. Once the stakeholders are identified, project managers are tasked to analyse these stakeholders in order to determine their expectations, role and strategic potential. Thus, the project managers transcend beyond merely identifying stakeholders by determining their needs and expectations such that they can be managed, influenced and balanced. In addition, Burke (2006: 44) states that for this to happen the project managers "should create an environment where the stakeholders are encouraged to contribute their skills and knowledge". According to McGregor (2012: 290), an enabling environment is grounded in building rapport, demonstrating the ability to connect with other stakeholders in order to create a climate of trust and understanding.

In the case the Cornubia project, eThekwini Municipality was the originator, while the owner was all of government but especially the Human Settlements Departments at the local, provincial and national levels. The project champion was eThekwini with Graco as the implementing engineers. Residents are both the customers and beneficiaries of the project. eThekwini Municipality has adopted an integrated human settlement approach to housing which advocates the building of housing and all the relevant housing infrastructure such as water, sanitation and electricity (eThekwini Municipality, 2016). An integrated approach to housing is human-centred and sustainable in nature, involving road and transportation routes, health, schooling and other related infrastructural developments (eThekwini Municipality, 2017). Integrated human settlements take into account the economic, social and environmental needs of residents (Monto *et al.*, 2005: 50). The notion of integrated human settlements has been defined by the BNG policy as "well-managed entities in which economic growth and social development are in balance with the carrying capacity of the natural systems on which they depend for their existence and result in sustainable development, wealth creation, poverty alleviation and equity" (Department of Housing, 2004: 1). Through the aim of integrated human settlements, humanity and dignity are restored with the central purpose being to address spatial inequalities and to provide comfort and security for all (UN-Habitat Agenda, 2004: 1)

Embedded in stakeholder management is the stakeholder model whereby different classes are identified such as latent, expectant and definitive (Venter and Bricknell, 2012: 256–257). Latent stakeholders have power and interest in the project. Expectant stakeholders are differentiated from latent ones by the higher power and interest they possess and hence they are expected to go beyond responding to the needs of their clients. The model's classification is definitive and stakeholders are given priority on the project due to their power and vested interests (ibid.).

The RDP stipulates that such provision should take account of funding and resources constraints. There are different approaches to housing, from public, private, non-profit or civic sector initiatives. Joint partnership across all sectors of housing has proved to work well in the provision of housing. One of the successful approaches used around the world is cohousing (Phillips, 2015). Cohousing is essentially collaborative housing with residences managing their neighbourhoods. Cohousing serves limited populations and represents a community development approach that attempts to meet several needs. It includes the particular process as a key to the success of the community development project.

There are characteristics of cohousing according to the CohoUsing organisation: participatory process in which the future participant is involved in the design of the community so that it meets their needs; neighbourhood design in which the physical layout and the presentation of the buildings represent the sense of the community with the intention of creating a strong sense of community; and common facilities (Phillips, 2015). CohoUsing is designed for daily use, including a common kitchen, dining area, sitting area, children's playroom and laundry, exercise room and two guestrooms except in small urban areas (Phillips, 2015). Residents manage their own cohousing communities and also perform much of the work required for maintenance of the property. They are characterised by a structure and decision-making that are non-hierarchical (Phillips, 2015). Most of the cohousing residents make consensus decisions. There are several benefits of cohousing projects such as reduced cost of living, social capital, low crime and affordability.

The delivery of housing can be through the supply-side approach or the demand-side approach (Macedo, 2009: 256). Through supply-side programmes, the government assists by building or subsidising new housing for those who meet the criteria. The demand-side provision, on the other hand, advocates that the existing housing stock is occupied by families who need shelter and receive government assistance (Phillips 2015: 317). In South Africa, the BNG policy put an emphasis on utilising housing as an instrument for the development of sustainable human settlements where more diverse housing forms, informal settlement upgrading, and accrediting municipalities for housing delivery are emphasised (National Planning Commission, 2011: 243).

A partnership approach to housing delivery

Mozolo (2016: 75) reports that "the Cornubia Integrated Human Settlement is one of the three national priority projects and is strategically situated in the Northern Corridor of eThekwini and lies adjacent to uMhlanga in the East, Mount Edgecombe in the south, Ottawa in the west and Waterloo in the north. This settlement is bordered by the N2 motorway, the M41 arterial and Ohlanga River, seven kilometres south of King Shaka International Airport" (Maharaj, in Mzolo, 2016: 75). She also points out that partnerships can founder. Unless they are genuinely based upon shared interests, with an agreed mechanism for negotiating differences, partnerships have the ability to be destructive, especially for weaker partners. In the context of Cornubia, there were three models of partnership, as outlined by Mackintosh (1992, cited in Mayo 1997: 4–5): synergy, budget enlargement and transformational. Through the synergy model, partners combine their knowledge, resources, approaches and operational cultures and as such are able to achieve more together than they would by working on their own.

At Cornubia, partner organisations such as eThekwini Municipality, Tongaat Hulett Developments (THD), and the engineers and project managers of various phases were locked in the process of exchanging models aimed at ensuring that the project was a success. The major partners/stakeholders are THD and eThekwini Municipality. The efficient management of financial resources is central towards the delivery of a huge project such as Cornubia. Above the synergy model, the budget enlargement model is pivotal in ensuring the actual plan to house homeless people takes place with adequate financial injection and management. Through collaboration, different partners can utilise additional funds that they could not access on their own (Mackintosh, 1992, in Mayo, 1997: 4).

It is the government's responsibility to deliver essential services such as houses; hence, the eThekwini Municipality and the Kwa-Zulu Natal (KZN) Department of Human Settlements pooled financial resources for housing delivery at Cornubia. Phase 1A was completed with 486 houses being built and given to deserving residents who are now charged with ensuring that their houses are maintained and basic amenities such as water and electricity are paid for. Synergy and budget enlargement culminate in the transformational partnership arrangement (Mackintosh, 1992, in Mayo, 1997). For their socio-economic survival, the residents of Cornubia have settled in their new homes and have demonstrated creativity in terms of initiative by establishing income-generating activities such as Spaza shops and taking up employment opportunities in nearby firms.

A partnerships can be considered a "modality that promotes routine interaction in given policy among governmental and non-governmental actors, and in which there is no monopoly by public actors of either problem definition or methods of implementation" (Culpepper, 2002, cited in Canzanelli, 2016: 2). The private sector partner gains a relatively stable, long-term investment opportunity. In the case of Cornubia, THD was the seller of the land for construction of low-income houses and further plans through its social corporate responsibility to initiate communal farming for residents. Revenues are in the form of either a fee for service, paid by the government, or fees collected from users, as in the case of highway tolls or waste collection. The state actor benefits from public–private partnership (PPP) because it helps to improve service delivery. It is also a cost-effectiveness strategy to increase investment in public infrastructure, reduce public risks and make better use of assets (Canzanelli, 2016: 2). The cost–benefit assessment and environmental impact assessment conducted by KPMG (2015: 8) concluded that

Cornubia represents the largest joint development initiative between eThekwini and THD, with huge potential to be a fully fledged PPP. The report estimated that "the project will yield affordable and sustainable housing and tenure options for a range of income groups with the potential to accommodate more than twenty-five thousand dwelling units and house one hundred thousand people" (Real Consulting, 2015).

As the part of the Integrated Human Settlement development strategy of eThekwini and KZN province, the multi-million-rand project is designed as a mixed-income, mixed-use development, incorporating residential, commercial, industrial and open space uses. Thaver (2016: 9) adds that the Cornubia development is regarded as a catalytic intervention undertaken jointly by the eThekwini Municipality and THD to establish the first fully integrated human settlement in the country. Cornubia operated through PPH whereby PHD sold 659 hectares of land to eThekwini municipality for the construction of low-cost housing. According to Tongaat Hulett (2014 cited in Mozolo 2016: 76), the THD "is applying a variety of industrial, commercial and market-residential uses to complement and support the lower-income housing'. This project will be implemented at different stages for 20 years (Tongaat Hulett cited in Mzolo 2016: 76). Accordingly, this would open spaces for gardens, landscaped parks, rehabilitated wetlands and the Durban Metropolitan Open Space System (DMOSS) (Tongaat Hulett cited in Mzolo 2016: 75).

Background of Cornelia housing project

The Cornubia development is perceived as an integrated human settlement and a catalytic intervention undertaken jointly by the eThekwini Municipality and THD (Mzolo, 2016). eThekwini Municipality (2016) views the PPP as an active joint working arrangement between local government and the private sector in the programmes of local government. Considering the housing challenges in post-apartheid South Africa, which are compounded by the racial and spatial planning policies, Cornubia represents a holistic spatial development with mixed-used incorporating residential, commercial and industrial sites coupled with social facilities such as schools, clinics, police stations, a post office and a shopping centre. The Cornubia Integrated Human Settlement is one of the three national priority projects strategically situated in the Northern Corridor of eThekwini and lies adjacent to uMhlanga in the east, Mount Edgecombe in the south, Ottawa in the west and Waterloo in the north (Tongaat Hulett, 2014: 1). The settlement is bordered by the N2 motorway, the M41 arterial and Ohlanga River, seven kilometres south of the King Shaka International Airport (Maharaj, in Mzolo, 2016: 75).

Tongaat Hulett (2014 cited in Mzolo 2016: 83) reports that 15,000 subsidised houses including 10,000 houses which will be sold by the eThekwini Municipality will be built on 1,200 hectares. Mzolo (2016) further reports that the housing development will be linked to social infrastructure, commercial and industrial developments. The development is aimed at affording people from lower socio-economic backgrounds to live "closer to employment opportunities by systematically aligning various financial, human, institutional and managerial resources in order to improve provision of service delivery"(Mzolo (2016: 83). According to Mzolo (2016: 83), "the implementation of Cornubia Integrated Human Development is managed through intergovernmental relations which includes all three spheres of government namely national, provincial and local". Mzolo (2016: 83) further reports that "the implementation of the programme was to ensure that key components of the programme give effect to the strategic goals of the constitutional obligations of government and its priority of making a better life for all". Mzolo (2016) notes that the first phase of the project comprising 482 housing units has been completed and allocated to beneficiaries from various informal settlements around eThekwini.

Beneficiaries occupying double-storey, semi-detached units were given freehold tenure (Tongaat Hulett, 2014: 1–2). Cornubia was developed using a holistic approach that includes all those who live in the area and its surroundings. The development includes retail, commercial, bulk industry and residential components and is thus an integrated human settlement development which aims to uplift people from low socio-economic levels through job creation, which is aligned with financial, human and managerial resources (Tongaat Hulett, 2014).

Methodology

This chapter used triangulation research techniques, comprising individual interviews, observation and document analysis (Bless *et al.*, 2017). Individual interviews were conducted with 20 recipients of houses at Cornubia. The participants were selected purposively. Different ethnic and racial groupings such as Xhosa, Zulu, Coloureds and Indians were engaged during the interview period. Another set of interviewees was purposively selected from eThekwini Municipality's officials, KZN Department of Human Settlements and project managers from THD. A set of questions was developed to facilitate the interviews of different stakeholders such as the Municipality, KZN Department of Human Settlements, THD and beneficiaries of the project.

The author and trained research assistants visited the Cornubia community three times to collect data from beneficiaries of the project. Interviews with residents were approximately 20 to 30 minutes while interviews with officials lasted between 30 and 40 minutes. The interviews, especially with residents, were conducted in IsiZulu and translation where necessary was provided to have a comprehensive picture of the role, opportunities and challenges encountered and stakeholders' participation in planning, implementation, monitoring and evaluation of the Cornubia Housing Project.

Findings and analysis

Stakeholders' participation and their roles

The Cornubia project comprised various stakeholders who played a pivotal role in grounding the project from the initial planning in 2004 to the completion of Phase 1A by 2014. eThekwini Municipality is a key and central stakeholder mandated to house its citizens who are unemployed and homeless, staying in transit camps, renting at the backyards and those earning less than R3,500 per month. The Municipality as the principal stakeholder was instrumental in purchasing the land from THD for the purposes of building houses for the needy residents of eThekwini Municipality. Although it is not the mandate of the Municipality to build houses, it is to the municipal level that citizens direct their grievances. Poor service delivery, especially houses, has triggered numerous strikes with some being violent and destructive to public infrastructure.

The roles played by various stakeholders are also the determinants of the nature of the participation at various phases of the project. The official participants grounded the Municipality's role in the project as vital not only in terms of ensuring smooth planning, implementation and monitoring but also regarding monitoring the progress and evaluation of work completed based on the planned schedule. In addition, the Municipality was charged to register relevant beneficiaries in collaboration with the local Councillors. Transportation to relocate to their new home was also provided to people from different transit camps. Through the Municipality's Human Settlements Department, the technical experts, projects managers, private sector (Tongaat Hulett) and the KZN Department of Human Settlements were brought together to envision this integrated human settlement.

eThekwini Municipality committed itself to creating a quality living environment and, through its New Integrated Housing Development, planned to build 4,700 new subsidised low-income houses in 2017, with the target of building 23,000 houses by 2021/2022 (eThekwini Municipality, 2017: 42). These houses are made possible through the subsidies provided by the KwaZulu-Natal Department of Human Settlements. The subsidy targets low-income earners, particularly first-time homeowners who meet the set criteria. In South Africa, subsidies are grouped into two, namely Human Settlements Development Grants (HSDG) and Finance Linked Individual Subsidy Programme (FLISP). In HSDG, individual housing projects are allocated subsidies especially for beneficiaries who have been identified from housing lists developed by provinces and municipalities. Under FLISP, subsidies are transferred to provinces and then to individual housing projects (Palmer *et al.*, 2017: 244). Since Cornubia is a national project, it gives eThekwini Municipality an opportunity to mobilise experts in the field of infrastructural development, more in road and housing construction. Thus, central to the functions of the Municipality is the entrenchment of inclusive and interactive governance, promoting citizen participation and housing service delivery. However, the challenge for the eThekwini Municipality is to fulfil its "utilitarian" (Amtaika, 2013: 3) mandate without creating an "entitlement culture" (Ramphele, 2008: 261) and further undermining the potential of the people to advance their own development.

eThekwini Municipality and THD played a central role from the initial planning and the execution of 486 houses as part of the pilot project. However, evidence from all the participants showed that the beneficiaries had limited participation in project phases of Cornubia. The rationale for the non-participation was due to the fact the people earmarked to access houses were identified from various communities, informal settlements and transit camps. Despite this challenge, people played a pivotal role by enlisting themselves in the Municipal Department of Human Settlements through their local leadership and designated selection committee.

Benefits and opportunities for stakeholders

Vulnerable people in the region of eThekwini Municipality are getting houses within the area. The employment opportunities for the residents are very high as it is an industrial area. The provision of identifications has made the registration of residents easier to get access to industries and other opportunities. Residents are getting opportunities to start their lives and new social networks. Cornubia emerged as one of the contested areas for infrastructural development with abundant employment opportunities. Since its inception in 2004, a variety of companies mushroomed manufacturing various products such as blinds and carpentry facilities as well as a warehouse for storage. The area contestation according to the Councillor is due to the fact that everyone wants to be in charge, wants a stake in the Cornubia development, and this is compounded by the survival of the fittest. However, the local Councillor lamented that currently these firms absorbed only 10 per cent instead of 50 per cent employment.

In the New Integrated Housing Development, eThekwini's council set the goal of building 6,400 new serviced low-income houses in 2015/16, totalling approximately 32,000 by 2016/2017 (eThekwini Municipality, 2017: 251). Considering that the Municipality's total population of approximately 3.8 million resides in informal settlements, compounded by challenges such as access to adequate sanitation, clean, and safe energy (ibid., 252), Cornubia is one of the housing programmes aimed at redressing the housing backlog in the informal settlements. Employing the partnership approach in the delivery of houses provides an opportunity structure upon which the eThekwini Municipality, in collaboration with other spheres of government and the Department of Human Settlements at the provincial and national levels, is empowered to fulfil this constitutional mandate. The success of the project depended on departments, such as KZN Agriculture, Environmental Affairs and Rural Development, providing an environmental authorisation for Phase 1 of the Cornubia mixed land use phased development (Department of Agriculture, Environmental Affairs and Rural Development, 2011: 1). Under the leadership of the eThekwini Economic Development and Investment Promotion Unit, KPMG in conjunction with Tongaat

Hulett and Cornubia Building Tomorrow conducted a cost–benefit and macro-economic impact assessment of Cornubia. KPMG was mandated to test the economic and financial feasibility of the development and its long-term contribution to the growth and prosperity of the eThekwini Municipality (KPMG, 2015: 2). The report found that the development had a large impact on job creation in eThekwini during both the construction and operational phases. In the long term, nearly 285,000 new employment opportunities will be created due to the commercial activities associated with Cornubia, representing a healthy 12 per cent of total employment in the province. This will be achieved through 39,000 direct jobs, 144,000 indirect jobs and an additional 45,000 jobs in the rest of the province, as well as 54,000 jobs resulting from the economic impact of salaries and wages paid to employees at the development.

A house, according to the *Twenty Year Review, South Africa 1994–2014* (The Presidency, 2014: 68), is an asset that offers an entry point to social, commercial and work opportunities, thus offering a sense of full citizenship. Along this line, Cornubia is strategically located, surrounded by commercial companies earmarked to afford local residents job opportunities. According to the KZN's Department of Agriculture, Environmental Affairs and Rural Development (2011:14), Cornubia involves more than R8 billion investment in roads, bridges and infrastructure where houses for over 200,000 people will be built and more than 100,000 new sustainable jobs created.

Challenges faced by stakeholders

Similar to any project or programme on such a large scale, some challenges were encountered during the project cycle especially during the implementation period. The initial planning and the actual implementation of the Cornubia Housing Project involved various partners with a common interest (i.e. to house people from the informational settlements and transit camps). Participants were asked to share the challenges faced during the planning and implementation as well as monitoring and evaluation of the project. The project manager from Tongaat Hulett highlighted the deviation from the original plan drafted in the Cornubia Framework Plan as one of the major problems. There was a six-year gap between the programme design and implementation of the housing programme. Thus, the programme was conceptualised in 2004 and the implementation only commenced in the middle of 2010. The construction of houses was completed in 2014, hence the participants interviewed had three years of experience as residents of Cornubia. The implications of this delay meant people became impatient and embarked on numerous strikes and demonstrations demanding houses and transparency in the allocation process.

Despite the deviation and commencement gap, the delay in terms of completing the programme was identified as another daunting challenge confronting the programme. The implication for this delay was dire as it entailed the eThekwini Municipality having to bear the additional costs in order to complete the project. Initially, R43 million was budgeted to complete the project. However, Tongaat

Hulett's Project Manager reviewed that, due to delays, R16 million additional costs were incurred. The re-alignment of roads was labelled as the causal factor for the delay. This implies that the total cost of Cornubia became R59 million, money which could have been utilised to construct more houses for the people.

Officials from the KZN provincial DoHS highlighted several challenges especially during the implementation phase. For instance, the land was not suitable for building houses due to poor topographic and geotechnical conditions. The land earmarked for the building was agricultural land, where sugarcane was grown by Tongaat Hulett.

According to the officials interviewed, this had financial implications resulting in the unnecessary delay in starting the project. Emanating from these technicalities, eThekwini was tasked to redesign the original housing and infrastructure plan resulting in an additional cost of R15 million as part of addressing the situation. Admittedly, the land was not suitable for the construction of houses, roads and other infrastructure. Unfortunately, the poor condition was detected late and the Municipality was blamed for the failure to test the land during the design phase.

Other challenges identified by officials related to the noise contours which resulted in changes to the design layout during the implementation phase. The setback was that the Municipality was forced to reduce the number of housing units from 486 to 482. The project was also delayed because of strike action by workers contracted to different phases of the housing construction. The study by Mzolo (2016: 83) confirmed that the industrial strike was triggered by a wage dispute between workers and their employers.

eThekwini Municipality is the major stakeholder at Cornubia Housing Project. Considering the housing backlog at eThekwini, allocation of houses to deserving beneficiaries by the housing allocation committee was a formidable challenge. Although the programme targeted vulnerable people around the eThekwini area, it attracted people from other provinces such as the Eastern Cape. Sadly, 420,000 families were in need of proper housing and the programme was only able to accommodate 482 families (*eThekwini Metro News*, 2016: 70). The allocation of the units did not commence smoothly as some of the beneficiaries did not have the required documents, such as identity documents or affidavits stating that the beneficiaries were unemployed or earning a certain salary.

Interviews with the Councillor revealed that the allocation process had some complications resulting in non-occupation of 43 units. These houses were then occupied illegally by the uMkhonto weSizwe Military Veteran Association.[1] In order to evict the veterans, a court interdict was initiated by the Municipality, who then had to take the veterans to court. There were delays in construction of important educational and health infrastructure such as schools and clinics, and community halls, which resulted in residents struggling to access such facilities.

People who qualify for access to housing would be those who have never benefited from the RDP houses in South Africa, pensioners, people with dependants (children or grandchildren to stand as beneficiaries) including those who earn less than R3,500. Those in this salary bracket are the most likely to occupy houses in Cornubia as part of the criteria outlined in the National Housing Code (Mzolo, 2016). The houses are double-storey and do not accommodate people who are physically challenged as the bedrooms are on the upper level.

In the case of Cornubia, the participation of communities was complex and limited. All the participants reported that they did not participate in the planning, implementation and monitoring, and evaluation of the project. However, the empirical data revealed that the participation of beneficiaries was limited due to their places of origin most of which were far removed from the project site. The non-participation of people is in contrast to the ANC's (1994: 23) housing principle, which emphasises that housing provision should involve and empower communities. In addition, Juta *et al.* (2014: 1121) argue that participation should contribute to the development efforts of communities by empowering community members, implementing poverty alleviation strategies and fostering partnerships between stakeholders. Draai and Taylor (2009) highlighted that communities should be engaged throughout the different stages of development projects. According to Shai (2017: 59), such engagements by communities permit "the transfer of skills, knowledge and ownership of the process to local people". Although poor people have more to gain when they acquire government subsidised houses, they often have limited participation in such projects. This is evident from the empirical data that beneficiaries of the Cornubia Housing Project where they were the weakest participants in the project.

Conclusion

The chapter has explored the role of various stakeholders in the process of planning, implementation, monitoring and evaluating the Cornubia Housing Project. Interviews with key stakeholders such as officials from the Municipality, KZN provincial government and Tongaat Hulett revealed that a partnership approach to the delivery of low-income houses at Cornubia was effective, with the Municipality taking the leading role. Despite problems encountered in rolling out this project, officials interviewed expressed satisfaction with the delivery of houses to deserving beneficiaries. Considering the housing backlog and the prevalence of informal settlements in the eThekwini region, Cornubia has been viewed by the Municipality as a success not only in terms of providing 486 houses but also in providing associated services such as water, electricity, road access, stormwater control and sanitation. Compared to the RDP prototype house, which was a narrow, simplistic one-size-fits-all public housing focus, there is a tremendous improvement in the Cornubia Housing Project. Thus, Cornubia qualifies as an integrated human settlement development with planned public transportation, health and educational infrastructures such as clinics and schools.

On the issue of stakeholder participation, eThekwini Municipality and THD took an active role in terms of the planning, implementation, monitoring and evaluation of various phases of the project. However, the chapter revealed that the participation of beneficiaries was limited because most were located far from the project site. Although poor people have more to gain through accessing houses, they also have a lot to lose. This is evident from the empirical data that beneficiaries of the Cornubia Housing Project are both the recipients and the weakest participants in the project. The challenge for local leadership, however, is to build social cohesion among beneficiaries of the project from different cultural backgrounds, and racial and ethnic orientation. It is therefore recommended that for people to access socio-economic opportunities available in Cornubia, the formation of vibrant resident structures and effective participation should be promoted. Findings of the study revealed that Cornubia has potential benefits for people especially in the provision of houses, employment, economic opportunity and social integration.

Note

1 An association formed by the military wing of the African National Congress.

References

African National Congress (ANC), 1994. *The Reconstruction and Development Programme: a policy framework.* Johannesburg: Umanyano Publications.

Amtaika, A.D. 2013. *Local Government in South Africa since 1994: leadership, democracy, development and service delivery in a post-apartheid era.* Durham: Carolina Academic Press.

Atuahene, B. 2014. Lack of communication is an injustice in land restitution. *Mail and Guardian.* https://mg.co.za/article/2014-07-18.

Binns, T., Dixon, A. and Nel, E. 2012. *Africa Diversity and Development.* London: Routledge.

Bless, C., Higson, C. and Sithole, S.L. 2017. *Fundamentals of Social Research Methods: an African perspective*, 5th edn. Claremont: Juta and Company Ltd.

Burke, R. 2006. *Project Management: planning and control techniques*, 5th edn. Canada: Burke Publishing.

Canzanelli, G. 2016. *Public Private Partnership: from the contractual to the multi-stakeholders cooperative model.* SLS LEDA Paper No. 23, www.ilsleda.org/usr_files/papers/public_private__059463.pdf, [accessed 12 June 2018].

Cross, C. 2006. Attaching urban poverty with housing: towards more effective land market. Paper presented at the Urban Land Seminar, Durban, South Africa.

Community Law Centre and Socio-economic Rights Institute of South Africa, 2013 http://www.seri-sa.org/images/Minding_the_Gap.pdf.

Department of Agriculture, Environmental Affairs and Rural Development, 2011. *Directorate: environmental services.* Pietermaritzburg: Department of Agriculture, Environmental Affairs and Rural Development.

Department of Housing, 2004. *Breaking New Ground: a comprehensive plan for the development of sustainable human settlements.* Pretoria: Government Printers.

Draai, E. and Taylor, D. 2009. Public participation for effective service delivery: a local government perspective. *Journal of Public Administration*, 44(1.1), pp. 112–122.

eThekwini Metro News, 2016. Cornubia: a model of social and economic integration, p. 7.

eThekwini Municipality, 2016. *eThekwini Municipality Integrated Development Plan, Annual Review 2016/2017.* Durban: eThekwini Municipality Corporate Policy Unit.

eThekwini Municipality, 2017. *Integrated Development Plan: 5-year plan 2017/2018–2021/2022*. Durban: eThekwini Municipality Corporate Policy Unit https://console.virtualpaper.com/asegagasini-metro/09december_26january2017/2016121301/#1/.

Fox, W. 2007. Project management life cycle. In W. Fox, and G. Waldt (Eds.), *A Guide to Project Management*. Cape Town: Juta and Co. Limited.

Gibson, J.L. 2010. Land redistribution/restitution in South Africa: a model of multiple values, as the past meets the present. *British Journal of Political Science*, 40(1), pp. 135–169.

Harrison, P.M., Huchzermeyer, M. and Mayekiso, M. 2003. *Confronting Fragmentation: housing and urban development in a democratic society*. Cape Town: UCT Press.

Johnson, K. and Jacobs, S. (Eds.), 2012. *Encyclopedia of South Africa*. Scottsville: University of KwaZulu-Natal Press.

Joseph, S.L. and Karuri-Sebina, G. 2015. *Housing to Human Settlement: evolving perspectives*. Johannesburg: South African Cities Network.

Juta, L.B., Moeti, K.B. and Matsiliza, N.S. 2014. Community participation in South Africa: an assessment of the N2 Gateway Housing Project in Langa/Joe Slovo Township. *Journal of Public Administration*, 49(4), pp. 1113–1125.

KPMG, 2015. *Cost–Benefit and Macro-economic Impact Assessment of Cornubia Report*, February 2015.

Macedo, J. 2009. Housing and community planning. In R. Phillip and R.H. Pittman (Eds.), *An Introduction to Community Development*. London: Routledge.

Mayo, M. 1997. Partnerships for regeneration and community development: some opportunities, challenges and constraints. *Critical Social Policy*, 17, pp. 3–26.

McGregor, A. 2012. Project communication. In O. Venter (Ed.), *Project Management in Perspective*. Cape Town: Oxford University Press Southern Africa.

Montiea, B. 2011. Continuing rise in urban population creates challenges for urban housing efforts' network. *Human Settlements*, Issue No. 3, pp. 14–15.

Monto, M., Ganesh, L. and Varghese, K. 2005. *Sustainability and Human Settlements: integrated human settlement synthesis*. London: Sage Publications.

Mzolo, N.P. 2016. *Evaluating the Implementation Process of the Cornubia Housing Programme Phase 1A in the eThekwini Municipality*. Master's thesis in Public Administration in the Faculty of Management Science at Stellenbosch University.

National Planning Commission, 2011. *National Development Plan (NDP), Vision for 2030*. Pretoria: The Presidency, Republic of South Africa.

Network, 2011. *Human Settlements*. Randburg: Wema Investments Pty.

Ngcukaitobi, T. 2018. *The Land Is Ours: South Africa's first black lawyers and the birth of constitutionalism*. Cape Town: Penguin Books.

Palmer, I., Moodley, N. and Parnell, S. 2017. *Building a Capable State: service delivery in post-apartheid South Africa*. Claremont: UCT Press.

Parliament of the Republic of South Africa, 1994. *White Paper on the Reconstruction and Development Programme*. www.gov.za/sites/default/files/governmentgazetteid16085.pdf.

Phillips, R. 2015. Housing and community development. In R. Phillip and R.H. Pittman (Eds.), *An Introduction to Community Development*. London: Routledge.

Ramphele, M. 2008. *Laying Ghosts to Rest: dilemmas of the transformation in South Africa*. Cape Town: Tafelberg.

Real Consulting, 2015. *Social Impact Assessment: Cornubia phase 1*. www.rhdhv.co.za/media/Cornubia%20Phase%202%20EIA/C%20-%20Specialist%20Studies/C7%20-%20Social%20Assessment/Cornubia%20Ph%202%20SIA%2017%20feb%202015%20.pdf.

Republic of South Africa, 1994. *White Paper: a new housing policy and strategy for South Africa*. Pretoria: Government Printer.

Republic of South Africa. 1996, *Constitution of South Africa* (No. 108 of 1996). Pretoria: Government Printer.

Schiderman, T. 1992. Housing standards: can they be made appropriate? *Appropriate Technology*, 19(1), pp. 5–9.

Schiderman, T. and Lowe, L. 2002. Developing appropriate housing standards and procedures. In S. Ramaya and C. Rakodi (Eds.), *Building Sustainable Urban Settlements: approaches and case studies in the developing world*. London: ITDG Publishing.

Shai, L. 2017. *Leadership and Governance in Service Delivery at The Greater Tubatse Municipality, Limpopo Province, South Africa*. MA in Public Administration. Master's thesis, University of Pretoria, Pretoria

South Africa, 2004. *Breaking New Ground: a comprehensive plan for the development of sustainable human settlements*. http://abahlali.org/files/Breaking%20new%20ground%20New_Housing_Plan_Cabinet_approved_version.pdf [accessed 21 March 2018].

Swartz, M. 2009. RDP housing: Northern KwaZulu Natal. Interview, 29 September.

Tennyson, R. and Wilde, L. 2000. *The Guiding Hand: brokering partnerships for sustainable development*. Wales: The United Nations Staff and The Prince of Wales Business Leaders Forum.

Thaver, D. 2016. Cornubia to benefit region. *The Sunday Times, Property News*, 9 October 2016, p. 9.

Tongaat Hulett, 2014. *Cornubia: celebrating 20 years of building dreams*. www.thdev.co.za/news/page/11/.

The Presidency, 2014. *Twenty-Year Review, South Africa 1994–2014*. www.thepresidency-dpme.gov.za/news/pages/20-Year-Review.aspx.

Un Habitat, 2004. *Habitat Agenda – Human Settlement Country Profile: South Africa*. www.un.org/esa/agenda21/natlinfo/countr/safrica/human_settlements.pdf [accessed, 21 June 2019].

Venter, R. and Bricknell, L. 2012. Stakeholder management. In O. Venter (Ed.), *Project Management in Perspective*. Cape Town: Oxford University Press Southern Africa.

World Bank Group, 2018. *An Incomplete Transition: overcoming the legacy of exclusion in South Africa*. Claremont: UCT Press.

7 Enhanced women's participation in state subsidised housing programmes[1]

A case of Federation of Urban Poor in iNanda, Durban

Vincent Myeni and Phumelele Khumalo

Introduction

The exclusion of women from participating in matters that affect their lives has for many years been one of the social challenges which characterise both rural and urban communities in many countries including South Africa. Women's exclusion can be seen in areas of employment opportunities, politics, societal matters, the economy and developmental programmes implemented by both private and public sectors. The challenge of women's exclusion is entangled in triple forms of oppression: the apartheid, the capitalist system, cultures and traditions (Maharaj, 2000).

In the South African context, the marginalisation of women became clear when the apartheid government during mass industrialisation refused to provide housing permits to urban women as opposed to their male counterparts. This practice marginalised women as they could not access housing because of their gender (Ndinda, 2007).

The non-involvement of women in the planning and construction of their houses has been deemed as the reason why they suffer the consequences of dysfunctional housing projects. Making things even worse was the fact that policies also restricted black women from owning land (Moser, 1987). Furthermore, traditional financial institutions had structured their housing finance systems in a manner that obstructed women from having access to bank loans (Ndinda and Uzodike, 2008). Unfortunately, these challenges resulted in women suffering quite a number of challenges in their daily lives. First, this meant that women could not have financial stability that could help them build their future and that of their children. It was for this reason that most of them opted to live under appalling housing conditions, or they lived in informal settlements (Kabajuni, 2009). Second, due to lack of their involvement, women were left disempowered and therefore did not appreciate the housing assistance which was offered by the government because they did not have a sense of ownership (Ndinda and Uzodike, 2008). Subsequently, beneficiaries sold the state subsided houses and went back to informal settlements as they had no sense of belonging or that their housing needs were not adequately addressed.

In view of the fragmentation and unsustainable housing conditions experienced by women and poor communities in general, the government formulated policies and programmes, such as the Reconstruction and Development Programme (RDP), which were meant to create a conducive environment for the participation of community members in housing projects (Vijayamohanan *et al.*, 2009). The government also aimed to encourage a sense of self-reliance in community members by way of encouraging the participation of non-government organisations (NGOs) and community-based organisations (CBOs) to facilitate the delivery of services to poor people (MacNeil, 1994). These approaches were developed to close the marginalisation gap which developed during apartheid (Williamson *et al.*, 2006).

This chapter looks at the incorporation of women's participation as a key component in developmental programmes in post-apartheid South Africa. In unpacking this aspect, the study used the following objectives: to assess the level at which women in Piesang River participated in the delivery of their houses, the method used by women to participate in the process of housing delivery and the challenges which were experienced by women and other role players as the project unfolded. The study used the delivery of housing as a yardstick to measure the objectives. Within the housing delivery landscape, the enhanced People's Housing Process (ePHP) was used as a tool which was implemented by the government to deliver housing in black communities. This was done with the purpose of empowering those who were previously marginalised. The chapter also looks at the efforts which the government, women and civil society made to improve housing conditions for women.

Study area

The study was conducted in Piesang River, which is located in iNanda Township. The site was chosen for this study because it is one of the areas where the ePHP has been used as a tool to deliver housing. Women were the main beneficiaries of the project. The area is about 23 kilometres away from the Durban central business district (Khumalo, 2013) and was named after the geographical feature, the Piesang River. The land was privately owned by a sugarcane farmer. People invaded this piece of land in the 1980s and settled on it informally. On several occasions, residents were evicted from the land but they refused removal until the area was regularised to form part of the Piesang River Development Trust for housing upgrade (Khumalo, 2013). The area was characterised by a high rate of unemployment and frequent exposure to flooding during the rainy season as some people were settled near the river and residents were too poor to build houses that were resistant to flooding events. According to the Federation of Urban Poor (FedUP) (Slums Dwellers International, 2007), the government and CBOs like FedUP started with the process of upgrading informal settlements in the area from 1995 until the late 1990s.

Research method

This study was conducted using the qualitative method of data collection. Semi-structured interviews and focus group discussions were used as instruments for data collection. Purposive sampling was used to identify four officials for semi-structured interviews. The officials included the Project Manager who represented eThekwini municipality. His contribution to the study was mainly on the nature of the relationship between the municipality and FedUP and stages which were used to implement the project. Three officials from uTshani Fund were also interviewed. First, a Partnership Administration Manager provided information on the nature of the relationship between her organisation and eThekwini municipality. Second, a Technical Consultant provided information on the extent to which FedUP members participated in the implementation of the housing project. Finally, a Technical Community Planner provided information on the facilitation and town planning support which was given to the women during the planning and construction phases of the project.

Out of 60 women who formed membership of the FedUP saving scheme, snowball sampling was used to identify 24 women who participated in the study. Two focus groups each with 12 members – women who were beneficiaries and also members of the FedUP savings club – were formed. Women were separated in order to control the discussion easily, and to compare and verify the findings in cases of disparities. The study targeted women who were 18 years and above. Interestingly, the youngest woman who participated in the study was 44 years old and the oldest was 62. The study area is settled by black people only. Women provided information on the project as a whole, from the initiation, planning, implementation to close-out phases.

Historical overview of women's access to housing (1924 to 1990s)

The historical overview of women's struggles and their participation to access housing in South Africa compels this chapter to look first at the concept of the right to the city. This is due to the fact that cities are viewed as key areas of economic growth and innovation, and often provide opportunities for human development (UN-Habitat, 2010a). It is for this reason that many people migrate from rural to urban areas in search of better economic and educational opportunities. When urbanisation happens at a massive rate, the government is more likely to experience social, economic, infrastructural, environmental and institutional challenges. Furthermore, people tend to demand citizen recognition, democratic reforms and inclusion of those who are marginalised in the benefits of modern developments (Goebel and Dodson, 2011). Therefore, the narrative of the right to the city as being supported by progressive groups and scholars, including the Habitat International Coalition advocates, among others, for equitable access to basic services like housing, the right to democratic participation, environmental justice and freedom to choose cultural and religious practices in the urban space (Marcuse, 2009).

The literature on the issue of access to the city using a gendered lens shows that African women did not have equitable access to housing in urban areas compared to their male counterparts. This has been perpetuated by a number of challenges which include the manner in which African women have been viewed in both patriarchal traditional and modern Western laws (UN-Habitat, 2010b). For a long time in South African history, African women have found it difficult to deal with barriers which prevent them leaving rural areas to participate in the economic activities in the urban areas (Goebel and Dodson, 2011). Women began to mount challenges when they were viewed as a mechanism for the reproduction of male labour, needed for mining, farming and other manufacturing industries that existed in the early days of industrialisation in South Africa.

The 1923 Urban Areas Act in particular tried to keep African women away from urban areas by demanding either signed permission from a guardian or for her to be a relative of a particular man who had worked in the city for a number of years. The housing stock (hostels, servants' quarters at whites' homes or informal squatter settlements) which was provided by the state for African workers was limited to males only (Todes and Walker, 1993). This rendered women as illegal urban residents for some decades. Things began to change in the early 1930s when there was a need for women's labour due to an increase in industrial production (Marks, 1991). As women began to join the urban market, in practical terms they entered at lower employment levels and their wages made it impossible to either own or rent formal housing in their own names. This meant that the only option available to urban women who were without male partners was informal settlements (Todes and Walker, 1993).

In Cape Town in the 1950s and 1960s, stricter controls were enforced than anywhere else in the country. According to Lee (2009), many unmarried women were chased out of the city. Women had to be married or had to be legally dependent on a legal urban man for them to qualify even for council or public housing in Cape Town (Lee, 2009). From the 1950s onwards, organisations like the African National Congress Women's League and the Federation of South African Women actively fought for women's equality and against the pass laws of apartheid South Africa (Gasa, 2007). The increasing number of women's organisations which fought for women's right to the city became even more apparent in 1956 when more than 20,000 women marched to Pretoria against the pass laws. According to the World Bank (2011), women became involved in the struggle for access to housing and the right for squatting on vacant land to form informal settlements. Some women also decided to join trade unions so that their employment could be safe. It became politically difficult for the ruling party (the National Party) to govern especially in the city. This resulted in the changes in township policy through which municipal housing was made available to women who were either wives to working men or were working in the city.

Between the 1970s and 1980s, South African youth and women were at the forefront of nationwide protests. They expressed their frustration during funerals, they wrote petitions to political leaders, took part in marches with lawyers organised for those who were arrested during protests, and shelter in a form of protection was provided for young activists (Cherry, 2007). During those years, many women saw their role being extended from domestic to a national call to liberate the country from oppression. Motherhood was seen as another tool to be used to protect their children as mothers. Women's activism gave rise to some elite women being referred to as "Mothers of the Nation". The likes of Winnie-Madikizela Mandela, Albertina Sisulu and Lilian Ngoyi were the first women to receive such an accolade (Stevenson, 2011).

In 1986, the apartheid government repealed the influx control laws and this was the beginning of the support for self-help housing. Furthermore, council houses were sold to homeowners and some to women (Todes and Walker, 1993). This led to a mass influx of people to the cities, which also led to an increase in informal settlements. Again, women found informal settlements as the most appealing form of housing because it was not difficult for them to own shacks as opposed to access to formal housing. The challenge with informal settlements was that there was an inadequate supply of basic services like electricity, water and sanitation. Furthermore, women were vulnerable to social ills like violence and crime. The social problems and lack of services compelled women to continue with the fight to have access to council housing. The fight became more prevalent in July 1990 when women who stayed in informal settlements in Soweto took to the street naked to protest against being forced to have sex with councillors whenever they needed access to formal housing in the township. This day was called "naked women's protest" (Mentjes, 2007). This day signified two important aspects of women's access to housing: first, the difficulties that women had to endure before they could have access to housing in the cities; and second, it shows the power of unity behind a common cause of women (Mentjes, 2007).

This historical overview shows the struggle that African women went through so that they could have access to housing and allied services in the city before the dawn of democratic change in 1994. The transition to a democratic government elected in 1994 introduced a constitution which sought to get rid of all the imbalances of the past including access to housing.

Theoretical framework on women's access to housing

Section 26 of the South African Constitution stipulates that "Everyone has the right to have access to adequate housing" (Republic of South Africa, 1996). It is on this basis that the study was carried out to check if women's participation was integrated into matters, like housing, that concerned their lives. The welfare approach which was introduced between the 1950s and the 1960s in developing countries was concerned with women's development. This approach focused on developing women exclusively in their reproductive roles and assumed the role of men as being productive (Moser, 1998). The purpose of the welfare approach was to empower women and bring them to development as better mothers. This was done through training programmes which were organised to train women in skills deemed necessary for mothers who were housewives and not in employment (Kabeer, 1994). This was because family welfare was placed in the hands of women. It is said that this approach was top-down in nature and its programmes promoted a culture of dependency instead of helping women to be self-sufficient (Kabeer, 1994). It is for this reason that Collins (2000) stresses that women should be able to define who they really are so that they free themselves from the danger of marginalisation. Self-definition will assist women to understand themselves, and that would boost their self-confidence before they commit to a collective effort.

The heterogeneity of women was the focus of this study because in most cases women's success depends largely on the support of other women, and therefore the study emphasises the collective effort by women in changing their lives for the better. Generally, it has been shown that individual capability in a collective action plays a very important role in making women feel confident enough to stand on their own (Connell, 2009). One of the tools which have been used by women empowerment activists to bring women together to fight for equality and their recognition is the concept of feminism. Feminists' images and statements have been used to draw attention to gender issues. The most popular forms of feminism include liberal, social, radical and postmodern feminism (Connell, 2009). This study focused on postmodern feminism as a way to understand women's participation in the planning and construction of their houses.

Postmodern feminism relates well with a gender and development (GAD) approach because it stresses the fact that, as much as women are different from men, they are also different from one another. The GAD approach emerged in the 1990s with the aim of analysing the social relations and interaction between men and women. This approach focused on the social construction of gender-specific roles, responsibilities and expectations between women and men (Rathgeber, 1999). Apart from understanding the gender roles of men and women, the GAD approach also seeks to emphasise the importance of equal powers among all role players in development, as opposed to one role player dominating over another. For the purpose of this study, the emphasis is based on the fact that given the gender imbalances of the past due to patriarchal and apartheid practices, the post-apartheid regime should recognise the positive contribution of women in the developmental agenda of this country, especially on issues like housing that directly affect them.

Another theory which informed the study is participatory planning theory. This theory emphasises the participation of all stakeholders in all stages of a project. These stages include the sharing of information from the early stages of the project, consultation with all stakeholders, collective decision-making and acting together and supporting one another during the implementation of the project (Wilcox, 1994). One of the focus areas of this theory is that power must be decentralised so that resources and opportunities can be distributed to all role players of the project, including marginalised sections of society, including women (Thomas and Bendapudi, 2004). The concept of power decentralisation is very important because it works not only as a catalyst to enhance opportunities for women but as a cornerstone for good governance which fosters citizen participation and gender equality. The participation of the beneficiaries of the project bears fruits which are beyond the physical. For instance, besides the physical structure of a house, the social, economic and environmental aspects of development cannot be ignored. The house or the entire settlement must respond to global requirements of sustainable development. The current democratic government advocates for the creation of sustainable human settlements (Department of Human Settlements, 2004). Hence the preamble to the Housing Act of 1997 acknowledges that housing as shelter fulfils a basic human need, both as a product and a process: a product of human endeavour and enterprise, a vital part of integrated planning, a key sector of the national economy that is vital to the socio-economic well-being of the nation. Referring to housing as a process simply means that during the process of developing houses, there are resources which are used such as capital, labour and land (Khumalo, 2013).

In post-apartheid South Africa, the ANC-led government had to deal with the housing backlog and lack of services to help urban poor people. This was recognised in the Housing White Paper of 1995. In order for the state to deal with the challenge, a social contract between the state, communities and community-based organisations was seen as necessary. A guiding principle of housing development is that the state must encourage the support of individuals and communities including, but not limited to, co-operatives, associations and other bodies which are community-based, in their effort to fulfil their housing needs, by giving them support that would enable the transfer of skills and therefore empower the community (Ndinda, 2009). Municipal community partnerships are positioned to improve accountability and enhance responsiveness to the needs of the people. Moreover, these partnerships assist government especially at the local level to respond actively to the challenges that arise in their communities. For instance, this could include a positive response to the strengthening of democracy, social contract by promoting accessibility, enhancing representation, strengthening accountability and improving responsiveness (Khan and Cranko, 2002).

Local governments have a responsibility to build such partnerships because they are closer to the people. It was for this reason that local governments were tasked to provide services to communities in a sustainable manner, to provide democratic and accountable governance and to encourage the involvement of communities and civil society organisations in matters of local government (Republic of South Africa, 2000). To give a stronger voice to women, a National Policy on Women and Youth in Housing was introduced in 2009. This policy came after the realisation that the participation of women in the delivery of housing in South Africa has for a long time been faced with challenges linked to both patriarchal customary and discriminatory statutory laws (Khumalo, 2013). The main aim of this policy was to give a statutory platform to women and youth in the planning and construction of their houses. Precisely, it sought to:

- Promote and facilitate the empowerment and participation of women and youth in housing delivery;

- Enhance entrepreneurial development and increase the number of firms and small business enterprises providing services and products to the housing sector; and
- Build partnerships with key stakeholders from the non-government and private sectors in implementing the women in housing programme (KZN Human Settlements, 2009).

After the introduction of this policy, the province of KwaZulu-Natal (KZN) recorded the highest number of projects where the participation of women in ePHP was prioritised. For instance, the Department of Public Works in KZN awarded about 46 per cent of construction tenders to women from 2000 to 2010 (Khumalo, 2013). The Construction Industry Development Board reported that KZN was standing at 48 per cent with the highest number of women-owned construction companies which were active and registered with the board (Khumalo, 2013). eThekwini Municipality has introduced gender-related workshops and gender forums using the guidelines of the Gender Policy Framework for Local Government, which was developed in 2007. These initiatives were introduced to enhance women's participation in planning and development processes. Although the government has tried to institutionalise gender equality, it should be noted that such forums cover a fraction of women in urban areas, while the majority of women in the peripheries and rural areas are not covered (Todes *et al.*, 2010).

Tissington (2010) argues that, given the challenges posed by the growing population and the shrinking of financial resources, the focus should be to encourage people to play an active role in providing shelter for themselves, rather than leaving everything in the hands of the state. This could be achieved by instilling the culture of ePHP. According to the Housing Strategy of 1997, the government aimed to encourage and support initiatives emerging from local communities which are aimed at equipping and empowering people to drive their own economic empowerment initiatives with the purpose to develop their physical environment and the satisfaction of their basic needs (Department of Housing, 1995). This would go beyond the provision of financial resources to the creation of appropriate institutional frameworks and support structures.

The People's Housing Process (PHP) in eThekwini has been able to build more than 1,000 houses between 2002 and 2004 while it failed to deliver any house in 2005 and 2006 (Tissington, 2011). This failure prompted a need for change in the manner in which things were done previously. Hence, an upgrade to ePHP became necessary. The ePHP was adopted in July 2008. This policy replaced the previous People's Housing Programme. The ePHP broadened the definition of PHP as it allows for more flexibility and choice of the product while also retaining the central principle of people-centred development. The policy was adopted after long negotiations and discussions dating back from 2004 between the national Department of Human Settlements and a handful of NGOs such as Development Action Group, the Built Environment Support Group, Afesis-Corplan, uTshani Fund and FedUP (Himlin, 2008).

The ePHP maintained the principles of people-centred development by empowering beneficiaries, creating partnerships, mobilising and retaining social capital, directly involving women and youth in the decision-making process and encouraging housing that is responsive to social needs and community priorities (Tissington, 2011). The ePHP has been seen as an inclusionary process even for poor people through which they are able to contribute through sweat equity to replace their financial contribution.

The government used this programme to provide training and guidance to households so that they could develop skills to build their own houses. This process was adopted as a housing support programme which aimed at encouraging households to actively participate in the process within their affordability range. The participation of women was seen as another strategy which could be used towards the government's goal to eradicate informal settlements (Ndinda, 2004). Women must be seen as agents of change. They may not have a strong financial capacity as compared to their male counterparts, but their positive contribution in building the country by providing lasting solutions and indigenous knowledge should not be underestimated (Myeni, 2005). It is important that women are understood as both individuals and a collective.

Results on the level of participation and its impact on women

Based on the qualitative research method which was used to collect data, the study was able to obtain information on various aspects of the ePHP and the participation of women in the projects. The study found that women participated from the early stages to the end of the project. They were all interested in learning new skills, as they always asked questions about the project. Their participation enabled them to learn skills like problem-solving, ethical research, financial management, innovative thinking and conducting productive meetings. They were trained by the uTshani Fund (an NGO) right from the beginning of the project. Field workers were trained on how to do enumeration before they could go out to collect data using questionnaires. According to women and the training providers (NGOs), the main purpose for training women was to sustain FedUP as an organisation that represents the interest of poor people in urban areas.

The Piesang River is one of the housing projects that is a community-driven development. It is, therefore, a good platform for the state to play a facilitation role especially given the shortage of financial resources from the government to provide housing for everyone. This necessitates that the state should support community-based development initiatives (Macedo, 2009). This is because housing is one of the most important elements that human beings need for self-actualisation. It forms part of the basic needs that the human species requires for its sustainability. It is discouraging to note that ePHP has, as another form of housing delivery, been disregarded despite playing an important role in creating sustainable human settlements. It has the power to instil a sense of belonging, ownership, pride and self-reliance. It also encourages different and influential partners to come together and deliberate on matters that take the community forward. Women's empowerment is an essential part of nation-building because it essentially addresses the socio-economic challenges which affect communities at large (Ndinda, 2004).

From a focus group point of view, women were asked to provide historical information on the project area and how the community of Piesang River came about. This discussion included the community housing conditions prior to and post the upgrading project. Women informants indicated that they were motivated by a collective vision to have better houses than the shacks they stayed in. Households sizes and the number of shacks that needed to be upgraded formed part of the discussion. What set this project apart from other state-funded projects was that the savings of the women enabled the project to build bigger houses compared to those that were delivered using pure state housing subsidy.

The facilitation support which was offered by the uTshani Fund empowered women in a number of ways. For instance, the participation of women who were members of FedUP was guided by the technical facilitator. Women received support with regards to the design of their houses, the position the houses were going to take and the local layout plan. The facilitator also guided the interaction of women and external stakeholders about the project. This support boosted the confidence in women. They were able to take pride in what they could achieve through their contribution. The most important lesson from the ePHP is that it promotes the participation of beneficiaries throughout all phases of the project. According to Macedo (2009), the success of the ePHP housing delivery methods lies in the recognition of the importance of the strength of community organisations and local government.

The method used by women to participate in the process of housing delivery

On the issue of the method employed by women to participate in the project, women indicated that they formed a savings club where all members were expected to contribute some money towards the upgrading of their houses. Women used to meet weekly and monthly to collect money from members. The savings scheme worked more or less the same as stokvel.[2] Records of every saving would be kept by each beneficiary and they would get the same amount that they put in. To keep all women together, weekly meetings were held every Sunday afternoon. The purpose of the meeting was to keep all members of the saving group focused on one goal – housing upgrade – and to give moral support to one another as women. The challenge which threatened the existence of the group is that those women who have had their houses built lacked the interest to sustain their membership in the group. They hardly attended meetings, and if they chose to come, they would come late as opposed to those who were yet to benefit from the club. The non-participation or late arrival of those who had benefited was counter-productive because the group could not take important decisions due to the fact that they could not constitute a quorum, and when they took decisions, they would be challenged by those who did not come.

During the actual construction of their houses, women participated in various roles including mixing the concrete and or laying foundations. In terms of professional capacity, they also made use of professionals from uTshani Fund and other experienced professionals from within the community. Those who were physically unable and absent from meetings sent people to represent them during the construction phase of the project. Women indicated that their participation assisted them to gain knowledge and expertise which they could use in their daily life situations.

The ePHP as a state-assisted self-help housing programme sought to provide support to people so that they could organise the construction of their own houses (Khan, 2002). The advantage of this approach is that it clarifies the roles and responsibilities for both government and community. Usually, the government is expected to facilitate the provision of land and housing-related infrastructure. On the other hand, households need to contribute towards the construction of the top structure (Khan, 2002). The advantage about the ePHP is that it supports various funding mechanisms, namely, community contributions (savings club), capital funding (state housing subsidy), capacity-building funding (provided by NGOs for consumer education and capacity building through skills transfer), equity funding and bridging finance (provided by municipality in a form of grants for land packaging and social amenities) (Losier, 2009).

The challenges experienced by women and other role players in the ePHP

The implementation of the project brought challenges experienced by women involved in upgrading their houses. The first challenge was access to and ownership of land. The challenge with land is that it is expensive and the savings could not afford the land. According to the Project Manager hired by eThekwini to implement the project, the Piesang River housing project had a variety of problems. Beneficiaries of the housing project have not yet been issued their title deeds because land ownership has not been resolved. In addition to land ownership, issues of layout and a town planning scheme were not considered because there was a lot of political influence in the project. Politicians focused on building houses for the people and proper procedures were not followed. These problems have delayed the project close-out phase because of the critical nature of outstanding problems that remained unsolved (Khumalo, 2013). The other challenge was the fact that women complained that they unknowingly built on land which had municipality infrastructure on it. The infrastructure (including water pipes and electric cables) poses danger to them and especially children (Khumalo, 2013).

The sustainability of the savings club depended on recruiting more women who had a dream to upgrade their shacks one day. This was one of the challenges which the savings club had to deal with. Once the newly recruited members heard that they had to contribute some money, they pulled back because they did not trust one another. However, after some time, when the FedUP women began to build houses, other women started to join the group. The dream behind the club was to encourage poor communities to own resources and knowledge which underpins the organisation's approach to the delivery of basic services and deepening of democracy (Khumalo, 2013). In trying to mitigate the negative impact of trust and high drop-out rates, women in the group decided to start a local and regional information exchange programme. This programme allowed members of FedUP from different communities to visit other communities to witness activities and progress which had been accomplished by other communities. At the municipal level, officials from other municipalities would be called to come and witness the work of the achievement of the host municipality in cooperation with FedUP (Khumalo, 2013).

The relationship between FedUP and the local councillor took another turn especially when FedUP members built a $50\,m^2$ house as opposed to the municipality which built $40\,m^2$ houses. People started to question the variation especially those who were not a member of the group. The local councillor had to explain the reason why the houses looked different (Khumalo, 2013).

Conclusion

In conclusion, women's access to housing has been marred by a number of challenges which have been linked to patriarchal, traditional statutory laws which have treated housing needs for women differently from those of their male counterparts (Todes and Walker, 1993). In response to the patriarchal statutory laws of the apartheid regime, with the purpose of keeping women away from the city, women organised themselves and fought against the apartheid government so that they could have access to housing. Women's movements intensified in the post-apartheid era leading to mass rural to urban migration by women in search of employment opportunities. The majority of these women could not afford formal housing and the only option available to them was informal settlements. The post-apartheid era saw the introduction of a new housing delivery strategy, leading to the construction of many houses through the RDP. The ePHP allowed the participation of women in the delivery of housing projects unlike other housing programmes that have been implemented in the country. Irrespective of the challenges experienced by women in Piesang River (iNanda), their partnership with government and NGOs assisted them to achieve their dream of improving their housing conditions. Based on the outcome of the project, the local government should develop a strategic move that seeks to support community-based initiatives and be clear on how people should participate in decision-making processes. Effective mechanisms must be put in place so that the participation of all relevant stakeholders in planning settlement formation is ensured. The process must be democratic and inclusive in building of community and human capital. Again, the use of built environment professionals to conduct a feasibility study should be a prerequisite. This would avoid cases where people build over municipal infrastructures such as water and sanitation pipes and power lines, endangering the lives of those that live in such structures.

Notes

1 Part of this chapter is based on the Master's thesis of Phumelele Khumalo (2013).
2 From a South African point of view, a stokvel is a savings or investment society to which members regularly contribute an agreed amount and from which they receive a lump sum payment.

References

Bank, L.J. 2011. *Home Space, Street Styles. Contesting Power and Identity in a South African City*. New York: Wits University Press.

Cherry, J. 2007. We were not afraid: the role of women in 1980s Township uprising in the Eastern Cape. In Gasa, N (ed). *Women in South African History.* Cape Town: Human Sciences Research Council.

Collins, P.H. 2000. *Black Feminist Thought: knowledge, consciousness & the politics of empowerment*, 2nd edn. New York: Routledge.

Connell, R. 2009. *Short/introductions: gender*. Cambridge: UK Policy Press Publishers.

Department of Housing, 1995. *The Housing White Paper.* Republic of South Africa.

Gasa, N. (Ed.), 2007. *Women in South African History: they removed boulders and crossed Rivers*. Pretoria: Human Sciences Research Council Press.

Goebel, A. and Dodson, B. 2011. Housing and marginality for female-headed households: observations from Msunduzi Municipality Pietermaritzburg, South Africa. *Canadian Journal of African Studies*, 45(2), pp. 240–272.

Himlin, B. 2008. *People's Housing Process, Enhanced.* South Africa: Planact, SANGOnet.

Kabajuni, A. 2009. *Urbanization and Gender: attention to gender equality in efforts to improve the lives of slums dwellers.* Centre on Housing Rights and Evictions, United Nations Division for the Advancement of Women, EGM/BPFA-MDG/2009/E.P8.

Kabeer, N. 1994. *Reversed Realities: gender hierarchies in development thought.* London: Verso.

Khan, F. and Cranko P. 2002. Municipal-community partnerships. In S. Parnell *et al.* (Eds.), *Democratizing Local Government: the South African experiment.* Landsdowne: University of Cape Town Press.

Khumalo, P. 2013. *Assessing Women's Participation in the Planning and Construction of Their Houses: a case study of the Piesang River People's Housing Project.* Master's thesis, University of KwaZulu-Natal, Durban, South Africa.

KZN Human Settlements, 2009. *Research Report on The Involvement of Women and Youth in Housing.* Pietermaritzburg: KZN Human Settlements. www.kzndhs.gov.za/Uploads/documents/Resource_Centre/Reports/Research%20Report%20Women%20and%20Youth%20Involvement.pdf.

Lee, R. 2009. *African Women and Apartheid: migration and settlement in urban South Africa.* London and New York: Tauris Academic and Palgrave Macmillan.

Losier, T. 2009. *The Struggle for Land and Housing in Post-Apartheid South Africa.* The San Francisco Bay Area. Independent Media Centre.

Macedo, J. 2009. Housing and community planning. In R. Phillips and R. Pittman (Eds.), *Introduction to Community Development.* New York: Routledge.

MacNeil, T. 1994. Government as partners in community economic development. In B. Galaway and J. Hudson (Eds), *Community Economic Development: perspectives on research and policy*. Toronto: Thompson Educational Publishing Inc.

Maharaj, A. 2000. *The Role and Participation of Women in the Integrated Development Planning Process with Special Reference to the North Location Council Area in KwaZulu Natal*. Unpublished Master's thesis in Town and Regional Planning, University of KwaZulu-Natal, Durban, South Africa.

Marcus, P. 2009. Postscript: beyond the just city to the right to the city. In Marcus, P., Connolly, J., Novy, J., Olivo, I., Potter, C., Steil, J. (eds) 2009. *Searching for the Just City: debates in urban theory and practice*. London and New York: Routledge.

Marks, S. 1991. Patriotism, patriarchy and purity: Natal and the politics of Zulu ethnic consciousness. In V. Leroy (Ed.), *The Creation of Tribalism in Southern Africa*. Berkeley and Los Angeles: University of California.

Mentjes, J. 2007. Naked women's protest, July 1990: "we won't fuck for houses". In N. Gasa (Ed.), *Women in South African History*. Cape Town, South Africa: HSRC Press, pp. 347–367.

Moser, C.O.N. 1987. Women, human settlements and housing: a conceptual framework for analysis and policy making. In C.O.N. Moser and L. Peake (Eds.), *Women, Human Settlements and Housing*. London: Tavistock.

Moser, D.N. 1998. The asset vulnerability framework: reassessing urban poverty reduction strategies. *World Development*, 26(1), pp. 1–19.

Myeni, V. 2005. *Assessing Local Job Creation and Employment Sustainability Within Greenfields Housing Projects*. Unpublished Master's thesis, University of KwaZulu Natal, Durban.

Ndinda, C. 2004. The notion of "sweat equity" has been promoted as an integral part of subsidised housing in South African Housing policy. It's tougher for females, though. *Africa Insight*, 34(2/3), pp. 58–64.

Ndinda, C. 2007. *Women Participation in Housing Delivery: the case of eZilwelweni, South Africa, Journal of Development Southern Africa*, 2007, Vol 24 Issue 5.

Ndinda, C. 2009. But now I dream about my house: women's empowerment and housing delivery in urban KwaZulu Natal, South Africa. *Development Southern Africa*, 26(2), No. 2, pp. 317–333.

Ndinda, C. and Uzodike, U.O. 2008. Accessing housing finance in south Africa: the role of women activism. *Wagadu*, 6, Special Issue: Women's Activism for Gender Equality in Africa.

Rathgeber, E.M. 1999. WID, WAD, GAD: trends in research and practice. *The Journal of the Developing Area*, 24(4), College of Business Tennessee State University.

Republic of South Africa, 1996. *The Constitution of the Republic of South Africa*. Juta's Pocket Statutes.

Republic of South Africa, 2000. *Local Government: Municipal Systems Act (32 of 2000)*. www.gov.za/sites/default/files/gcis_document/201409/a32-000.pdf

Slums Dwellers International. 2007. FeDUP. https://www.sasdialliance.org.za/about/fedup

Stevenson, J. 2011. The mamas were ripe: ideologies of motherhood and public resistance in a South African township. *Feminist Formations*, 23(2), pp. 132–163.

Thomas, K. and Bendapudi, R. 2004. *Participatory Planning, Center for Good Governance*. ww1.sasanet.org/documents/tools.

Tissington, K. 2011. *A Resource Guide to Housing in South Africa 1994–2010: legislation, policy, programmes and practice*. Socio-Economic Rights Institute of South Africa.

Todes, A. and Walker, N. 1993. Women and housing policy in South Africa: a discussion on Durban case studies. In *Shelter, Women and Development: first and third world perspectives. Proceedings of an International Conference*. College of Architecture and Urban Planning, The University of Michigan, 7–9 May 1992.

Todes, A., Sithole, P. and Williamson, A. 2010. Including women: (dis)junctures between voice, policy and implementation in integrated development planning. *Urban Forum*. Vol 21, (1) pp 69–84.

UN-Habitat, 2010a. *The State of the World's Cities 2010/11: bridging the urban divide*. London: Earthscan.

UN-Habitat, 2010b. *The State of African Cities: governance, inequalities and urban land markets*. Nairobi: UN-Habitat

Vijayamohanan, P.N., Asalatha, B.P. and Ponnuswamy, B. 2009. *Women in Development: dissecting the discourse.* Prasanth Nagar, Ulloor: Centre for Development Studies.

Wilcox, D. 1994. *The Guide to Effective Participation*, funded by Joseph Rowntree Foundation, UK.

Williamson, A., Sithole, P. and Todes, A. 2006. Decentralizing voice: women participation in integrated development planning process in KwaZulu Natal, South Africa. Paper presented at Conference on the Place of Participation in a Democratizing South Africa, IFAS, HSRC and CUBES, Wits.

World Bank, 2011. *Gender, Equality and Development.* World Development Report, Washington DC.

8 Citizenship, gender and the technologies of governance

An interrogation of the low-income housing programme in KwaZulu-Natal

Sithembiso Lindelihle Myeni and Tafadzwa Chibvongodze

Introduction

The post-apartheid South African state has always been characterised as a "developmental" one, where the government led by the African National Congress (ANC) has made deliberate efforts to strengthen state–citizen relations by facilitating citizens' access to crucial social goods and services such as housing. The provision of affordable housing to some marginalised women, for instance, has certainly advanced their socio-economic status and promoted women's participation in the local economy. This chapter argues that while housing delivery in South Africa has been utilised by the state in the (re)production of socio-democratic citizenship, it has also been instrumental in shaping the "politics of governing from a distance".

We show that the Jozini rural housing subsidy has played an important role defining certain labels that give the state impetus to intervene and govern the private lives of its citizens. We further argue that the provision of housing to South African citizens goes beyond achieving socio-democratic principles but serves to problematise poverty and seeks ways to intervene in the everyday life of those characterised as "poor".

This chapter is divided into three sections. The first section explores the notion of the "developmental state" within the South African context. Special attention is given to the democratisation of South African society and the strengthening of constitutional rights not only through electoral participation but also by improving access to public and social goods such as electricity, water and particularly housing. We consider the Reconstruction and Development Programme (RDP) and National Development Plan by the ANC government as some of the roadmaps to the "developmental state" project and roadmaps to the democratisation of South Africa. The second section analyses how the democratisation process in South Africa is shaped around service delivery. We choose housing delivery as a prism to critically explore the crafting of the socio-democratic citizenry. We argue that while housing delivery in South Africa has been utilised by the state in the (re)production of socio-democratic citizenship, it has also been instrumental in shaping the politics of democratic participation. We use Foucault's "discourse of power" and Lefebvre's theory of "production of space" to demonstrate how the construction of "gender", "citizenship" and the governance of the so-called "poor" in the new democratic dispensation has intersected with the actual production of rural housing low-income houses. In the last section, we support our assertions by relying on empirical evidence from qualitative data collected from government officials, members of traditional leadership institutions and beneficiaries of a low-income rural housing programme in KwaZulu-Natal province, the Jozini rural housing subsidy.

The South African developmental state

The idea of a developmental state in contemporary political and economic discourse was first explicitly introduced by "Chalmers Johnson in 1982 in his seminal book *MITI and the Japanese Miracle: The Growth of Industry Policy 1925–1975*" (Burger, 2014). The concept of a developmental state was associated with the spectacular rise of the Japanese state economy during the tension between the world views of the USA and USSR. Kuye and Ajam (2012: 52) argue that "the developmental state has always been associated with industrialised countries of East Asia (such as Singapore, Malaysia and Hong Kong) as well as Scandinavian corporatist models such as Norway". Accordingly, the developmental state is a state that emphasises "the role of the state either in directly intervening to stimulate economic growth or through creating conditions that influence the nature and direction of growth" (Kuye and Ayam, 2012: 52). This means the government plays a large, active and significant role in the economy in support of selected, mostly private sector industries. Government intervention in the developmental state is directed towards control over the financial sector and effective state-owned enterprise (Chang, 2011). Van Dijk and Croucamp (2007: 665) define a developmental state as "a state where politics have assured that power, autonomy and capacity are centralised in order to achieve explicit developmental goals".

International and local scholars have identified major components and characteristics that define the developmental state. Leftwitch (1995: 405–419) crafted a stylised model of the developmental state to be based on six components: (1) "a determined developmental elite, a bureaucracy with authoritative and pivotal influence in developing policy, often at the expense of both political and legislative elites"; (2) "relative autonomy of the developmental state from class, regional or sectoral interests, within a dense web of ties to non-state and other state actors (internally and externally)"; (3) "a powerful, competent and insulated economic bureaucracy"; (4) "a weak and subordinated civil society; (5) the effective management of non-state economic interests, with state power and autonomy consolidated before national or foreign capital becomes influential"; and (6) "repression of civil rights, legitimacy and performance". This means that it is possible for a developmental state to be successful even in an authoritarian and democratic state (Van Dijk and Croucamp, 2007; Chang, 2011).

According to Koma (2010: 112–113), a developmental state has the following characteristics, which can be applied to South Africa:

> (1) It excels in public administration and intervenes in the economy to promote social development. The local sphere of government constitutes an integral part of public administration that also ought to excel in regard to the provision of public services. (2) A strong state capacity is critically important as a distinguishing feature of a developmental state. It is achieved through the creation of an inexpensive, efficient and effective public service, staffed by the nation's brightest and best officials functioning without constraints, and capable of being innovative in addressing the social and economic needs of the citizens. (3) It is concerned with integrating the dual economy by addressing the socio-economic needs of the entire population, especially poor people, marginalised people and those who are historically disadvantaged; and is a well-managed and democratic state, that builds its legitimacy on its capacity to simultaneously foster productive economic activities and economic growth, qualitatively improving the living conditions of its people and reducing poverty.

Maserumule (2007: 214) pointed out that for a developmental state to realise its social imperatives, a strong public service system is needed to enhance government capacity to effectively implement the development programmes and agendas of government. According to him, the only way to develop a strong public service system is through the establishment of an appropriate intellectual capital, which is about the quality and relevance of knowledge to its people. He concluded that in a developmental state public servants

> are the servants of the people and the champions of the poor and the downtrodden; their sense of service delivery is always focused on eradicating poverty and social deprivation and they look at their careers in the public service as a calling and not as an opportunity to accumulate wealth or self-serving elitism.
>
> (Maserumule, 2007)

This emphasises that one of the fundamental imperatives of a developmental state is that of establishing and maintaining state capacity. Overall, the social imperatives in a developmental state are about enhancing the quality of life of the citizenry through the provision of social services.

Those who have toyed with the idea of a developmental state suggest that a nation intending to foster sustainable development should adopt participatory democracy principles in every development process they intend to implement. In the context of South Africa's ambitions to attain the status of developmental state, the adoption of policies such as the RDP and the Integrated Development Programme post-1994 signalled the embracing of participatory governance and institutionalisation of a bottom-up approach to development. As enshrined in the

ANC's freedom charter and later in the constitution of South Africa, the notion of participatory governance centres on the democratic government relinquishing some of its administrative powers to ordinary citizens through structures of the local government. However, in this chapter, we question if notions of participatory democracy have been realised.

Understanding governmentality and the subject

According to Foucault (1995: 221), governmentality is an exercise of power "by which, in our culture, human beings are made subjects". He further notes that it "seeks to fashion and guide the bodily comportments and inward states of others and of self and of others" (ibid.). It thus follows that government sets the rules to achieve the maximum benefits for the governed. In return, the governed need to obey the rules established by the government, hence there is a symbiotic relationship between the governor and the governed. According to Foucault (1995), the production of governable subjects occurs simultaneously with the production of truth or knowledge which should stand as the rationality of regulating social behaviour. Foucault (1991) rightly maintains that certain:

> "practices" do not exist without a certain regime of rationality.... If I have studied "practices" ... it was in order to study [the] interplay between a "code" which rules ways of doing things ... and a production of true discourses which serve to found, justify and provide reasons and principles for these ways of doing things.
>
> (Foucault, 1991: 79)

Foucault (1994) further argues elsewhere that:

> there can be no possible exercise of power without a certain economy of discourses of truth which operates through and on the basis of this association. We are subjected to the production of truth through power and we cannot exercise power except through the production of the truth.
>
> (Foucault, 1980: 93)

Moreover, exercising power over subjects through self-regulation ensures that it becomes acceptable, and is seen as a good act and a norm by those being ruled. This argument is well put by Foucault (1995) who states that:

> what makes power hold good, what makes it accepted, is simply the fact that it does not only weigh on us as a force that says no; it also transverses and produces things, it induces pleasure, forms knowledge, produces discourse. It needs to be considered as a productive network that runs through the whole social body, much more than as a negative instance whose function is repression.
>
> (Foucault, 1995: 120)

For instance, in the context of spatial control, biopower is administered through objects such as regulatory signs (a good example would be that of "do not litter" signage). Such objects function not only to establish surveillance on space but also guarantee that the ruling class establishes the "governmentalities" of space through "consent". Like Foucault, Gramsci (1977) also identifies the importance of "consent" in the production of governable spaces. Gramsci considers space as a discourse in which social relations and practices are produced and enacted (Jessop, 2005: 424). Similarly, neo-Gramscian writer, Goonewardena (2005) asserts that the production of hegemony cannot be achieved without the production of space. Moreover, he argues that space is a medium of hegemony as it can be used to mirror the ideologies of the ruling elites.

The question of space being ideological is also raised by Lefebvre (1974: 210), who argues that while "ideologies … do not produce space, they are in space". Furthermore, Lefebvre (1974) notes that space is heavily embedded with power and knowledge ready to be used in producing hegemony and vice versa. In exploring Gramsci's contribution to the discourse of governmentality, we therefore analyse his influence on Lefebvre, specifically in the conceptualisation of Lefebvre's spatial triad. Lefebvre's spatial triad consists of three interrelated aspects of space: representations of space (conceived space), representational space (lived space) and spatial practices (perceived spaces). Likewise, Kipfer (2013: 198) has argued that traces of Gramsci's concept of hegemony are seen in each aspect of Lefebvre's spatial triad and more crucially in his critique of everyday urban life.

The institutionalisation and normalisation of hegemony can never be fully achieved without a well-crafted production and top-down appropriation of what Lefebvre refers to as the "representation of space". He considers these representations of space or "conceived space" as closely "tied to the relations of capitalist production and to the order which those relations impose, and hence to knowledge, to signs, to code, and to 'frontal' relations" (Lefebvre, 1974: 33). The conceived space is described by Merrifield (2000) as being a platform where ideology and power are embedded. It is in the representations of space (or conceived space) that ideology and knowledge are used in intervening in the lives of ordinary citizens by the state, political elites and technocrats. Therefore, we contend that the consolidation of power and hegemony comes full circle in the "representational space" which, according to Merrifield (2000: 174), is "directly lived space, the space of everyday". This aspect of this space is "directly lived through its associated images and symbols of its users and inhabitants … and it overlays physical space, making symbolic use of its objects" (Lefebvre, 1974: 39). We consider the production of this representational space as directly linked to the production of social identities and spatial dispositions. Our observation also relates to that of Simone (2008), who argues that it is in the "representations" and "representational" space that attachment of identity to spatiality takes form. In his understanding of the appropriation of city spaces, Simone (2008: 70) asserts that "spaces are linked to specific identities, functions, lifestyles and properties so that the spaces … become legible for specific people at given places and times".

According to Lefebvre (1974), "perceived spaces" or "spatial practices" represent a "continuum midway between small-scale individual practices and large-scale social processes and institutions". He further asserts that people always appropriate space according to the broader social, economic and political realities they find themselves in. Similarly, like representations of space and representational space, spatial practices embody the ideologies, socio-cultural beliefs, knowledges and symbols which inform the "spatial territoriality" of individuals. While Foucault's conception of governmentality is widely accepted as an analytical tool to understand the relationship between the governor and the governed, it is criticised for re-enforcing the centrality of state power in governance (Joseph, 2010).

The politics of rural housing in South Africa: producing governable subjects

The Jozini rural housing subsidy like many projects of its kind has been used by the state as a tool to create what Foucault refers to as "governable subjects". We evince that state-led initiatives such as the Jozini low-income housing scheme have played a critical role in defining certain labels that give the state the impetus to intervene in and govern the private lives of its citizens. We further argue that the provision of housing to South African citizens goes beyond achieving socio-democratic principles but serves to problematise poverty and seeks ways to intervene in the everyday lives of those characterised as "poor" (also see Escobar, 1995). Escobar (1995) criticises state-directed development and service delivery programmes, arguing that far from mobilising people to rise against poverty they have systematically transformed poor people into objects of knowledge, management and governance.

Consequently, to control and intervene in the population, we argue that through the housing policy the South African government directly or indirectly produced a simplified and schematic model of the reality in which they want to intervene. To this end, while the provision of housing aimed to address the prevalence of material poverty among previously disadvantaged groups, it also functioned as a process of conditioning state–citizens relations. Indeed, in both apartheid and democratic South Africa, the production of space through housing practices has not only intersected with identity formation but also with how the state exercises power over its citizens. Parnell and Hart (1999) suggest that housing programmes initiated by pre- and post-democratic South African government were less to do with solving the housing crisis among poor people, and more about serving the interests of capital and the state.

Commenting on South Africa's self-help housing practices initiated during the urban crisis of the 1970s and certainly under the ANC's RDP, Parnell and Hart (1999: 367) argue that the self-help housing strategy in Johannesburg, for instance, was "a prevailing method of social engineering, whose acceptance or rejection reflects perceived political and economic advantages for the state and the private sector, and ... not a simple response to a shortage of affordable shelter among the poor".

In projecting Parnell and Hart's (1999) analysis onto our case of the Jozini rural housing subsidy in the province of KwaZulu-Natal, we note that it has the nuances of social engineering masked as a poverty alleviation initiative. More importantly, in the next section, we will show that the Jozini rural housing subsidy project like any programme of its nature has to a certain extent been used as a method of garnering voters' empathy if not support.

Context of the study and study methodology

In terms of geographical location, Jozini municipality is situated in the northern part of the KwaZulu-Natal province and is one of the five local municipalities under uMkhanyakude District Municipality. Jozini's population is largely rural and thus like most rural areas in South Africa it is characterised by a high incidence of poverty, lack of service delivery and underdevelopment. According to the 2011 census, Jozini is the most populous local municipal area within the uMkhanyakude district with a population of 186,502 people (Statistics South Africa, 2019). We note that in the context of rural housing the crafting of participatory democracy relies on the inclusion of the utilisation of traditional institutions in executing any developmental programme.

This study was underpinned by empirical data from in-depth interviews with Department of Human Settlements officials, members of traditional leadership institutions and community members as beneficiaries of the Jozini subsidy. We look at how the intersectionality of rural housing policy, participation and governance has shaped state–citizen relations in post-apartheid South Africa. The interviews were conducted between 2014 and 2015 with 12 purposively sampled participants that had a deep understanding of Jozini's social, political and housing processes. The empirical data was analysed in relation to key themes that emerged from the participants' accounts. The themes were identified and organised using NVIVO 10 data analysis software.

Rural housing subsidy and participatory democracy in Jozini: resuscitation of "indirect rule"?

In the early sections of this chapter, we discussed how the post-apartheid government construed participatory practices as critical mechanisms in the reversal of social exclusion and establishing a progressive relationship between the government and those who are governed. We note how the ANC-led government formulated policies such as the RDP and Integrated Development Programmes to nurture grassroots involvement and participation in the planning of the development process. The adoption of these policies followed the democratic decentralisation of governmental powers to elected local leaderships and more importantly to traditional authorities (Ntsebeza, 2004). Our findings suggest that, in the context of providing housing in rural Jozini, the post-apartheid government has made progressive efforts to promote democratic participation and assist rural communities to steer their own development through traditional leadership institutions.

The politics of naming in governing

One of the officials from the Department of Human Settlements responsible for the implementation of the Jozini rural housing subsidy states that traditional leaders and institutions occupy a crucial role in fostering inclusivity of rural communities in the Jozini rural subsidy scheme, since they are familiar with the needs of their communities. He notes that the Department of Human Settlements developed innovative ways of creating an inclusive and democratic environment for participation. Naming of communities' subsidy schemes after their respective traditional leaders is on one of those methods of stimulating the communities' sense of inclusivity and belonging:

> In 2008, the Department of Human Settlements began implementing the Jozini low-income housing scheme. To promote an effective implementation of the programme it felt that the inclusion of local communities in this developmental process was necessary. Since the implementation of the programme was done through traditional authorities who in most cases are familiar with the needs of their communities, we suggested that the programme be named in line with their traditional councils. So, you will find that most of the projects under the Jozini low-income housing scheme are named in line with *Amakhosi* [traditional leaders]. For instance, we have the *KwaMathenjwa* Phase 1 Housing Project, which is named in line with *iNkosi Mathenjwa* and we have *Mngomezulu* Phase 1 Housing Project named in line with *iNkosi Mngomezulu.*
>
> (Interview, Department of Human Settlements Official #1)

We find the naming of the rural housing subsidy schemes after traditional leaders not only a gesture but also an important technique of attaching the community's cultural identity to the scheme. Our argument is augmented by the official from the Department of Human Settlements, who notes that the naming of housing projects according to traditional leaders or councils elicits feelings of cultural ownership of the housing projects by communities. He further outlines that this sense of ownership ensures that communities commit to becoming the rightful managers of rural housing processes, while the state takes a back seat in their development. While we argue that the naming of housing projects after traditional leaders is an innovative way of encouraging the full participation of rural communities, we also assert that it is a tool of producing governable citizens.

Put in other words, the implementation of the Jozini housing subsidy scheme replicates a colonial type of "indirect rule", in which the state attains a panoptical governance of its citizens through traditional institutions (also see Mamdani, 1996). We argue that to govern its rural populace, the present-day South African government like erstwhile colonial administrators uses local traditional authorities to politically institutionalise their ideas and claim their presence in the mundane lives of their citizens. While Mamdani (1996) sees the use of tribal authority by those in power as an effective method of exercising hegemony through self-governance, we assert that this political strategy has had a far-reaching impact on how the South African government implements and delivers its rural housing programme. Indeed, by placing traditional leaders (*Amakhosi*) at the helm of housing delivery processes, the state manages to carve out symbolic representations that speak to cultural inclusivity and the communities' indigeneity. Therefore, it is important to discuss the role of traditional authorities in assisting the state in not only establishing effective and responsive technologies of governance but also in shaping a seemingly democratic relationship between the state and its rural citizens.

Fostering indigenous knowledge systems in participatory practice: the ambivalence of democratisation

The involvement of traditional authorities in the provision of housing goes beyond attaching their name tags to the housing delivery process, to seeking their input in the selection of intended beneficiaries. Another official from the Department of Human Settlements described the Jozini low-income scheme as primarily driven by the local communities' indigenous knowledge system (IKS). For him, the communities' IKS, which is accessed through traditional institutions, is pivotal in assisting the state to gain a deeper social understanding of the community. He notes that on commencement of any housing projects, the department together with traditional leaders set up project steering committees (PSCs) comprising members familiar with the areas where projects are intended to be rolled out. He argues that the PSCs epitomise the government's effort to decentralise power and place it in the hands of communities and at the same time invoke an ethos of community participation. The official had this to say about traditional leaders' role in governing housing delivery through PSCs:

> When the Department of Human Settlements through local municipalities identify land for housing, we establish Project Steering Committees, because everything in as much as we are educated you know we may have knowledge in terms of academic stuff but we still need an indigenous knowledge … in order for us to ensure that there is a balance … we form a project steering committee and that project steering committee constitutes of the people that reside within an area and the way it is formed it is democratically elected so they conduct elections where we have the community coming together to say who are the people they nominate and then they pick those names and then they vote accordingly and that becomes the PSC. The PSC is responsible for identifying and selecting potential beneficiaries of the rural housing subsidy. We have managed to effectively distribute houses to poor community members identified by traditional leaders. So one can say traditional leaders have made these schemes a success.
>
> (Interview, Department of Human Settlements Official #2)

While some of the participants indicate that the South African governments' use of traditional leaders in the Jozini rural housing subsidy scheme has facilitated poor people's access to rural housing and public participation, others thought otherwise. For instance, one politician who participated in our interviews was sceptical about the credibility of PSCs and their role in rural housing provision. Instead, he argues that PSCs are another form of indirect rule where some powerful political elites collaborate with traditional leaders to promote their political ideas and coalesce allegiances. He narrates a past instance in which a certain member of the executive council (MEC) in the province of KwaZulu-Natal illegally bypassed the municipality and other departmental structures and facilitated a strategic provision of houses to certain traditional leaders.

> The MEC provided houses directly to the traditional authorities [chiefs] in the areas and they were not controlled by the municipality in any way. The Chiefs controlled housing provision and the municipality did not play any role during that process. I guess all what happened was for political reasons. Identifying beneficiaries during this period varied according to the different traditional authorities. It was largely depending on how politically active they were and who they were politically aligned to or with. As a result, many people did not get these houses because they did not support the dominant political party that led the traditional council during that period. If you did not give support to the political party that a particular Headman dominated, the Headmen would be informed; as a result you can be left out from receiving a house.
>
> (Interview, Politician #1)

According to Croese (2016), state-led housing delivery programmes are usually hijacked by political elites who use it to fulfil their political ambitions, reward their supporters and punish opponents. In her study of state-led housing delivery in Angola, Croese (2016) convincingly argues that the Angolan National Urbanism and Housing Programme, a state initiative, represents a case where housing delivery effectively became an instrument of patrimonialism, in which political elites through local institutions get to decide "how, by whom and to whom" housing should be delivered (Croese, 2016: 94). Similarly, state-led housing delivery in South Africa follows the operatives of patronage where politicians indirectly influence political behaviour. One of the community members who participated in our study had this to share:

> There is an outcry from the people where you find for example a person that is known and can afford but you will find that he/she was able to receive a house. He works, he has a house but because he is politically active you will find that he will get a house from the scheme even though he is not poor at all. The people that are sincerely poor in the area will not get a house because they are not politically active and neither do they support the dominant political party.
>
> (Interview, Community Member #1)

We argue that this patrimonial distribution of houses along political affiliations not only creates unequal patterns of access to housing but also perpetuates material poverty among some of the most vulnerable members of the society. Indeed, in the case of the Jozini rural housing subsidy, the allocation of housing using one's political orientation and patronage has excluded disabled people and women from accessing housing. One participant described an instance where a disabled citizen was excluded from receiving a house and benefiting from a housing process:

> There is another person who is disabled, but because of their political alignment they are still living in poverty without a house. The house opposite where this person stays there is a big house belonging to Mr Nyawo who was an artisan. He has renovated his house, he has livestock, but he still has an additional house from the municipality within his homestead because he was politically aligned and active.
>
> (Interview, Community Member and Beneficiary #2)

It can be noted from the above interview extract that far from empowering its intended "beneficiaries", the Jozini housing project like any of its nature in South Africa functions as instrument of amassing power and politico-social allegiances by political elites and traditional leaders. We also understand the Jozini housing project as an interface of accumulation where practices of corruption and racketeering promote situations of personal gains among various actors.

Stifled participation: navigating invited spaces

It is without doubt that the Jozini rural subsidy scheme has mitigated the housing problem among rural communities; however, the findings also point to the exclusion of community members when it comes to deciding who gets to benefit from the scheme. One participant criticised how traditional leaders go about selecting potential beneficiaries, arguing that it is done without consultation with community members. As such the whole process of means testing is left concentrated in the hands of the few. He shows his concern about the lack of participation in the decision-making and about the silencing of other voices when selecting intended recipients of rural housing.

> The traditional leader has the right to intervene, where he is aware of a person who is not deserving of a house. What we do get from the traditional leader is that there are people who are left out of the list. At times what the traditional leader says is what is followed. She or he has the power to put or remove people from the list.
>
> (Interview, Community Member and Beneficiary #3)

We regard the Jozini rural housing project as illustrating what Gaventa (2005) refers to as an "invited space" where important decision-making in the development process is steered by those that are powerful and are considered technical experts. In the case of Jozini low-income housing, we assert that the shaping of a state–citizen relationship through housing follows an unequal distribution of power that borders along gender, traditional societal structures and professional classification. We note that power seems to be concentrated in the hands of the state, traditional leaders and contractors, whereas community members to a certain extent serve as subjects upon which this power is exercised. Cornwall (2008) notes that the spaces that communities are invited to participate in are commonly circumscribed by essentialised stereotypes of community concerns and capabilities, leaving little scope for rural communities and particularly women to participate as citizens. He adds that for people living in poverty or subjected to exclusions, the experience of entering a participatory space can be extremely intimidating.

Cornwall and Coelho (2007: 11) have asserted elsewhere that power relations permeate every dimension of the participatory sphere, where powerful technocrats lay the guidelines of how the intended beneficiaries are supposed to participate in their own development process. They further capture the ambivalence of participatory democracy by arguing that participation in public or invited spaces is usually "framed by those who create them and infused with power relations and cultures of interactions carried into them from other spaces". In analysing the micro-politics of participation, Gaventa (2005) regards spaces of participation as spaces of power in which "forms of overt or tacit domination silence certain actors or keep them from entering at all". For Chaudhuri and Heller (2002), the mere production of participatory spaces does not necessarily mean everyone will participate equally in them. In many cases gender roles assume a crucial place in the allocation of housing in rural Jozini and determine who gets to access housing. In the next section, we posit that the Jozini low-income scheme acts as an interface where, due to their perceived subservient position in rural South Africa, women have little or no say on how houses are allocated.

The gendered nature of housing delivery in the Jozini low-cost housing scheme

In analysing our research findings, we found the Jozini low-income housing scheme to be a gendered one. Consequently, we consider it as reflective of the broader societal gender inequalities that border along societal status and more importantly gender lines. For example, we note that while the women of Jozini are equally represented and participate in PSCs, their input falls short in challenging the patriarchal representations of housing. According to Meth and Charlton (2017) men are normally considered heads of household and have used the materialities of a house to assert their authority and masculine identity at the expense of women. The patriarchal representations of housing make it difficult for society members to conceive of women as fit to own a house and head a household. While one of the participants highlights that the view that women cannot own houses and head household is slowly being challenged, some community members still hold on to those perceptions:

> In previous times a woman could never be considered as the head of a household in Mathenjwa, but this has now changed, and a woman can leave home to have her own house without a man. Whereas previously if she didn't have a husband, then her boy child would be the head of that household, but the idea that women can be head of household is something that is yet to be accepted by other community members.
>
> (Interview, Community Member and Beneficiary #3)

The above finding speaks to Lefebvre's (1974) views on "representational space" and "representations of space", where in this context we would argue that the housing scheme acts as an interface that the local people of Jozini use to project, negotiate and re-enact their cultural identities and gender norms. We contend that the Jozini housing process has reproduced and entrenches the normative patriarchal and cultural dominance of men over women. Reading from Lefebvre's (1974) writings on representations of space and representational spaces, we perceive the Jozini housing subsidy scheme as a form in which these aforementioned types of space assume shape. Indeed, like representations of space and representational spaces, the Jozini rural subsidy scheme is a platform where certain people due to their gender are either included or excluded in accessing houses. To reiterate Simone's point mentioned in the previous section of this chapter, we suggest that the Jozini low-income scheme has produced and reproduced, "spaces [that] are linked to specific identities, functions, lifestyles and properties so that the spaces ...] become legible for specific people at given places and times" (Simone, 2008: 70). This gendered access to housing not only violates women's constitutional right to have access to housing, it also accentuates their precarious state of impoverishment and powerlessness. One of the traditional leaders we interviewed narrated an ordeal where several women involved in street trading could not access housing because they were earning an income from their informal business practices:

> I remember that some women who sold goods on the road. When we looked at the amount of money they earned and saw that it is not a lot, they earn R500 and sometimes R400, we tried to register them to receive a house, but we were told by the government department that they do earn money. It was now coming from the government department saying that they were earning something.
>
> (Interview, Traditional Leader, 2014)

We contend that women's lack of access to housing in Jozini is aggravated by their reluctance in challenging male domination in the rather gendered allocation of housing. However, we sympathise with these women and use Foucault's reasoning to argue that the absence of agency among the women of Jozini is systematically influenced by a panoptic patriarchal Zulu society. The process of "panopticism", which forms the basis of self-discipline, control and surveillance, has restricted the participation of Jozini women in the housing scheme in various ways. For instance, culturally rural Zulu women are less likely to lend their voices in democratic or participatory spaces that are dominated by males. Challenging male views can also be problematic. Their reluctance to participate is greatly governed by self-discipline inculcated through socialisation and the socially constructed norms that in the Zulu culture women should assume a subordinate role among males. Kapoor (2005: 1212) demonstrates the pitfalls of participatory democracy:

> Panopticism has an important implication for participatory development since participation is public and public participatory space can be a panoptic one. Under the watchful eyes of the community, participants perform roles by playing to an audience, living up to an expectation, or acting out a socially sanctioned duty. Thus, for example, the village leader performs the authority figure, the facilitator acts as the benevolent arbiter, the woman performs her prescribed gender role, the minority group accentuate its status as "dependent" or "victim".

Similarly, Chaudhuri and Heller (2002: 2) problematise the notion of participatory democracy as ignoring power imbalances existing between various social groups. They are sceptical of scholars and policy-makers who put a lot of trust in and romanticise participatory democracy as a system that contributes to the empowerment of those at the bottom. Instead, they assert that the notion of participatory democracy with its limitations is especially problematic

> in developing democracies where basic rights of association are circumscribed and distorted by pervasive vertical dependencies (clientelistic relationships), routine forms of social exclusion, the unevenness and at times complete failure of public legality, and the persistence of pre-democratic forms of authority.
>
> (Chaudhuri and Heller, 2002: 2)

Conversely, we conclude that given the ambivalence of participation, achieving equal access to housing remains an elusive dream.

Conclusion

This chapter argues that while housing delivery in South Africa has been utilised by the state in the (re)production of socio-democratic citizenship, it has also been instrumental in shaping the politics of democratic participation and the state–citizen relationship. We show that the Jozini rural housing subsidy plays an important role in defining certain labels that give the state the impetus to intervene in and govern the private lives of their citizens. We further argue that the provision of housing to South African citizens goes beyond achieving socio-democratic principles but serves to problematise poverty and seeks ways to intervene in the everyday life of those characterised as "poor". We forward an argument that rather than mobilising people to rise against poverty, state-directed development and service delivery programmes such as the Jozini rural housing programme have systematically transformed poor people into objects of knowledge, management and governance. The chapter used Foucault's thoughts on power and governmentality and Lefebvre's theory of "production of space" to demonstrate that the Jozini low-income housing scheme is one of many tools of governmentality that the state uses to govern from a distance, while emitting their ideas, aspirations and political construction of "gender", "citizenship" and the governance of the so-called "poor" in the new democratic dispensation, which has intersected with the actual production of state-financed low-income houses. By using empirical evidence from qualitative data, the chapter contends that although the acquisition of low-income housing represent a person's claim to citizenship and a political obligation to redress gender inequalities, it has been used by the state as an instrument to produce governable subjects.

Acknowledgements

The financial assistance of the National Research Foundation in collecting data under the South African Research Chair Initiative for Applied Poverty Reduction Assessment in finalising this chapter is hereby acknowledged. Opinions expressed and conclusions arrived at are the authors' and are not necessarily to be attributed to the NRF.

References

Burger, P. 2014. *How suitable is a "developmental state" to tackle unemployment, inequality and poverty in South Africa?* SALDRU, School of Economics, University of Cape Town. www.econ3x3.org/sites/default/files/articles/Burger%20P%202014%20Developmental%20State%20FINAL.pdf

Chang, H. 2011. Institutions and economic development: theory, policy and history. *Journal of Institutional Economics*, 7(4), pp. 472–498.

Chaudhuri, S. and Heller, P. 2002. *The Plasticity of Participation: Evidence from a Participation Governance Experiment*. Department of Economics, Columbia University, Mimeo.

Cornwall, A. 2008. Unpacking "participation": models, meanings and practices. *Community Development Journal*, 43(3), pp. 269–283.

Cornwall, A. and Coelho, V. 2007. *Spaces for Change? The Politics of Participation in New Democratic Arena*. London: Zed Books.

Croese, S. 2016 State-led housing delivery as an instrument of developmental patrimonialism: the case of post-war Angola. *African Affairs*, 116(462), pp. 80–100.

Escobar, A. 1995. The problematization of poverty: the tale of three worlds and development. In S. Schech and J. Haggins (Eds.), *Development: A Cultural Studies Reader*. Oxford: Basil Blackwell, pp. 79–92.

Foucault, M. 1991. Questions of method. In G. Burchell, P. Miller and C. Gordon (Eds.), *The Foucault Effect: Studies in Governmentality*. Chicago: University of Chicago Press, pp. 73–86.

Foucault, M. 1995. *Discipline and Punishment: The Birth of the Prison*. New York: Random House.

Gaventa, J. 2005. *Deepening the Deepening Democracy Debate*. Institute of Development Studies, University of Sussex, Sussex.

Goonewardena, K. 2005. The urban sensorium: space, ideology and the aestheticization of politics. *Antipode*, 37(1), pp. 46–71.

Gramsci, A. 1977. *Selections from the Prison Notebooks*. Edited and translated by Hoare, Q. and Smith, G. London: Lawrence and Wishart.

Jessop, B. 2005. Gramsci as a spatial theorist. *Critical Review of International Social and Political Philosophy*, 8(4), pp. 421–437.

Joseph, J. 2010. The limits of governmentality: social theory. *European Journal of International Relations*, 16(2), pp. 223–246.

Kapoor, I. 2005. Participatory development, complicity and desire. *Third World Quarterly*, 26(8), pp. 1203–1220.

Kipfer, S. 2013. City, country, hegemony: Antonio Gramsci's spatial historicism. In M. Ekers, G. Hart, S. Kipfer and A. Loftus (Eds.), *Gramsci, Nature, Politics*. Sussex: Wiley-Blackwell Publishers.

Koma, S. 2010. The state of local government in South Africa: issues, trends and option. *Journal of Public Administration*, 45(1.1), pp. 111–119.

Kuye, J. and Ajam, T. 2012. The South African developmental state debate: leadership, governance and a dialogue in public sector finance. *African Journal of Public Affairs*, 5(2), pp. 48–67.

Lefebvre, H. 1974. *The Production of Space*. Massachusetts: Blackwell Publishers.

Mamdani, M. 1996. *Citizen and Subject: Contemporary Africa and the Legacy of Colonialism*. Kampala: Fountain Publishers.

Maserumule, M. 2007. Conflicts between directors-general and ministers in South Africa 1994–2004: a "postulative" approach. *Politikon*, 34(2), pp. 147–164.

Merrifield, A. 2000. Henri Lefebvre: a socialist in space. In M. Crang and N. Thrift (Eds.), *Thinking Space*. London: Routledge.

Meth, P. and Charlton, S. 2017. Men's experiences of state sponsored housing in South Africa: emerging issues and key questions. *Housing Studies*, 32(4), pp. 470–490.

Ntsebeza, L. 2004. Democratic decentralization and traditional authority: dilemmas of land administration in rural South Africa. *The European Journal of Development Research*, 6(1), pp. 71–89.

Parnell, S. and Hart, D. 1999. Self-help housing as a flexible instrument of state control in 20th-century South Africa. *Housing Studies*, 14(3), pp. 367–386.

Simone, A. 2008. People as infrastructure: intersecting fragments in Johannesburg. In S. Nuttal and A. Mbembe (Eds.), *Johannesburg: The Elusive Metropolis*. Johannesburg: Wits University Press, pp. 68–90.

Statistics South Africa, 2019. *Census 2011*. Pretoria: Statistics South Africa. www.statssa.gov.za/publications/P03014/P030142011.pdf.

Van Dijk, H. and Croucamp, P. 2007. The social origins of the developmental state: reflections on South Africa and its local sphere of government. *Journal of Public Administration*, 42(7), pp. 662–675.

9 Revisiting land challenges in housing urban poor people in post-apartheid South Africa

An insight into Durban

Lovemore Chipungu and Knowledge Zungu

Introduction

Urban land and housing provision for low-income groups is a universal policy concern in most cities of less developed countries. This is inevitable in today's urbanising world where housing is competing for a place in the urban economic and spatial landscape. Ever-increasing urbanisation is associated with the proliferation of large cities that are becoming home to growing populations. More people now live in towns and cities rather than in rural areas. Existing evidence shows that globally 54 per cent of the world's population lived in urban areas in 2014. This is a significant trend given that in 1950, only 30 per cent of the world's population lived in urban areas and this figure is expected to increase to 66 per cent by 2050 with nearly 90 per cent of the increase concentrated in Asia and Africa (United Nations, 2015: 1–12). Of major concern is the fact that high levels of urbanisation are being experienced in less developed countries that are home to some of the world's fastest growing cities. Asia and Africa are urbanising faster than any other region in the world. By 2050, their total urban population is projected to become 56 per cent and 64 per cent urban, respectively (United Nations, 2015: 11).

According to a UN-Habitat report (2011c), housing in Africa is a holistic and multi-dimensional concept that represents the physical environment. The key interdependent components that interact in any housing sector are land, infrastructure, finance, labour and building materials – all these components are shaped and organised by the legal, regulatory and institutional framework in which they operate. Land is identified as a core component for housing affordability; therefore, making it accessible and affordable would go a long way to making housing affordable for the majority of urban dwellers in Sub-Saharan Africa. It has been observed that "urban land for housing development is increasingly scarce, poorly regulated and therefore expensive" (UN-Habitat, 2011c: viii). The availability of reasonably priced urban land is important to increase the supply of low-income housing and limit the emergence and growth of new informal settlements.

This chapter revisits the urban land challenges for housing urban poor people by interrogating the South African situation. As a young democracy in Africa,

South Africa is not immune to the housing problems bedevilling low-income countries and especially affecting urban poor people. This chapter looks at post-apartheid South Africa and examines the extent to which access to land remains a hindrance to decent housing among urban poor people. With its focus on Durban, the chapter uses empirical data obtained through qualitative and quantitative research methods – mainly through mapping, interviews, and observations. Critical insight into administrative mechanisms related to land and housing is based on information which was obtained from key informants in the Municipality and the provincial government. In addition, other stakeholders outside the public sector were consulted in order to create a holistic view of the circumstances impacting on land and housing. This information was complemented with secondary data in the form of municipal maps and reports. This chapter is divided into six sections: introduction; conceptual framework; a historical overview on South African low-income housing; a case study of Durban; a discussion section; and a conclusion.

Urban land and housing: a conceptual framework

Neoliberalism is a complex mix of liberal economics, public choice theory and normative beliefs concerning the role of the state and the primacy of markets. At the centre of this ideology is a strong belief in the rule of law, the market as the key determinant of service provision and a shift towards less government intervention. Allmendinger (2001: 172) observes that the need for neoliberalism stemmed from post-war welfare states that created a dependency culture, which requires a change in attitude through encouraging the idea that inequality is an inherent and natural part of life. Therefore, what is required is a strong, deregulated state whose function is to police the market and provide stability through minimising dissent. Allmendinger (2001: 173), quoting Gamble (1988: 8) sums up neoliberalism as “a free economy and a strong state”. In the same vein, Harvey (2005: 2) notes that neoliberalism is advanced by liberating individual entrepreneurial freedoms and skills within an institutional framework characterised by private property, free markets and free trade.

The influence of neoliberalism in housing emerged in the early 1970s out of debates between the liberals and neo-Marxists and was championed by major international agencies led by the World Bank. Jenkins and Smith (2001: 481) observed that neoliberalism borrows most of its ideas from liberalism but zeros in on the enabling market perspective, and the structural adjustment programme. Purely from a housing perspective, this theory was influenced by Turner’s liberal ideas, which opposed the construction of permanent public housing by governments in developing countries (Turner, 1976). Pugh (2001) argues that the World Bank in particular regarded government construction of housing as unaffordable, ineffective and excessively dependent on subsidies. This approach was considered unsustainable. Hence, as Pugh (2001: 404) observes, the rationale was to completely change the housing production process with a focus on creating measures to support “affordability, cost recovery and replicability”, which were justified on the basis that giving "hand-outs" (in the form of government subsidies) to beneficiaries induced large-scale rural–urban migration which in turn aggravated the housing problem.

Neoliberalism is anchored on three key tenets, namely, economic, social and political. It argues that markets are the most rational means of distributing social goods and services. This creates individual rights, responsibilities and opportunities as the state defers its functions to the market (Dodson, 2006: 2). The advent of neoliberalism as the basis for government policy in land and housing delivery has witnessed the "rolling back" of the state, whose role is limited to the injection of capital and the provision of land and infrastructure. When the World Bank spearheaded neoliberalism in the early 1970s, it promoted site and services schemes where beneficiaries' sweat equity and other internal resources (such as community support and finance) were invested in the construction and development of houses (Van der Linden, 1986).

Historically, neoliberalism was partly associated with the imposition of structural adjustment programmes, which saw a substantial retreat of the state from engagement in service provision (Baken and Van der Linden, 1992: 72). It was assumed that market efficiency and economic growth would eventually lead to poverty alleviation through trickle-down mechanisms. This approach was seen as the "new emphasis area and was an important component for land market assessment and a new tool for urban management" (Baken and Van der Linden, 1992: 74).

Neoliberal housing policies shift the responsibility for housing supply from governments to private consumers through loan repayments as opposed to subsidies. It is argued that the neediest people are not ignored in the process since once the housing demands of other groups were met privately, increasing housing supply would open opportunities for poor people. In this regard, housing was perceived as straddling the intersection of social policy, urban development and fiscal management (Pugh, 1991: 290).

It is from this perspective that Keivani and Werna (2001: 192) advocate that the epicentre of neoliberalism in housing rests on the reconfiguration of the state's effectiveness by limiting its economic allocative function to the social sector with a focus on supporting settlement-wide actions as expressed in the enabling approach. Pugh (2001: 401) notes:

> The state should create the legal, institutional and economic framework for economic productivity and social effectiveness. Housing development would depend on the quality and effectiveness of its economic, financial, legal and institutional framework – including its relation to the wider national and international economies.

In essence, this meant relying on the efficiency of markets. However, there is an over-emphasis on the workability of markets to the extent that Harvey (2005: 2) argues that, in their absence, they are supposed to be created and, where necessary, by force. However, focusing purely on markets is not enough to produce tangible progress in housing production and consumption. Hence, the settlement-wide approach identifies structural issues that are impediments to the success of market mechanisms.

The conceptualisation of housing through housing instruments was essential since this formed the enabling environment that was conducive to housing development. As Pugh (2001: 411) points out, these instruments were key constituents for the development of the housing sector. On the other hand, Zanetta (2004: 25) contends that this perspective fits housing within the broad objectives of economic development and macro-economic performance with the intention of maximising macro-economic linkages through financial, fiscal and economic links. Hence, these instruments assist in revalorising market mechanisms, redefining urban policies and eliminating barriers that restrict the productivity of urban economic agents both at formal and informal levels. It is on the basis of these developments that one can concur with Peck and Tickell's (2006: 33) conclusion:

> Rather than rolling back the frontiers of the state, neoliberalism involves the rollout of new state forms, new modes of regulations, new regimes of governance with the aim of consolidating and managing both marketisation and its consequences.

The neoliberal approach has been criticised for not being explicit in some of its proposals. One such critical issue pertains to the land market. Ward (1991: 9) notes that in theory the need to improve the efficiency of the land market was emphasised in the *Fitzwilliam Memorandum*. In practice, however, it was not clear how such markets could be improved for the benefit of low-income groups since the acquisition of land by urban poor people in less developed countries is not done through formal markets. Therefore, efficient land markets can only operate to further satisfy the high-income market (Baken and Van der Linden, 1992). If poor people are to participate in such markets, state intervention should not be ruled out. Housing development in less developed countries is highly political and therefore cannot be depoliticised. This notion is captured by Grindle (1980: 15) who notes that national decisions in less developed countries largely depend on the proportion of individual and collective demand-making and representation of interests. Therefore, housing issues at whatever level are sites of contestation where competing interest groups seek to impose their definition of what the main housing problems are and how they should be addressed. Such decisions cannot be left completely to the whims of the market, especially where vulnerable groups are involved (Jacobs *et al.*, 2003: 442). This, in turn, calls for the need to understand the contextual underpinnings of these factors from different countries – hence the South African case.

Land and housing in South Africa – a historical retreat

Urban development in South Africa is closely associated with the discovery of minerals – especially gold and diamond that attracted hundreds of thousands of black workers from all over the African continent. The mining economy relied on cheap, unskilled labour – a situation that led to the development of the compound model of housing, which in principle also evolved to be a mechanism for labour control (Maylam, 1990; Duncan, 1993; Lombard, 1996). Tighter controls were required to deal with indiscipline, desertion, theft and uncertainty of the labour force. As Maylam (1990) observes, by 1900, mines had become centres of urban development where a lot of people were attracted to work in various sectors of the urban economy.

During the development of locations or townships in the nineteenth and twentieth centuries, housing policies tended to be diverse, largely shaped by each town's local economy, while the emphasis remained on compound-type accommodation (Maylam, 1990). There was no developed policy or system for housing the urban black population before 1920, apart from the compound housing for workers at the mines, docks, factories, harbour and commercial businesses (ibid.). Townships established in all towns (such as Kliptown, Western Native Township, Sophiatown, Martindale, Eastern Native Township, Newclare and Alexandra), accommodated only a small proportion of blacks who lived outside the compounds, with the rest living in private leasehold or freehold townships or rented backyard quarters in the central areas of towns (Maylam, 1990). Wilkinson makes an interesting observation about the developments of the time by noting that in the 1920s:

> the only efforts to regulate or improve the generally very poor housing conditions of blacks living in urban areas were sporadic forays by the larger local authorities to clear the so-called "plague spots" and a few half-hearted efforts to establish municipal "Native locations", invariably far removed from the rest of the town.
>
> (Wilkinson, 1998: 217)

Despite these challenges, early settlements were characterised by low-density, detached housing, particularly in burgeoning white suburbs, while blacks, on the other hand, were housed in cramped mine and municipal compounds (Pirie, 1988, cited in Parnell, 1988: 308).

Another interesting observation is that in spite of these challenges that were burgeoning in the housing sector, housing policy never came to the scene to rescue this scenario. Instead, racial capitalism embodied within the "Stallard Principle" became the order of the day. Christopher (1994: 38, cited in O'Malley, 2005) substantiates this point noting that the state through the Housing Act (No. 35 of 1920) enabled funds to be "made available to local governments in order to build housing for poor people. The resultant estates were required to be racially segregated, separated from one another by open spaces and with separate access roads".

By the time the National Party came into power in 1948, housing strategies were already fragmented and had been subsumed within policies directed at the implementation of an evolving Apartheid doctrine (Lombard, 1996). During this era, "housing delivery was strictly controlled through state provision of public-rental housing and hostel accommodation in dormitory townships" (ibid: 6). Morris (1981: 69, cited in Maylam, 1990: 69) expounds that the housing policy in the 1950s aimed "to remove blacks' freehold rights in urban areas, segregate the races, control movement and reduce the economic burden of blacks on the state and on local authorities".

The principle of residential segregation was entrenched through the Group Areas Act (No. 41 of 1950), which enforced the recommendations of the Urban Areas Act of 1923. This was achieved through the construction of vast black townships sited as far as possible from white residential areas, but reasonably close to industrial areas. In addition, these townships were "designed and sited in a way that they could be cordoned off in the event of riot or rebellion, and the resistance suppressed in open streets" (Hindson, 1983: 71, cited in Maylam, 1990: 70).

However, more interesting was the apartheid government's need to control the urban population by eliminating surplus "natives" to the reserves or Bantustans (Department of Native Affairs, 1951: ii, cited in Wilkinson, 1998: 219). This targeted several "black spots" on the perimeters of some of the larger centres, which had their origins in irregular sales of land to blacks. This, in essence, relegated the issue of land, tenure and housing for blacks to the homelands, whose nominal regimes had neither the capacity nor the resources to respond adequately to the overwhelming demand (Lemon, 1991: 24–25, cited in Lombard, 1996). Smit (1992) and Lombard (1996) added that in fast-growing townships like Soweto, homeownership rights were restricted to a 30-year leasehold tenure – thus effectively abolishing the existing system of 99-year leaseholds.

This period also witnessed the government's withdrawal from providing rental housing stock for the low-income groups – a situation that resulted in these groups pursuing alternative means of accessing housing through land invasions and the building of backyard shacks in formal townships (Lombard, 1996). The situation created an opportunity for the private sector to engage in low-income housing. Among such organisations that became actively involved in the urban land and housing debate, as either pure private organisations or government affiliates, were the Urban Foundation, the South African Housing Council and the Independent Development Trust. Their roles in the housing sector in the period prior to democracy are summarised in Table 9.1.

Land and housing delivery in post-apartheid South Africa

The South African housing policy was born out of the conflict and misconceptions of the pre-1994 period. This inevitably saw the Reconstruction and Development Programme (RDP, enacted in 1994) as the major vehicle through which housing could be provided progressively. In essence, the RDP became a flagship policy framework for integrated socio-economic progress. In the housing sector, the name RDP has become an emblem for any housing scheme, especially

Table 9.1 Private sectors involved in the housing debate

Organisation	*Focus on housing policy*
Independent Development Trust (1990)	Replaced the government as an enabler, setting the framework within which role players would operate. Its role was also to manage and distribute capital subsidy schemes established in 1991. The capital subsidy schemes were informed by World Bank housing strategies that focused on improving housing finance institutions and land markets (among others).
The South African Housing Council (1990)	Advocated for the recognition of informal housing (but not squatting, illegal land invasion and occupation of private property). It also proposed that individuals receive government support in the form of subsidies, home ownership, and site and services.
The Urban Foundation (1976)	Sought to mobilise free market processes in housing provision by encouraging state withdrawal from total monopoly.
National Housing Forum (1992)	Advocated for a unitary housing policy, serviced sites, well-located land and municipal services.

Source: adapted from various documents by author, 2016.

among low-income people. However, it must be emphasised that although the RDP has been the leading policy guide, it is also supported by a plethora of policies whose content and focus are directed towards specific gaps and housing needs of the country. Most of them are derivatives of the 1994 White Paper on Housing, which aimed at establishing viable and economically integrated communities. The various policies and guidelines passed over the years are summarised in Table 9.2.

In order to operationalise these policies, the South African government identified specific strategies as shown in Table 9.3. At the core of these strategies is the subsidy scheme that has since evolved to be an overarching instrument in housing delivery.

In addition to the above, the South African housing production system is guided by a number of legislations that empowers the three spheres of government (national, provincial and municipal) and other institutions in the delivery of housing. Among such key legislations are the National Housing Act of 1997 (which has been undergoing many amendments), the Prevention of Illegal Eviction from and Unlawful Occupation of Land (Act No. 19 of 1998) and the Municipal Systems Act (Act No. 32 of 2000).

Through proper harnessing of resources available, the South African government has delivered 3,230,000 subsidised housing units mainly to low-income people since 1994 (South Africa Development Report, 2011: 26). This concerted effort by the government has seen significant and fundamental improvements in people's access to decent housing coupled with better physical infrastructure and social and economic facilities. The government's proactive action has been directed not only towards the urban areas, but also to rural areas where the

Table 9.2 An overview of housing policies in South Africa

Policy	*Year*	*Description*
Reconstruction and Development Programme	1994	Framework for integrated and coherent economic progress with the aim of eradicating imbalances created by apartheid such as inadequate housing.
White Paper on Housing	1994	A holistic policy that touches on all aspects of housing such as tenure, sanitation, infrastructure, socio-economic facilities, institutions and strategies.
People's Housing Process (PHP) – revised as the Enhanced PHP of 2008	1998	Aims to assist communities in achieving decent housing through sweat equity by encouraging NGOs to assist beneficiaries with planning and implementing housing projects.
Breaking New Ground	2004	Shift from focus on quantity to quality and choice of the housing through innovative and demand-driven housing programmes and projects with the overall aim of eradicating informal settlements by 2014.
Social Housing Policy	2005	Creates an enabling environment for institutions that provide housing for low- to medium-income people but that exclude immediate individual ownership.
Inclusionary Housing Policy	2007	Aims to create a more racially integrated and income inclusive residential environment.
National Housing Code	2009	Sets out policy principles, guidelines, norms and standards, which apply to the government's various housing assistance programmes.

Source: adapted from various documents by author, 2016.

populace has benefited largely through rural subsidy schemes (Rust, 2002). As already noted above, this success has been mainly underlined by the aggressive mobilisation of housing finance, which saw subsidies being utilised in every sector of housing production. For instance, the Department of Human Settlements received R22 billion for housing delivery in the 2011–2012 budget with a further R100 billion being allocated to other allied departments involved in bulk infrastructure development (South Africa Development Report, 2011: 28). This, admittedly, has made South Africa the leading country in the world that has managed to deliver housing on such a large scale in a relatively short period. However, despite such overwhelming evidence of success, the country is still reeling under an estimated backlog of 2.1 million housing units (Gerber, 2018).

Despite these positive developments, a number of challenges confront urban land delivery in South Africa. Through the Department of Rural Development and Land Reform, the government focused on acquiring rural and agricultural land through the land reform programme. Only the Housing Development Agency (HDA) is able to acquire urban land for low-income housing in South Africa. The HDA acquired a total of 16,837.3 hectares of urban land by 2018

Table 9.3 Key strategies for housing implementation in South Africa

Strategy	*Description*
Subsidies	There are currently five forms of subsidies: project-linked, consolidated, institutional, individual, and rural subsidies, and the enhanced extended discount benefit scheme.
Partnership	Based on the concept of a public–private–social partnership meant to allow mobilisation and harnessing of combined resources, efforts and initiatives of communities, the state, and commercial and private sectors.
Mobilisation of housing finance	Focuses on the mobilisation of additional resources to supplement government subsidies through private investment, formal credit and individual savings.
Land management	Focus is on the speedy release and servicing of land in order to secure access to freehold land for development, e.g. setting up of provincial land tribunals to resolve land disputes thereby fast-tracking housing development.
Complementary grants	These are national grants for the provision of bulk infrastructure and services such as the Consolidated Municipal Infrastructure Programme meant to ensure equitable access to affordable municipal services.

Source: compiled from different sources by author, 2015.

and released it for human settlement projects (Housing Development Agency, 2018: 28). There is no legislative framework that forces private owners to sell urban land hence the HDA cannot acquire many hectares of well-located urban land. The willing seller, willing buyer principle makes urban land expensive and difficult for the government or the HDA to acquire for low-income housing.

Land and housing delivery in Durban

Like other metropolitan municipalities, eThekwini has a good track record in the provision of decent housing to its low-income households in need of subsidised housing units. Existing statistics show that to date the Municipality has delivered approximately 186,000 low-income subsidy houses or homes, and 2,640 Community Residential Units as part of the hostel upgrading project. In addition, 22,200 rental housing units were transferred to tenants who rented those units (eThekwini Municipality, 2017: 98). Despite these efforts, the housing backlog in the Municipality is still very high, as at December 2016 the existing housing backlog was 387,000 housing units. Considering the current prices to construct a housing unit, the Municipality would require between R51 and R85 billion to clear the current backlog (ibid.). Another of the biggest challenges that contribute towards the housing backlog is access to land.

The same institutional environment that prevails in the country equally shapes land and housing delivery in eThekwini. Generally, for public housing schemes, the municipality initiates land acquisition for low-income people through its Land Assembly Department. This involves critical key stages, detailed below.

Land audit

The land audit is conducted by the Land Assembly Department. This begins by requesting a hand plan (i.e. development plan) from surveyors and a land record report. The report is then taken to the town planners within the Housing Unit for feasibility studies to be conducted on that piece of land. This is the first step in investigating the land, the services and servitudes on the land, and everything else that needs to be considered. One of the participants pointed out that a land feasibility report must be prepared by the planning section in order to advise on the suitability of the land acquisition (fieldwork, 2013).

A desktop study has to be carried out by the planning section on an identified vacant piece of land. Important aspects considered during the desktop study include the land's location, registration number, possible constraints (including environmental issues, Durban Management Open Space System, steep, soil testing, etc.) and topography. When the study is completed, a report is compiled and submitted to the Public Sector Housing Department for pre-screening. The pre-screening process involves municipal line departments who comment on the proposed project on the piece of land in question and advise on the services they will provide.

Land valuation

At this stage, a professional land valuer is appointed by the municipality and the landowner in order to determine the value (or price) of land under consideration.

Offer and sales agreement

Once parties agree on the price and payments are done, a conveyancer is appointed to attend to the transfer of the land to the municipality. The land is then cleared and handed over to the projects section to commence the construction process.

Apart from purchase and sales agreements with private landowners, the municipality enters into other agreements with state-owned entities and the Ingonyama Trust Board (ITB) and these are listed in Table 9.4.

However, it must be noted that land acquisition processes are normally very slow, especially when land transfer takes place between the municipality and provincial or national governments or state-owned entities (Author, field interviews, 2013). The South African Cities Network (2014) pointed out that land transactions with state-owned entities take up to ten years or more in some cases, due to centralised decision-making and limited engagement on forward planning and projects. In Lacey Road (Sydenham, Durban), the Municipality negotiated with the Department of Public Works for eight years to release the land, so as to

Table 9.4 Land acquisition agreements

Type of agreement	*Key aspects considered*
Purchase and sales agreement	The land is negotiated for and bought from a private owner. The municipality enters into this agreement with the owner to acquire land.
Land availability agreement	This is when an agreement is reached with other government entities when they make land available to the municipality. The municipality also enters into this agreement with the ITB when they sign a memorandum of agreement, whereby the municipality receives the power of attorney for that particular land to build low-cost housing.
Development rights agreement	This is an agreement signed by the municipality and ITB when the ITB gives the municipality the right to develop land for low-income housing. However, ownership of land remains with the ITB and it is the only institution in this case obliged to give title deeds to beneficiaries as the landowner.
Donation agreement	This type of agreement transpires where someone fails to pay rates on land to the municipality, or when the privately owned land is invaded and the owner(s) decides to donate the land to the municipality.

Source: author, fieldwork, May 2013.

upgrade the informal settlements on the side of the road (South African Cities Network, 2014: 80). With private landowners, the land acquisition process can take up to three years or more, as was the case in Cornubia (Durban), where it took almost four years.

In some instances, as a last resort, urban land is acquired from private owners in Durban through the land expropriation process. According to the Expropriation Act (No. 63 of 1975), this process involves lodging an application with the Member of the Executive Committee for Human Settlements for consent to expropriate. Once consent is granted, a notice of expropriation is advertised in the Durban *Metro* newspaper. A conveyancer is appointed to register the expropriation with the Deeds Office and obtain an expropriation number. A compensation agreement is then prepared and the purchase price at market value, together with the solatium and interest being paid into the conveyancer's trust account. The transfer is then effected and the land is transferred to the municipality and cleared for development. This is a long process that can take a minimum of six months (Author, field interviews, 2013).

Land acquisition challenges for low-income housing

Durban, like any other city in the developing world, also faces a number of challenges when it comes to the acquisition of land for housing low-income households and these include: difficulties associated with finding suitable and well-located land; the cumbersome land acquisition process; disputes over land ownership; and topographical issues.

The issue of finding a suitable and affordable vacant piece of land within urban restructuring zones in close proximity to employment, economic opportunities, recreational areas and social services is one of the biggest challenges low-income households face in Durban. In most cases, land that is suitable for housing development is located far from the central business district (CBD) or is even outside the urban development line where it is not expensive. Where land is available within urban restructuring zones, it is expensive and beyond the reach of urban poor people if acquired without government subsidies. An overview of land prices prevailing in Durban shows that 1,000 m^2 of land in the Point area (Durban Waterfront, CBD) can cost up to R10 million, yet the same size of land in Morningside (a mere 5 km from the CBD) can cost up to an R1 million while in Mayville (approximately 7 km from the CBD) can cost R80,000 (data gathered by the author in 2016). These prices are dictated by locational factors, which unfortunately hits poor people hard and thwarts the government's effort to acquire such land since it renders it uneconomical.

This situation is aggravated by the topography in Durban, which is characterised by steep slopes in the west and moderately flat seaside plains in the east (eThekwini Municipality, 2011: 12). Steep slopes are vulnerable to natural disasters, expensive to construct low-income housing on and expensive to maintain. The costs associated with the cut and fill, earthwork, retaining walls and erosion prevention (among others) are often prohibitive. The Municipality's *2012/13 Integrated Development Plan* (eThekwini Municipality, 2013) noted that the topography of Durban incorporates 98 km of coastline, 18 catchments, 16 estuaries, and 4,000 km of rivers (eThekwini Municipality, 2013: 21). Related to topographical issues is the fact that approximately 75,000 hectares of land in the Municipality fall under the Durban Management Open Space System, which is environmentally sensitive, and habitat to various animal and plant species. Hence, this land is protected by legislation and development is restricted. Should development occur in such areas, it is too expensive for low-income projects. Hence conducive topographical conditions in the south, characterised by a flattish coastal band, carry much of the current urban development and transportation corridors while an inland band of undulating topography accommodates a mix of township developments (eThekwini Municipality, 2011: 13).

This situation is complicated by institutional requirements which further impose conditions on development. The National Water Act (No. 36 of 1998) clearly states that "no person may establish a township unless the layout plan shows, in a form acceptable to the local authority concerned, lines indicating the maximum level likely to be reached by floodwaters on average once in every 100 years" (National Water Act, Section 143, cited in Khoza, 2009: 10). The preparation of floodlines serves as a tool for planning and managing flood impacts for developments (National Water Act, cited in Council for Scientific and Industrial Research, 2000; Khoza, 2009; eThekwini Municipality, 2011). In line with the Act, the Municipality requires that all new developments and extensions to existing properties provide information relating to the 50- to 100-year floodlines. Unfortunately, the shortage of land in Durban has forced the government to construct some low-income housing units along floodplains. This is evident in some parts of Ntuzuma Township, where flood plains pose hydrological risks of flooding adjacent houses (Khoza, 2009: 3).

Land for urban development (especially for housing) comes in the form of a package largely associated with the provision of infrastructure. The Municipality provides physical and social infrastructure to its citizens through funding from the urban settlements development grant and the municipal infrastructure investment framework. Provision of such infrastructure is based on the Social Facilities Accessibility Model, which uses the level of demand required to provide citywide facilities (eThekwini Municipality, 2013).

In the 2010/11 financial year, the Municipality contributed R10,000 for the provision of bulk infrastructure per site in low-income housing projects. Currently, there is a huge backlog in the provision of physical infrastructure and, depending on the availability of financial resources, it will take years to address. For example, there are 301,448 households without electricity but the Municipality can only afford to provide electricity to between 9,000 and 13,000 households per annum. At this rate, it will take between 23 and 37 years to clear this backlog (eThekwini Municipality, 2013: 25).

The 2016/17 financial year proposed a total consolidated budget of R41.6 billion for the city's programmes and projects. This budget (among other things) was supposed to cater for various infrastructural needs such as upgrading 1,400 pre-1994 housing units and provide for 37,500 water connections, 90,000 electricity connections and 24,000 sanitation connections (eThekwini Municipality, 2016). This is further elaborated in the *2018/19 Integrated Development Plan*, where R2.2 million was set aside to address the infrastructure and service needs backlog (eThekwini Municipality, 2018c).

However, this situation is exacerbated by the fact that most of the low-income housing is undertaken on green fields located far from the CBD. This has cost implications when it comes to the provision of infrastructure. The average benchmark infrastructure cost per site for greenfield low-income housing projects within 400 m to 1 km of public transport trunk routes costs between R8,699 and R14,267, while for upgrading informal settlement projects within the same distance it ranges between R9,996 and R9,148 (eThekwini Municipality, 2012).

It is equally important to acknowledge that there are also limitations associated with funding mechanisms in place, which in turn impacts negatively on the provision of land for low-income housing developments. The Municipality relies on funding from both the provincial (through housing subsidies) and national (through the urban settlements development grant) governments. The Municipal Council also allocates funding to deliver low-income housing. In the 2018/19 financial year, the Municipality allocated R2.2 billion to the new low-income housing developments and interim servicing of informal settlements (eThekwini Municipality, 2018a: 30). This is a mere drop in the ocean since the city requires between R51 billion and R85 billion to swiftly eradicate the low-income housing backlog (eThekwini Municipality, 2017: 98). Urban poor people contribute little if anything towards infrastructure development since these costs are covered by government subsidies. For instance, the first 65 kwh of electricity is free for low-income households using less than 150 kwh per month (eThekwini Municipality, 2018b: 7). Thousands of low-income households benefit from this subsidy, which is one of the rate rebates on consumption of housing infrastructure (eThekwini Municipality, 2013). This situation has been worsened by illegal connections for water and electricity (mostly in informal settlements such as Mayville, part of Cato Manor) since this increases the Municipality's infrastructural costs due to unplanned and unaccounted for consumption. However, even where there is accountability for consumption of infrastructure among poor households, their inability to contribute towards the payment of basic services due to high levels of poverty still leaves the burden on the shoulders of the Municipality (eThekwini Municipality, 2013).

Another competing challenge relates to existing mechanisms for the delivery of land for housing development. Under the current system of market regulation, some governments departments are forced to acquire land at market prices and through long and cumbersome procedures (Baken and Van der Linden, 1992: 22). Durban Municipality experiences challenges in securing rights to land that is owned by state entities and other spheres of government. For this reason, the Municipality partnered with the HDA to acquire land on its behalf for human settlement projects. Ironically, the worst delays are experienced in acquiring land from the government and state-owned companies, which at times can drag for more than eight years. The slow and cumbersome land acquisition process, as already noted above, further bogs this down.

The last challenge relates to disputes over land ownership emanating from both legal and illegal land acquisition processes normally associated with land invasions (South African Cities Network, 2014). One such notable dispute was between the Municipality and the Passenger Rail Agency of South Africa (PRASA), which owns 984.82 hectares of land in Durban, over a property on uMngeni Road near the Durban Station. This land was initially owned by the Municipality, which later donated it to PRASA for the expansion of their operations. Part of the condition was that PRASA was supposed to return the land to the Municipality if not used. Unfortunately, PRASA did not only use the land but also refused to hand it back to the Municipality resulting in tension, communication breakdown and delays in the process.

Similarly, land invasions, especially on municipal land, are a common phenomenon in Durban. The Municipality normally resorts to the use of legal action (through obtaining court orders) in order to remove land invaders. This results in bitter relations between the occupants and the Municipality, as law enforcement agencies are sometimes used to remove illegal occupants and, at the same time, processes to transfer that land to the Land Assembly Department for the development of low-income housing is delayed due to lengthy court processes arising from protracted legal challenges.

Discussion

The case of Durban to a large extent highlights similar challenges that South African cities are experiencing in the housing arena. However, this negative overview should not overshadow the fact that the country has also seen key intervention measures in trying to reach urban poor people as far as urban land and housing is concerned. The search for better opportunities has seen the urban space in South Africa being the recipient of most migrants from both within and outside its borders. To date, 63 per cent of the South African population is urbanised (Worldometers, 2019). Unfortunately, this high level of urbanisation has significantly contributed to the development of informal settlements, which increased from 300 settlements in 1994 to 2,628 in 2010 (South Africa Development Report, 2011: 27; *Delivery*, 2012: 29) which increased to 5.4 million by 2018 (Umraw, 2018). This increase can be partly attributed to the country's liberal laws, specifically the *Prevention of Illegal Eviction from and Unlawful Occupation of Land* (No. 19 of 1998), which to some extent protects people who engage in the development of informal settlements. The government is cognisant of the mammoth task and, over the years, it has managed to stabilise and provide basic services for people in informal settlements.

The inclusive nature of the South African government's intervention in land and housing development has seen the country achieving high levels of access to physical infrastructure. The government's commitment to such programmes is reflected in its budgetary pronouncement. For instance, in the 2016/2017 budget, the National Treasury allocated R37.7 billion (to run for three years) to the Department of Water and Sanitation to implement water and sanitation projects while R7.8 billion was put aside for electrification programmes for 60,000 households with non-grid access (Republic of South Africa National Treasury, 2017). In the water and sanitation sector, such high access levels have been boosted by the country's free basic water policy, which allows each household to receive the first 6,000 l/m of water free of charge. However, access to social and economic services in new housing schemes is still a problem since most houses built under subsidy schemes are not accompanied by such services because they are driven by the availability of land with a focus on providing the superstructure only (Goebel, 2007; South Africa Development Report, 2011).

South Africa also embraces both a Westernised and innovative response to urban land and housing demand. This is characterised by large-scale housing production and upgrading of informal settlements. Unfortunately, the "hand-out" approach has fundamentally contributed towards the current dependency syndrome among households who sit back waiting for the government to deliver. In addition, the high level of expectation created by the government has indirectly contributed to the increase in the number of informal settlements. Rather than investing their time and money in building houses, most households would rather wait for over 20 years to be allocated a house by the government. It is therefore not surprising that since 1994 only 3 per cent of the country's new housing stock has been provided through the People's Housing Process (Bolnick, 2010).

Above all, inadequate capacity to deliver on the part of South Africa has seen some underperforming provinces barely exhausting their annual financial budgets despite endless protests of poor service delivery. So gross is the problem of incapacity that the government spends R2 billion annually on municipal capacity support. In the 2016/17 financial year, poor planning and budgeting at the municipal level resulted in municipalities spending only 86.8 per cent (i.e. R24.6 billion) of the infrastructure grant (Republic of South Africa National Treasury, 2018). The situation has been aggravated by widespread corruption, which manifests itself in the form of poor-quality housing (Goebel, 2007).

Conclusion and recommendations

The case of South Africa depicts a country rich in resources and supported by a plethora of policies, which in the housing arena touch on every aspect of housing delivery strategies. Yet, in reality, the country's housing delivery system is heavily tilted towards subsidy housing schemes provided by the government with very little participation from beneficiaries. Ever-increasing spatial concentrations of low-income households due to rapid urbanisation has seen phenomenal growth of informal settlements and pressure for the provision of basic services. Available well-located land within the Municipality is either too expensive for low-income housing or incompatible for housing due to adjacent uses – a factor arising from poor planning. Yet, land that is reasonably cheap and accessible is only found on the periphery of the city or outside the urban development line – a factor that would create a replica of the apartheid city if developed. The situation is aggravated by the fact that land and housing delivery is highly dependent on the national housing subsidy scheme, which, to a large extent, limits densification options (eThekwini Municipality, 2015).

In this regard, concerted effort from all stakeholders in government, the private sector, civil society and the traditional leadership is required if the issue of urban land and housing is to be resolved amicably. Compulsory acquisition of land within the city's boundaries, if done within existing legal and economic means, would bring much relief to both the government and urban poor people. This, to a large extent, requires political will. The absolute efficacy of political will is found in leadership at the national political level that motivates and disciplines the multiple actors responsible for intervening in the land and housing market. However, elevating political will to this critical level does not necessarily relegate or undermine the complexity of other factors that also play influential roles. The resolution does not lie in creating antagonism over land as a natural resource – but in creating a holistic enabling environment, which should become a platform for interactive intervention by all stakeholders.

References

Allmendinger, P. 2001. *Planning in Postmodern Times.* London: Routledge.

Baken, R.J. and Van der Linden, J.J. 1992. *Land Delivery for Low Income Groups in Third World Cities.* England: Avebury.

Bolnick, A. 2010. *Informal Settlement Upgrading: Towards an Incremental People Centred Approach.* South Africa: Ikhayalami.

Council for Scientific and Industrial Research, 2000. *Human Settlement Planning and Design*, Vol. 2. Pretoria: CSIR Building and Construction Technology. www.csir.co.za/sites/default/files/Documents/Red_BookVol2.pdf.

Delivery, 2012. The Magazine for Local Government. No. 29. www.sadelivery.co.za.

Dodson, J. 2006. *Rolling the State? Government, Neoliberalism and Housing Assistance in Four Advanced Economies.* Brisbane: Urban Research Program, Griffith University.

Duncan, D. 1993. *The Origins of the "Welfare State" in Pre-Apartheid South Africa.* http://ebookbrowsee.net/david-duncan-the-origins-of-the-welfare-state-in-pre-apartheid-south-africa-pdf-d377417977 [accessed 20 August 2014].

eThekwini Municipality, 2011. *Preparation of Flood Lines.* www.durban.gov.za/City_Services/engineering%20unit/Coastal_Engineering_Stormwater_Catchment_Management/Catchment_Management/Pages/Floodline_preparation.aspx [accessed 9 November 2013].

eThekwini Municipality, 2012. *eThekwini Housing Sector Plan: The Housing Chapter of the IDP*. Durban: Department of Human Settlements and Infrastructure., Housing Unit.

eThekwini Municipality, 2013. *Draft Integrated Development Plan: 2013/14 IDP Review*. Durban: eThekwini Municipality. www.durban.gov.za/City_Government/City_Vision/IDP/Documents/eThekwini%20IDP%202013_14.pdf.

eThekwini Municipality, 2015. *Spatial Development Framework: Review 2015–2016.* Durban: eThekwini Municipality.

eThekwini Municipality, 2016. *eThekwini's 2016/17 Financial Year Budget Adopted.* www.durban.gov.za/Resource_Centre/new2/Pages/EThekwini%E2%80%99s-2016-17-Financial-Year-Budget-Adopted.aspx.

eThekwini Municipality, 2017. *eThekwini Municipality: Integrated Development Plan – 5 Year Plan: 2017/18 to 2021/22*. Durban: eThekwini Municipality.

eThekwini Municipality, 2018a. *Medium Term Revenue and Expenditure Framework 2018/2019 to 2020/2021*. Durban: eThekwini Municipality.

eThekwini Municipality, 2018b. *eThekwini Electricity Tariff Book 2018/19.* Durban: eThekwini Municipality.

eThekwini Municipality, 2018c. *2018/19 Integrated Development Plan.* www.durban.gov.za/City_Government/City_Vision/IDP/Documents/Draft%202017%202018%20IDP.pdf.

Gerber, J. 2018. R10bn budget slash for human settlements department. www.news24.com/SouthAfrica/News/r10bn-budget-slash-for-human-settlements-department-20180510 [accessed 9 February 2019].

Goebel, A. 2007. Sustainable urban development? Low-cost housing challenges in South Africa. *Habitat International*, 31, pp. 291–302.

Grindle, M.S. (Ed.), 1980. *Politics and Policy Implementation in the Third World.* Princeton: University Press.

Harvey, D. 2005. *A Brief History of Neoliberalism.* Oxford: Oxford University Press.

Housing Development Agency, 2018. *Annual Report 2017/2018*. Johannesburg: Housing Development Agency.

Jacobs, K., Kenny, J. and Manzi, J. 2003. Power, discursive space and institutional practices in the construction of housing problems. *Housing Studies*, 18(4), pp. 429–446.

Jenkins, P. and Smith, H. 2001. An institutional approach to analysis of state capacity in housing systems in the developing world: case studies in South Africa and Costa Rica. *Housing Studies*, 16(4), pp. 485–507.

Keivani, R. and Werna, E. 2001. Modes of housing production in developing countries. *Planning in Progress*, 55, pp. 65–118.

Khoza, M. 2009. *The Application of Floodlines in Land Use Control: a case study of Moreleta Spruit in Tshwane*. Bloemfontein: University of Free State.

Lombard, J.J.G. 1996. *Housing Strategies and the Urban Poor in South Africa: a brief critical evaluation*. Working Paper No. 80. www.ucl.ac.uk/bartlett/development/sites/bartlett/files/migrated-files/WP80_0.pdf.

Maylam, P. 1990. The rise and decline of urban apartheid in South Africa. *African Affairs*, 89(354), pp. 57–84.

O'Malley, P. 2005. *Analyses, Chronologies, Historical Documents, and Interviews from the Apartheid and Post-Apartheid Eras*. www.nelsonmandela.org/omalley/index.php/site/q/03lv01538/04lv01646/05lv01752.htm [accessed 19 January 2013].

Parnell, S. 1988. Land acquisition and the changing residential face of Johannesburg 1930–1955. *Area*, 20(4), pp. 307–314.

Peck, J. and Tickell, A. 2006. Concepualizing neoliberalism thinking Thatcherism. In H. Leitner, J. Peck and E.S. Sheppard (Eds.), *Contesting Neoliberalism: urban frontiers*. New York: Guildford Press, pp. 26–50.

Pugh, C. 1991. Housing policies and the role of the World Bank. *Habitat International*, 12(1–2), pp. 275–298.

Pugh, C. 2001. The theory and practice of housing sector for developing countries, 1950–1999. *Housing Studies*, 16(4), pp. 399–423.

Republic of South Africa National Treasury, 2017. *Budget Review 2017*. www.treasury.gov.za/documents/national%20budget/2017/review/FullBR.pdf.

Republic of South Africa National Treasury, 2018. *Budget Review 2018*. www.treasury.gov.za/documents/national%20budget/2018/review/FullBR.pdf.

Rust, K., 2002. *Housing Policy and Programme Review. Policy Evaluation. Department of Housing, Gauteng Provincial Government*. South Africa: Human Science Research Council.

Smit, D. 1992. The Urban Foundation: transformation possibilities. *Transformation*, 18, pp. 35–42.

South Africa Development Report, 2011. *Towards a People's History. Land Act, Dispossession, Segregation and Restitution*. Research Channel Africa. South African History Online. www.sahistory.org.za/.

South African Cities Network, 2014. *Case Studies on the Acquisition of Urban Land by Municipalities from State Owned Companies and other Organs of State*. Braamfontein: SACN.

Turner, J.F.C. 1976. *Housing by People: towards autonomy in building environments*. London: Marion Boyers.

Umraw, A. 2018. What the numbers say about SA's "squatter camps". huffingtonpost.co.za/2018/06/14/what-the-numbers-say-about-sas-squatter-camps_a_23459035/ [accessed 12 February 2019].

UN-Habitat, 2011. *Affordable Land and Housing in Africa, Volume 3*. Adequate Housing Series. Nairobi: UN-Habitat.

United Nations, 2015. *World Urbanization Prospects: the 2014 revision*. Department of Economic and Social Affairs, Population Division. New York: United Nations.

Van der Linden, J. 1986. *The Sites and Services Approach Reviewed*. Hants, England: Gower Publishing Co.

Ward, P. 1991. "Fitzwilliam Memorandum" on land markets and land price research. International research workshop: land value changes and the impact of urban policy upon land valorization processes in developing countries. Fitzwilliam College, Cambridge, 14–19 July. *International Journal of Urban and Regional Research*, 15(4), pp. 623–628.

Wilkinson, P. 1998. Housing policy in South Africa. *Habitat International*, 22(3), pp. 215–229.

Worldometers, 2019. *Worldometers.* www.worldometers.info/world-population/south-africa-population/ [accessed 12 February 2019].

Zanetta, C. 2004. *The Influence of the World Bank on National Housing and Urban Policies: the case of Mexico and Argentina during the 1990s.* London: Ashgate.

10 Housing for individual sovereignty through innovations in policy and practice

Sithembiso Lindelihle Myeni and Oliver Mtapuri

Introduction

Housing has remained one of the major challenges that most countries in the developing world continue to endure. Rapid urban population growth due to rural–urban migration and natural population growth including within the cities themselves, and the continuous transformation of rural areas into urban centres, has burdened urban infrastructure, which is not growing at the same pace. Housing and related facilities have thus emerged as some of the top challenges. The challenge is quite evident in most cities in Asia, Africa and Latin America. The amalgam of real challenges associated with housing is depicted by the increasing numbers of low-income housing of poor quality; the sprawling of informal settlements/slums/squatter settlements; the destitute or street families; poor or total lack of sanitation facilities such as clean water, drainage and sewer systems; and an inadequate provision of electricity and road infrastructure, among other basic services. South Africa's urban centres are characterised by many of these challenges and responsible authorities at local and national government levels have been working towards finding solutions to minimise and even eliminate the challenge of housing in both urban and rural spaces. In light of this, the government of South Africa initiated subsidised housing as one of the efforts to address the housing problem. The scheme meets increasing demand as the key shelter option for poor people living in and moving into metropolitan cities, and especially to those residing in informal settlements. This chapter revisits the production of subsidised housing within the contours of a neoliberal framework couched in a strong social agenda in South Africa.

The meanings of homeownership

While a house is generally regarded as accommodation, shelter or a home, the Department of Human Settlements (2010) regards it as a basic right enshrined in the 1996 Constitution, which recognises that everyone must have access to adequate housing and the government has the mandate to "take reasonable legislative and critical measures within its available resources to ensure that this right is realised" (Republic of South Africa, 1996: 11). In response to this constitutional call, the government of South Africa has promulgated a number of laws and policies in its quest to fulfil this right (Tissington, 2011), starting with the Housing Act of 1997, which gave birth to a variety of housing programmes meant to provide decent housing as well as access to tenure security, basic services, materials, facilities and infrastructure to poor households at affordable costs (Department of Human Settlements, 2009).

According to Gunter (2014), house ownership in an urban setting amounts to some form of economic empowerment. It is a common practice to see those who own houses renting them out to others in return for money, which then meets other needs. Fox and Goodfellow (2016) equate owning a house to owning an asset or capital that can be used or exchanged for cash or used to generate income. Owning a house also gives a sense of security which can contribute towards a sustainable livelihood. Ripstein (2017) also equates home or property ownership to sovereignty – a view also supported by Hart (1981), who described property rights ownership as a small-scale sovereign. Ripstein (2017: 243) thus notes that discussions around sovereignty "often appeal to the proprietary metaphors of ownership" noting that "early modern discussions of sovereignty viewed sovereignty in broad proprietary terms". As such, a sovereign was believed to be someone who was responsible for his/her own territory and was not answerable to anyone or any higher authority. In this case, the territory became his/her property, giving him/her power over all those who inhabited his/her territory as they automatically become his/her subjects. As such, ownership has elements of territoriality which imply that a person has localised hegemony over his "own territory", represented by his home. Home is a place to establish self-territorial determination and for the inculcation of local territorial allegiance from where belonging and nationhood find a foundation which is formalised by citizenship.

However, in liberalism, the notion of rights is often used with an inclination towards civil and political rights. Liberalism is in defence of private property rights under the guise of capitalism and is not concerned with the social and economic inequality that is normally rooted in feudal social relations (Thomas, 2010). Modern liberal defenders believe that there should be no limitations to the individuals' rights to accumulate private property. It is crucial to note that such a conception of the notion of rights is responsible for the unequal access to land and home ownership. Marx (1978) on the other hand is of the view that the notion of rights emerged together with the bourgeoisie's preferred mode of organising production and social relations. He argued that, because of the dominance of capitalism, the notion of equality in as far as rights are concerned can never be attainable. He views private ownership of productive assets as unjust and the basis for material and class inequalities, which then led to the divide between the wealthy and the poor groups in society. According to this view, those who own and control the means of production are against the equal distribution of the productive assets (for example homeownership) since this will render them powerless and subtract from their wealth. They thus fight to maintain the status quo and make more money from the poor landless/homeless groups.

While to the poor worker owning a house means empowerment and brings a sense of security, to the property owners a shortage of housing for the working class means more money and more value for their land and properties. For as long as capitalism is still alive, unequal distribution of and access to essential services like housing will remain (Marx, 1978; Thomas, 2010). This process is characterised by systematic acquisitions of property which is converted into housing in private territorial enclaves, that is, rich people de-housing poor people. De-housing involves the acquisition of properties by few hands that then gain monopoly power over those housing units with the self-ordained power to determine prices and keep poor people out of the housing market. Some poor people manage to enter the housing market through their own effort, and others through the government and/or philanthropic organisations. The formation of groupings, some of which are dominant and powerful, while others are unaggressive and inexpressive, creates incompatibilities in power, resources, money, influence, knowledge and information, leading to the dominance of one over the other. The unaggressive bear the brunt.

One of Marx's collaborators, Engels (1887, cited in Larsen *et al.*, 2016: 582) believed that "homeownership would in fact chain the worker in semi-feudal fashion to his own particular capitalist". According to Engels, private property rights were far from bringing any liberation for workers but constituted what he called "the chief institutional arrangement that made capitalist urban expansion possible", which includes numerous features of political economy (trade, wages, price, value, money) which he argued were responsible for the creation of inequalities, exploitation and injustices. Homeownership is thus driven by private property rights which in turn play a critical role in the creation of a society moulded by capital accumulation interests at the expense of those who cannot afford to own a home.

Hodkinson (2012: 428) notes that "for Engels there was no such thing as a housing crisis, only a crisis of capitalism in which housing conditions formed just 'one of the innumerable, smaller, secondary evils' caused by the exploitation of workers by capital". He also suggests that the only solution to the question is "to abolish altogether the exploitation and oppression of the working class by the ruling class through working class revolution and the expropriation of private property". Drawing insights from Engels, Harvey (2008) highlights how the elite groups complicate housing provision by introducing some financial instruments and dubious innovations in various sectors of mortgage finance, whose conditions are meant to make more capital for those elite groups. The effects of financial instruments tend to deepen inequality: the loan interest costs result in the original cost doubling if not tripling over extended periods of loan repayments, leading to impoverishment. These views can, therefore, be roped in to account for the housing situation in post-apartheid South Africa and the rest of the world and help explain some of the challenges associated with subsidised housing. The following section takes a look at the housing situation in post-apartheid South Africa.

Housing in South Africa

This section of the chapter discusses the housing situation, legislation and policies in South Africa. The discussion concentrates on two main eras: soon after independence (1994–2004) and 2005 and beyond. The latter period focuses on the Breaking New Ground (BNG) as promulgated in 2004 and presented in a number of housing programmes.

Post-apartheid housing (1994–2004)

Charlton and Kihato (2006) acknowledge that at the time South Africa gained independence its cities were characterised by a range of housing challenges, which included among others dire housing and services backlogs, inequalities in municipal expenditure and the spatial anomalies associated with the apartheid city among others. The fall of the apartheid regime witnessed a paradigm shift in housing policy. The incoming ANC government capitalised on the discriminatory policies and failures of the apartheid government by promising to bring to an end the housing woes that had affected the black population for a long period of time (Thomas, 2010). Its 1994 election campaign was centred on the promise that they would procure four-roomed houses for the electorate when voted into power (Tomlinson, 1998). The new government was committed to the "establishment of viable, socially and economically integrated communities situated in areas allowing convenient access to economic opportunities as well as health, educational and social amenities" (Tomlinson, 1998). Accordingly, South Africans were to have access to "a permanent residential structure with secure tenure, ensuring privacy and providing adequate protection against the elements; potable water; and sanitary facilities including waste disposal and domestic electricity supply" (Smit, 1999: 3).

In its quest to redress the wrongs committed by the apartheid regime, the ANC introduced a policy framework known as the Reconstruction and Development Programme (RDP). This policy was premised on the promise that the ANC government was going to construct one million houses for poor people in five years (ANC, 1994). The RDP was then accompanied by the "rights" mantra, which argued that access to decent housing was a basic right, and hence they were dedicated to housing everyone as part of their obligation to observe human rights and correct the wrongs of the apartheid era (Huchzermeyer, 2001). The provision of housing through RDP was also expected to create jobs, skills and economic activity, as actors in both the private sector and civil society were expected to play crucial roles in expanding housing delivery and financing capacity and at the same time promoting the growth of small and medium enterprises owned by black people whose activities were related to housing delivery. The ANC adopted at the time an approach to restore and secure homeownership and dignity for blacks and to empower them with skills during housing delivery.

One of the tasks of the Department of Human Settlements (DoHS) is to ensure that there is a realisation of the right to housing (South African Human

Rights Commission, 2000), amending pre-existing housing legislation as a step towards revamping the overall housing legislative framework (Cohen, 1995). It thus worked on legislation like the Housing Act of 1997 (Act 107 of 1997), the Housing Consumer Protection Measures Act of 1998 (Act 95 of 1998) and the Prevention of Illegal Eviction from and Unlawful Occupation of Land Act of 1998 (Act 19 of 1998). The preamble of these two policies was that everyone had the right to adequate housing. This witnessed the revoking of the Prevention of Illegal Eviction Act of 1998, which was set to be replaced by an act that prohibited arbitrary deprivation of property and at the same time recognising the rights of property owners to apply for evictions. While the Act prohibited arbitrary deprivation of property as a reversal of what was happening during apartheid, it also entrenched the right to property in the hands of the whites and this was inadvertently reinforced by the right of property owners to evict. These provisions affected blacks more than they affected whites, thereby increasing their vulnerability and insecurity.

The RDP resolved to pursue a gradualist approach in dealing with the housing shortage despite the urgency of the matter. It also came up with a framework for self-help and government-supported housing (Cohen, 1995). This arrangement saw the government providing housing inputs in accordance with the new housing legislation as spelled out by the White Paper on a New Housing Policy and Strategy, released in December 1994. Its vision was to increase by 5 per cent the share allocated to housing from the national budget with the expectation of eradicating the housing backlog in ten years. Provision of housing also included upgrading of informal settlements that surrounded the main urban centres, providing housing-related services, clean water, electricity, a toilet system, roads and a drainage system on top of uplifting the shanty houses into habitable and standard houses (Wilson and Marrs, 2004). The government did not manage to meet its target of a million houses in the first five years such that by 2000, in partnership with housing institutions, communities, the private sector and NGOs, it had managed at least 1,115, 300 houses with secure tenure which housed up to 5,776,300 poor people whose monthly income was R3,500 and below in both urban and rural areas (Department of Housing, 2001).

Despite this, the government was criticised for failing to realise its target of allocating 5 per cent of the national budget towards housing delivery, only realising a maximum of 1.6 per cent (Bond, 2000). In addition, over one million South Africans were still homeless and the number continued to grow (Gilbert, 2004). The government aimed to help poor people by increasing ownership without relying on apartheid construction firms and thus attempted to use subsidies to facilitate the emergence of black entrepreneurs. Upon realising that there was a shrinking of the funding to finance the programme, it involved the banks to finance low-income housing. It also aimed at raising employment in the construction of houses as a measure to mitigate the high levels of unemployment. These diverse goals, however, complicated the implementation. It has been argued that, in order to meet its target of one million houses in five years, the government effectively undermined quality and chose quantity as most of the houses were of poor quality in terms of workmanship. The housing units were less than 40 m² in size, covering a floor space of only 25 m² and with no partitions (Smit, 1999; Gilbert, 2004).

Housing delivery during this era was also made difficult by the challenges identified by Smit (1999: 2):

- Apartheid spatial engineering created inefficient settlement patterns for commuting and infrastructure provision;
- Role confusion and inefficiency in a myriad of housing institutions;
- Lack of clear policy direction;
- Absence of end-user finance for people with lower-middle and low incomes, despite a world-class financial sector;
- Complex, slow and frequently unsatisfactory tenure and land allocation procedures;
- Constraints in the housing construction sector (monopolies, limited capacity, bottlenecks and misfits between demand and supply capacity); and
- Complex socio-political issues such as high expectations, poor consumer education, non-payment for services, lack of special-needs housing and violation of women's housing rights.

Housing approaches/policies: 2004 to present

After ten years of independence, in 2004, the Department of Housing initiated an important shift in housing provision. The then Housing White Paper spoke of a housing programme with the aim of creating viable communities. Post-apartheid housing projects between 1994 and 2004 continued to take place on land that was racially set aside for townships and thus continued to reinforce segregation along class and race lines (Hucherzermeyer, 2003). The new approach by the Department of Housing emphasised the need for sustainable human settlements as well as achieving the integration of urban areas and ending economic exclusion (Breaking New Ground, 2004). This led to the introduction of the Comprehensive Plan for Sustainable Human Settlement, which was known as "Breaking New Ground" (BNG) by the cabinet in September 2004. The BNG plan retained the basic principles of the Housing White Paper and at the same time aimed to improve the quality of housing and housing environments as well as integrating communities and settlements. It also put in place new norms and standards for housing products, improving privacy and sustainability of human settlements. The plan also aimed at upgrading informal housing in line with the UN's Millennium Goals of improving the living conditions of those people residing in slums (Department of Human Settlement, 2010).

Housing subsidies

The National Housing Subsidy Policy has played an important role in the provision of houses to poor people in South Africa and is thus viewed as the cornerstone of the housing policy. The policy was promulgated to cater for the existing and projected backlogs and reduce housing and financial sector market distortions (Smit, 1999). Because of the high unemployment levels in the country, this arrangement offered one-off "capital" subsidies as opposed to interest subsidies. There were three ways in which people could access these subsidies: individual, project linked and institutional. Accordingly, the individual subsidy was meant to provide qualifying households with access to state assistance in facilitating the acquisition of an already existing house or a vacant serviced residential stand for the purpose of constructing a house through an approved mortgage loan. Institutional housing subsidies are those linked to some institutions (e.g. housing associations) and are meant to provide capital grants to social housing institutions to construct affordable rental units. They also facilitate the sale of housing units by the institution after a minimum period of four years of continuous occupation (Department of Human Settlements, 2010).

Although subsidies are mainly targeted at new housing projects, there are also funds available to top up subsidies where previous state investment in projects is not more than the current subsidy amount, while those who already own properties are not eligible (Smit, 1999). Upon inception in 1994, the subsidy amount was graded by income as follows: those who earned a monthly income of R1,500 were entitled an amount of R16,000, while those earning between R1,501 to R2,500 monthly were entitled to R10,000, and those earning between R2,501 to R3,500 were to receive R5,500 (Smit, 1999). However, these amounts in subsidies represent a compromise as they were not enough to cover the costs of completing a 40 m^2 house which was around R40,000 then. Beneficiaries were thus supposed to supplement with loans or savings – something that most households could not afford given the level of apartheid-induced poverty in the country.

Integrated Residential Development Programme (IRDP)

According to the Department of Human Settlements (2010), a review of the housing programmes outcomes since 1994 showed that low-income settlements, as was the case in the apartheid era, continued to be marginalised as they were located on the periphery of cities and towns and lacked access to a range of social and economic amenities. There was thus a need for a new plan in facilitating the development of integrated human settlements in convenient locations where the provision of urban amenities, including places of employment, was less difficult. To address this, the IRPD was instituted. The IRDP facilitates the acquisition of land and the servicing of stands for different land uses – commercial, recreational, schools and clinics, as well as residential stands for low-, middle- and high-income housing. The first phase of the programme is the provision of serviced stands and the second provides for housing construction to those qualifying for low-income houses as well as the sale of serviced stands to those who for various reasons do not qualify for the subsidies (Smit, 1999).

Upgrading of informal settlements

According to the Department of Human Settlements (2010), informal settlements normally experience rapid urbanisation but lack the resources, housing and related infrastructure needed for proper urbanisation. To deal with the challenges associated with these settlements, the government resolved to upgrade them as a step towards improving the living conditions of millions of poor people who stay in these settlements by providing them with secure tenure, access to basic services and housing. Ownership of a house with basic services and a secure tenure is a big step in a household's quest for improved social and economic circumstances. The programme was designed with the aim of bringing about social cohesion, stability and security in integrated developments, as well as creating jobs, and improving the economic well-being of communities which were previously side-lined in terms of having access to land and business services, formal housing and social and economic amenities. The programme was designed to benefit a range of people living in informal settlements who qualify for housing subsidies, households whose income is less than the minimum threshold and households headed by minors, among others. While upgrading in this context is *in situ*, it is important to note that in circumstances where the terrain is not suitable for human settlement (for example those prone to flooding, difficult/dangerous terrain, shallow undermining conditions and so forth), residents are relocated and settled elsewhere. Since the subsidy is normally not enough, beneficiaries are allowed to apply for housing construction assistance through other national housing programmes like Individual Subsidies, Enhanced People's Housing Process, Social Housing and so on (Department of Human Settlements, 2010).

Provision of social and economic facilities

This programme is meant to provide the basic social and economic facilities that are missing in some residential settlements. These include schools, clinics, community halls, recreational facilities and trading facilities, which were absent in most new housing projects and informal settlements. This provision is aimed at establishing quality, sustainable human settlements through funding primary social and economic amenities, where funding is not available from other sources. Funding is provided to all municipalities that lack the financial capacity to provide those services/facilities which are also meeting the basic requirements for consideration (Department of Human Settlements, 2010).

Rural housing subsidy

The Rural Housing Programme focuses on areas of communal land tenure and calls for the tenure rights to be confirmed first through the processes prescribed by the responsible authority. This programme is only available on a project basis but can also be flexibly applied to meet real needs. As a prerequisite for accessing this type of subsidy, beneficiaries are expected to provide evidence of undisputed land tenure rights and that they qualify for new order tenure rights on the piece of land which is allocated to them. The subsidy may also be used to develop internal municipal services or upgrade existing housing structures or services (where there are no alternative funds), build houses, or any combination of these options. This programme is in line with the objective of the BNG plan to create "sustainable human settlements for a needs-orientated rural development programme that caters for traditional technologies, appropriate funding mechanisms and addressing important issues of tenure security, livelihood strategies and the broader socio-cultural matters" (Department of Human Settlements, 2010: 17).

Stubborn demand and persisting challenges

Despite all the housing subsidy initiatives, upgrading of informal settlements and so on, housing challenges still continue to persist in South Africa. Tissington (2011) notes that despite providing 2.3 million housing units to almost 11 million South Africans between 1994 and 2010, the country is still experiencing a shortage of housing. Even the recipients of this housing programme are not satisfied with the dwellings, which are often located far away from places of employment resulting in people spending more money on transport. The government could not continue to dish out free housing to the people since the initiative was just a safety net for the poorest of poor people.

By 2010, there was evidence which showed that it was impossible for the country's existing housing policy and practice at the time to realise its target of eradicating informal settlements as well as the UN's Millennium Development Goal of slum-free cities. Between 1999 and 2004, only 10 per cent of households moved from informal settlements to formal dwellings (Lall *et al.*, 2007). The South African Institute for Race Relations (2014) notes that increasing poverty and high levels of unemployment push poor people to continue flocking to informal settlements in city peripheries as they are too poor to afford decent accommodation. This, in turn, suggests that employment creation can be a way of reducing urban informality if jobs can be created where people are, especially in rural areas.

Mukorombindo (2014) argues that the increasing population of households residing in slums is a clear indication that the government cannot meet the demand for houses in South Africa. Wilkinson (2014) reasons that despite this increase in informal settlements, government intervention has at least seen an improvement in living conditions when compared to the apartheid era. Among the critical challenges encountered in trying to realise these targets are factors such as a lack of a strategy to unlock well-located land for residential development in urban centres, little or no connection of bulk infrastructure/services to new residential settlements and an absence of services and upgrading programmes in existing informal settlements. Also included on the constricting factors is the lack of affordable, decent rental housing for those low-income earners who cannot afford their own houses or are staying away from home. It has also been argued that despite the progressive informal settlements upgrading policy since 2004, no informal settlement had been "fully" upgraded by 2010. Impeding new housing delivery and informal settlements upgrading are various challenges including politicisation of the programme, poor inter- and intra-governmental relations in the provision of bulk service connections to housing settlements, poor coordination and implementation of the programme resulting in delays, shortage of technical skills, over-reliance on the private sector, corruption and so on (Tissington, 2011).

Housing delivery is also hindered by the imperfect down-marketing of housing finance. About 86 per cent of South African households do not earn enough to afford a mortgage of more than R200,000 (Joffe, 2006). The challenge is also worsened by the ever-escalating prices of housing; restricted access to housing finance and the low supply of subsidised housing have also made it difficult for poor people to enter the formal housing market (Lall *et al.*, 2007). For example, it is very difficult for poor people to legally gain access to land especially in urban settings where the value tends to be inflated. There is also some resistance by many municipalities to allocate well-located land for low-income housing and this resistance stems largely from the high-income groups whose motive is to avoid a perceived devaluation of their properties when located close to low-income housing (Lall *et al.*, 2007). Sikota (2015) argues that one flaw of these housing delivery programmes is that they are not participatory. Gunter (2014: 96) attributes the continued housing shortage to "factors like high and rising costs of ownership, inability to apply for subsidised housing, irregular and low income have limited access to formal housing by the urban poor". The next section posits a theory of incompatibility.

Towards a theory of incompatibility

Homelessness is a product of inequality. For poor (unaggressive) people, owning a house means pouring all their life savings into housing. They are exploited during construction as wage labourers and through paying rent to their property owner as tenants as they remain enslaved to paying rent. Paying rent diminishes poor people's capacity to accumulate capital. Rent has elements of slavery. Therefore, housing is about equity, fairness and social justice. In the context of South Africa – it is also about redress.

It is only at home that a person has localised hegemony over his/her "own territory" and can set his/her own rules and regulations. Home has some regulatory effects on a homeowner including the one who is renting (on a limited scale as the property owner can prescribe his/her own rules). Home is a space for the establishment of self-territorial determination, individual sovereignty and local territorial allegiance leading to nationhood (sovereignty effects). Because of local territorial allegiance, the cumulative individual allegiances consolidate into national sovereignty. The negative effects of private property rights include de-housing effects (housing is a monopoly of the few); vulnerability effects (as represented by the circumstances of poor people in informal and similar settlements); and precarity effects (absence of tenure and landlessness makes the situation of unaggressive/poor people precarious).

The theory of incompatibility posits that in circumstances of unequal relations on the basis of power, standing in society, status, money, mandate, knowledge, information asymmetries and so on, it is the will of the dominant individuals or entities that will prevail over the unaggressive as a result of the incompatibility of their interests. The unaggressive are the weaker in society by circumstances of exploitation and manufactured disadvantage by the dominant. At any given time in any society, as has been since time immemorial, there will always be the dominant and unaggressive. The unaggressive could include for example children and elderly people (at times women in some patriarchal societies) at the micro level. At the meso level could be groups of elites, firms, non-governmental organisations, municipalities and so on. At the macro level, the dominant could be governments, multinational companies, the military and so on. While the interests of these individuals and entities could and can be reconcilable, they will always be incompatible. This theory applies in all circumstances in which asymmetries of all forms are present.

Conclusion

This chapter has shown that in as much as the South African government regards homeownership as a basic right for every citizen, and despite the many pieces of legislation and policies to meet this right, the housing challenges has not been dealt with resolutely. The chapter has demonstrated that most programmes have been very slow in realising their stated goals. In addition, subsidy programmes have not provided adequate funds to finance a house to completion because most beneficiaries of subsidy programmes do not earn enough to supplement the subsidies nor have access to alternative funding sources. The quality of housing also continues to be a concern. The powerful land/property holders have also resisted the government's move to parcel out land to landless/homeless people. The implication of this is that the legacy of apartheid continues to thrive with poor people residing in the periphery of urban centres. The chapter posits a theory of incompatibility which acknowledges asymmetries based on power, influence and status differentials to produce dominant individuals and entities to establish their hegemony over others.

References

ANC, 1994. *The Reconstruction and Development Programme: a policy framework.* Johannesburg: Umanyano.

Bond, P. 2000. *The Elite Transition: from apartheid to neoliberalism in South Africa.* London: Pluto Press.

Breaking New Ground, 2004. *A Comprehensive Plan for the Development of Sustainable Human Settlements.* www.capegateway.gov.za/Text/2007/10/bng.pdf.

Cohen, T. 1995. Land and housing. *South African Human Rights Yearbook 1995*, 6, pp. 131–147.

Department of Housing, 2001. *The South African Housing Policy: operationalizing the right to adequate housing*. Paper presented at Istanbul +5, New York, 6–8 June.

Department of Human Settlements, 2009. *National Housing Code*. Pretoria: Department of Human Settlements.

Department of Human Settlements, 2010. *National Housing Policy and Subsidy Programmes*. Pretoria: Department of Human Settlements.

Fox, S. and Goodfellow, T. 2016. *Cities and Development*. New York: Routledge.

Gilbert, A. 2004. Helping the poor through housing subsidies: lessons from Chile, Colombia and South Africa. *Habitat International*, 28, pp. 13–40.

Gunter, A, 2014. Renting shacks: landlords and tenants in the informal housing sector in Johannesburg South Africa. *Urbani izziv*, 25, pp. 96–107.

Hart, H. 1982. *Essays on Bentham: jurisprudence and political philosophy*. Oxford: Oxford University Press.

Harvey, D. 2008. The right to the city. *New Left Review*, 53, pp. 23–40.

Hodkinson, S. 2012. The return of the housing question. *Ephemera*, 12, pp. 423–444.

Huchzermeyer, M. 2001. Housing for the poor? Negotiated housing policy in South Africa. *Habitat International*, 25, pp. 303–331.

Hucherzermeyer, M. 2003. The legacy of control? The capital subsidy for housing, and informal settlement intervention in South Africa. *International Journal of Urban and Regional Research*, 27(3), pp. 591–612.

Joffe, H. 2006. Reporting on Wits University School of Public Development and Management Forum. *Business Day*, 6 June.

Lall, S.V., van den Brink, R., Leresche, K.M. and Dasgupta, B. 2007. *Subsidized Housing and Access to Land in South African Cities*. Pretoria: World Bank Publications.

Marx, K. 1978. On the Jewish question. In by R.C. Tucker (Ed.), *The Marx-Engels Reader*, 2nd ed. New York: WW Norton & Co.

Mukorombindo, Y. 2014. Eradicating informal settlements by 2014: a goal deferred. www.healthe.org.za/wpcontent/uploads/2014/05/2014_MUKOROBINDO_HUMAN_SETTLEMENTS_POLICY ANALYSIS_BRIEF-libre-2.pdf [accessed 15 June 2018].

Republic of South Africa, 1996. *The Constitution of South Africa (1996)*. www.justice.gov.za/legislation/constitution/SAConstitution-web-eng.pdf.

Ripstein, A. 2017. Property and sovereignty: how to tell the difference. *Theoretical Inquiries in Law*, 18, pp. 243–268.

Sikota, Z. 2015. *No Meaningful Participation Without Effective Representation: the case of the Niall Mellon housing project in Imizamo Yethu, Hout Bay*. Master's Thesis, Cape Town, University of the Western Cape.

Smit, D. 1999. Housing in South Africa: significant government achievement based on public–private partnership. *CDE Focus*, 5, November.

South African Human Rights Commission, n.d. *Access to Adequate Housing*. www.sahrc.org.za/index.php/focus-areas/access-to-justice-adequate-housing/access-to-adequate-housing.

South African Institute of Race Relations NPC, 2014. *84th Annual Report*. https://irr.org.za/about-us/annual-report/84th-annual-report.

Thomas, C.G. 2010. *The Discourses on the Right to Housing in Gauteng Province, 1994–2008*. PhD Thesis, Johannesburg, University of the Witwatersrand.

Tissington, K. 2011. *A Resource Guide to Housing in South Africa 1994–2010: legislation, policy, programmes and practice*. Johannesburg: SERI.

Tomlinson, M.R. 1998. South Africa's new housing policy: an assessment of the first two years, 1994–1996. *International Journal of Urban and Regional Research*, 22, pp. 137–146.

Wilkinson, K. 2014. Factsheet: the housing situation in South Africa. https://africacheck.org/factsheets/factsheet-the-housing-situation-in-south-africa/ [accessed 16 June 2018].

Wilson, N. and Marrs, D. 2004. Informal settlements are on the way out. *Business Day* (online edition). 3 September 2004.

11 A gendered discourse on women's access to housing in South Africa

Claudine Hingston

Introduction

Housing is a fundamental human need and it serves as a shelter as well as a space to eat, sleep, relax and nurture a family. According to UN-Habitat (2017), housing is at the centre of our lives and in many ways defines who we are and who we can become. Through the "Housing at the Centre" approach, UN-Habitat (2017) advocates for local and national governments to reflect on their urban decision-making and action, and on the pivotal role of housing in urban development. The Housing at the Centre approach is designed to help all levels of government achieve the realisation of the right to adequate housing for all, as defined by international legal instruments. This approach is underpinned by seven fundamental conditions – security of tenure, habitability, affordability, accessibility, location, access to basic services, and cultural adequacy (UN-Habitat, 2017). It is widely recognised that shelter satisfies a basic human need for physical security and comfort (Statistics South Africa, 2017). Moreover, the characteristics of the dwellings in which households live and their access to various services and facilities provide an important indication of the well-being of household members (Statistic South Africa, 2017). The right to adequate housing is a human right and is mentioned in a number of international human rights instruments and treaties such as the Universal Declaration of Human Rights (United Nations, 1948) and the International Covenant on Economic, Social and Cultural Rights (1966). For instance, the following is stated in Article 11 of the International Covenant on Economic, Social and Cultural Rights (United Nations, 1966):

> States Parties to the present Covenant recognize the right of everyone to an adequate standard of living for himself and his family, including adequate food, clothing and housing, and to the continuous improvement of living conditions.

After taking over power through a democratic election in 1994, the African National Congress government adopted the White Paper on Housing (1994) which stipulates that all South Africans should have access to a permanent residential structure with secure tenure. The White Paper on Housing (1994) further states that every effort will be made to realise this vision for all South Africans. This vision, however, has not been fully realised as, up to recent times, South Africa has a substantial number of homeless people and people that lack adequate housing. A joint research report on homelessness by the City of Tshwane *et al.* (2015) calls attention to a study on street homelessness by the Human Science Research Council between 2006 and 2010, which suggests that there may be between 100,000 and 200,000 street homeless people in South Africa's urban and rural districts, including adults and children. The research, however, acknowledges that formal statistics on homeless people is limited. Additionally, a substantial number of people in South Africa live in informal housings. Recent statistics by Statistics South Africa on housing reveal that 13.6 per cent of South Africans live in informal dwellings (Statistics South Africa, 2017). Informal housing is described by Statistics South Africa as a make-shift structure not erected according to approved architectural plans, such as shacks or shanties in informal settlements or in backyards. Thus, informal housing is in essence inadequate housing. According to People's Environment Planning (2016), there are currently about 12 million people in South Africa without adequate housing and the deficit continues to grow.

This study aligns more with the term "adequate housing" than "housing" as adequate housing is what is best suited for human needs and comfort. This chapter further aligns with the country's Constitutional Court (2000) interpretation of adequate housing. In the *Government of the Republic of South Africa vs Grootboom*, the Constitutional Court ruled:

> Housing entails more than bricks and mortar. It requires available land, appropriate services such as the provision of water and the removal of sewage and the financing of all these, including the building of the house itself. For a person to have access to adequate housing all of these conditions need to be met: there must be land, there must be services, and there must be a dwelling. The right of access to adequate housing also suggests that it is not only the State that is responsible for the provision of houses but that other agents within society, including individuals themselves, must be enabled by legislative and other measures to provide housing.
>
> (Constitutional Court of South Africa, 2000: para 35)

Since the inception of the White Paper on Housing (1994), there have been numerous shifts in South Africa's housing policy. These shifts always take cognisance of the South African Constitution, which enshrines the right of everyone to have access to adequate housing, regardless of factors such as gender, race and religion. In fact, after 1994, the principles of gender equality influenced policy and legislation formulation in areas related to the economy and development, such as access to employment, land, housing, water, health care and public works programmes, among others (Ministry in the Presidency Responsible for Women, 2015). Thus, South Africa's housing policy affords both women and men equal rights to housing. Despite this, women in South Africa still experience many challenges in accessing housing. These challenges stem from gender and social constructs that place women in marginalised positions. This study aims to contextualise women's access to housing in South Africa, examine factors that limit South African women's access to housing via a gender lens and suggest ways in which they can be addressed. This study is a desk research and therefore makes use of relevant secondary data.

The interpretivist paradigm was utilised in this study. According to Hennick *et al.* (2011), the interpretative paradigm recognises that reality is socially constructed as people's experiences occur within social, cultural, historical or personal contexts. As the interpretivist paradigm also allows researchers to be co-creators of the research knowledge (Henning *et al.*, 2004), it was deemed suitable for this study.

This study is couched as a gendered discourse. Discourse involves the use of texts to communicate. According to Lucke (1996), human subjects use texts to make sense of their world. In this same vein, the researcher attempts to make sense of women's access to adequate housing through text. Holmes and Marra (2010) note that people also draw on discursive resources to construct their social identities. They add that feminist linguists are known to have the knowledge and skills not only to identify, describe and critique discourses of femininity and masculinity but also to highlight discursive behaviours which penalise women in many social contexts (Holmes and Marra, 2010). The researcher argues that if discourse can be used to construct, it can also be used to expose and deconstruct. According to Venter and Marais (2010), discourse analysis has been recognised as an increasingly important analytical tool in housing policy research and is a key source of understanding housing processes. In this same vein, the researcher uses discourse to examine the gender dynamics of housing in South Africa. This study is therefore a gendered discourse aimed at contextualising women's access to housing in South Africa and the challenges they face.

This study further draws on intersectional feminism. Intersectional feminism is based on the understanding of how women's overlapping identities – including race, class, ethnicity, religion and sexual orientation – impact the way they experience discrimination and oppression (Maj, 2013). Hancock (2007) affirms that factors such as gender, class and race play a role in shaping lived experiences. Although South African women may have similar problems, their experiences differ because of their race and class. While this study attempts to contextualise and examine South Africa's women's access to housing in South Africa in general, it privileges black South African women, often referred to as African women. This is because they constitute the group that literature indicates to be the most affected by housing problems. According to Meth and Charlton (2017: 4), "race-based apartheid legislation made homeownership and occupation in cities, for black women in particular, hard to achieve". The historic and current patriarchal systems of property and land ownership and inheritance continue to impede black women's access to housing (Meth and Charlton, 2017). This situation is exacerbated by "persistent socio-cultural practices which often prevent rural women from holding land titles" and property, and "actual transformations in gendered access (by black women) to and control over land in post-apartheid South Africa" (Meth and Charlton, 2017: 4). Intersectional feminism thus lends an understanding that the diverse identities of South Africa women differentiate their experiences in various issues, including housing. This study utilised relevant information from various texts such as books, journals and online materials. The use of the term *African women* in this study is in reference to black South African women.

An overview of women's access to housing in South Africa

Before delving into a discussion on women's access to housing in South Africa, it must be noted that these problems are not limited to South Africa. Globally, women have constraints with regards to access to housing. As Venter and Marais (2006: 69) state, from 1970 onwards, feminist research began to question the relevance of the household as a unit without adequate recognition of women and female-headed households. Venter and Marais (2006) further note that "literature focusing on gender in the context of low-income housing acknowledges that inadequate housing tends to have a greater impact on women, who spend more time in the home and its immediate environment, than on men". Similarly, Gandhi (1987) states that despite women being the primary users of the house in performing domestic and paid labour, they have little control or right over houses. Gandhi further notes that in spite of wide-raging historicities, social differences, and political and ideological differences of different countries, there are some basic similarities in situations, obstacles and issues facing women, such as housing problems.

Moving on to South Africa, women's access to housing is rooted in the historical, social and economic context of South Africa. Todes and Walker (1992) state that housing policies have created sharp divides among different groups of South African women particularly based on class and historical access to housing. Pillay *et al.*, (2002) note that from the 1930s there were explicit laws and policies that controlled the mobility of women and "these laws made women dependent on their male partners or fathers for their rights to remain in urban areas" (UN Habitat, 2007: 14). This legacy resulted in a significant number of women residing in informal settlements and housing for families was via male-members households (Pillay *et al.*, 2002). Similarly, Todes and Walker (1992) state that rules governing housing allocation ensured that women's access to housing was almost entirely through men and that women were also constrained by their lack of earning power and by the Natal Code, which defined them as minors with no contractual powers. This "minority legal status of women under the customary law regardless of age or marital status resulted in women not being able to own property except with the consent of a male relative" (Pillay *et al.*, 2002: 9). It also resulted in many single women being forced to enter into convenience marriages and since up to 1988, women were married in community of property and they were subjected to their husband's marital power in controlling property, even after a divorce (Todes and Walker, 1992). This situation culminated in women being denied housing rights and having to make do with poor-quality housing on the outskirts of economic centres (Pillay *et al.*, 2002). This historic system coupled with patriarchal and discriminatory socio-cultural practices impacted black women's access to housing more negatively than any race group (Meth and Charlton, 2017). This lends credence to the intersectional feminism claim that women's experiences differ because of their identities.

Following the changes in the political landscape of South Africa after apartheid, new laws and policies that aimed to bridge gender and racial inequalities were introduced. The issue of housing access was considered and this was included in the South African Constitution. The Constitution affords both women and men equal rights. Section 26 of the Bill of Rights in the Constitution states that everyone shall have the right of access to adequate housing and accessibility and it prohibits evictions of persons from their homes and the demolition of their homes without a court order. This is outlined as follow:

1 Everyone has the right to have access to housing.
2 The state must take reasonable legislative and other measures, within its available resources, to achieve the progressive realisation of this right.
3 No one may be evicted from their home, or have their home demolished, without an order of the court made after considering all the relevant circumstances. No legislation may permit arbitrary evictions (Republic of South Africa, 1996).

The White Paper on Housing (1994), in accordance with the South African Constitution, stipulates that new policies should be sensitive to the elimination of discrimination in respect of gender, race and religion and is quite explicit with regard to eligibility criteria in respect of who the end-beneficiaries should be (Venter and Marais, 2006). According to the White Paper on Housing (1994), the government has specifically identified the need to support the role of women in the housing delivery process (Venter and Marais, 2006). A document on the right to adequate housing from April 2000–March 2002 (South African Human Rights Commission, 2002) calls attention to a statement made by the National Department of Housing that instituted measures do not discriminate against women and that the department is committed to women not only as beneficiaries but also as active participants and service providers in the delivery of housing. From the above, it appears that policy and legislature wise, there are no obstacles to women accessing housing. In a nutshell, on paper, women in South Africa seem to be on a par with men in access to housing. In reality, the situation differs.

In 2003, the Public Service Commission (2003) noted that housing policy directives that focus on gender equity are largely neglected in most provinces. Charlton (2004) identified some gender gaps in the housing policy such as that the particular needs of women who might be abused or vulnerable in some way are not prioritised and that gender-related issues post-occupation are not considered. Venter and

Marais (2006) further state that there have been a number of studies that have raised gender-related criticism about housing policies. In concurrence, Chenwi and McLean (2009) point out that although housing legislation and policies in South Africa have attempted to incorporate gender concerns and ensure women's participation in housing delivery, a number of inadequacies and gaps in the implementation of legislation and policies still exist. Apart from the gaps and inadequacies identified in policies, the social framework through which housing delivery takes place also results in inequities in access to housing. It is this social framework that this article is concerned with. The next section examines factors that limit women's access to adequate housing in South Africa.

Factors limiting South African women's access to adequate housing

This chapter acknowledges that there are many factors that inhibit women's access to housing. The factors examined in this chapter, however, will focus on gender-related issues within an economic, cultural and social context.

Economic issues

According to Pillay *et al.* (2002), women's economic realities have implications for their rights of access to housing. Black African women, in particular, are the hardest hit financially as they have a higher unemployment rate and earn less when employed. Their work pattern is also impacted by child care and other caregiving responsibilities that are unpaid and generally unrecognised (Pillay *et al.*, 2002). These "interrupted work patterns negatively impact on mobility and earnings in the workplace and ultimately on women's access to credit and ability to afford a house" (Pillay *et al.*, 2002: 8). According to Todes and Walker (1992), the rules of access for public housing require that lessees have income and can pay rent. This, in turn, affects African women the most, given their poorer access to employment. Although access to housing in the private sector exhibits no gender bias as it is based on the dictum "you get what you can pay for", economic factors tend to undermine the position of women in the private housing sector such as the high cost of entry into private housing and strict payment terms (Todes and Walker, 1992). This exerts a high financial pressure on women, thus discouraging many from accessing private property. Because of the economic factors associated with public and private property, many women, particularly African women, tend to turn to the informal housing sector because of its low entry cost. This low-cost housing, however, comes at a high cost as there is a poor level of essential service provision (water, electricity, sewage, roads and garbage collection) in informal settlements that affects women severely (Todes and Walker, 1992). Inadequate housing is perilous for women because of childcare needs, vulnerability to violence and risks of evictions (Chenwi and McLean, 2009). Furthermore, it increases their vulnerability to extreme weather events such as precipitation and related floods.

According to a report on the status of women in the South African economy (Ministry in the Presidency Responsible for Women, 2015), numerous studies have found that there is a substantial gender gap in the experience of poverty by men and women in South Africa and that women experience more intense poverty than men. For instance, Meth and Charlton (2017) note that female-headed households tend to experience poverty more than their male counterparts. Moving back to the report on the status of women, it further states that there are racial differences in female poverty rates as well and that while 63.4 per cent of African women lived below the lower bound poverty rates in 2012, this figure drops to 35.1 per cent for coloured women, and 1.6 per cent for white women, and this statistic has not changed much in present times (Ministry in the Presidency Responsible for Women, 2015). Thus, poverty rates among African women, particularly those in non-urban areas, are very high and this affects their access to adequate housing. This is indicative of intersectional feminism, which posits that women's experiences differ because of identities such as class, race and ethnicity. Unemployment and poverty also result in women staying in abusive relationships with partners they are dependent on, which in turn greatly affects their well-being in their homes. It is evident that black African women in South Africa are the most financially constrained group of women and this impedes their access to housing. This interplay between gender, class, race and economic status demonstrates the concept of intersectional feminism.

Culture, religion, patriarchy and violence

Culture, religion, patriarchy and violence are interwoven and all play a role in the oppression of women. The former South African Minister in the Presidency Responsible for Women, Susan Shabangu, alludes to this when she states that culture, social systems and religion have promoted patriarchy and the oppression of women and that discrimination of women has taken a variety of forms ranging from disenfranchisement to various forms of abuse (Ministry in the Presidency Responsible for Women, 2015).

Culture

South Africa has a strong legal framework in respect of gender equality and women's rights and it is one of the highest ranked countries in Africa in this respect (Statistics South Africa, 2011). There have been criticisms of the failure to translate this good stance into practice since patriarchy and gender discrimination are prevalent in South African society. As stated in the gender statistics report (Statistics South Africa, 2011), there are discriminatory practices, social norms and persistent stereotypes in the country that result in inequitable access to opportunities, resources and power for women and girls.

While providing for the rights of all, the Constitution of South Africa also provides for and protects the right to culture and recognises traditional leadership. This could be interpreted as protecting practices such as polygamy, spouse inheritance, *Ukuthwala* (the practice of abducting young girls and forcing them into marriage) and other customary practices which have the impact of undermining the constitutional guarantee of gender equality (Maluleke, 2012). Makulele (2012) further notes that although the provisions protecting the right to culture explicitly include a qualification stipulating that these rights should not be exercised in a manner inconsistent with any provision of the Bill of Rights, not much cognisance has been taken of it. Customary practices such as *Ukuthwala*, widow's rituals and others are entrenched, and in the villages where they are carried out, they compromise women's right to equality and are interpreted to mean that women, as opposed to men, do not have inherent rights (Maluleke, 2012). According to Pillay *et al.* (2002: 9), "discriminatory customary and religious laws and practices often work to the detriment of women's housing rights and patrilineal succession under customary law has had serious implications for women's rights to land and housing". Additionally, "customary land tenure practices are based on communal tenure with rights vested in male traditional leaders, and the allocation of land and housing by traditional authorities is to heads of households, who are almost always male" (Pillay *et al.*, 2002: 9). Thus, "women's right to land and housing is, as a result, dependent on their relationship to male heirs" (Pillay *et al.*, 2002: 9).

Pillay *et al.* (2002: 9) also note that the practice of polygamy has an adverse impact on women and housing and "cites a 1997 study by the Development Action Group which reveals that male hostel dwellers were accessing subsidy schemes with women in urban areas and then bringing wives from rural areas to live with them". This led to the urban women being "forced out of the common home and they did not qualify for a further subsidy" (Pillay *et al.*, 2002: 9). Since the identified cultural practices are still persistent and more entrenched in black communities, they further stifle the African woman's access to adequate housing, another indicator of intersectional feminism.

Religion

Religion is also instrumental in placing women in subordinated positions to men. As Raday (2003: 672) notes, "religious norms impose patriarchal regimes that disadvantage women". These include mandatory obedience to their spouse, inequality in inheritance rights and division of matrimonial property, non-eligibility for religious offices and few or no rights over their own bodies. Although not all religions are homogenous, they all to some extent endorse patriarchy and promote the idea of men being the dominant sex. Adherence to religious dictates places women in positions where they see themselves as secondary to men and men in turn view women as their property. Such religious dictates have played a part in limiting women's access to housing as the belief that the male is the head of the household and the decision-maker prevents women from actively becoming involved in housing decisions that will benefit them.

Patriarchy

Rakoczy (2004) argues that patriarchy as the rule of the father/male over women is a form of violence because of its negative effect on women's dignity and space in society. In most societies, including South Africa, patriarchal norms and values underpin gender relations. These norms can have serious consequences for women. The former Minister in the Presidency Responsible for Women, Susan Shabangu, alludes to this when she states that patriarchy is the philosophy underpinning women's subordination on one hand and male supremacy on the other hand. She notes that patriarchy is the oldest form of discrimination in the world and it seeks to systematically discriminate against women and impedes the efforts of the South African government to empower women (Ministry in the Presidency Responsible for Women, 2015).

Within the South African landscape, Meth and Charlton (2017: 4) state that with regards to "renting, owning (but not fully paid off) and occupying rent-free, men of all race groups in South Africa dominate as household heads", which in short is a patriarchal structure. Pillay *et al.* (2002) call attention to the notion that patriarchy has a negative consequence in the area of housing for women. For example, (Pillay *et al.*, 2002: 8) note that "most male partners register homes in their own names and this forces women to forge and remain in relationships to meet their housing needs". There is evidence that tensions do arise between men and women in the housing processes and there is "a predominance of male aggression enacted against women as a result of this tension. This tension has its roots in wider socio-economic relations, specifically persisting patriarchy, normalisation of violence and extensive poverty" (Meth and Charlton, 2017: 17). Further, "housing policy often favours couples while households headed by a single female are often excluded or discriminated against, as they do not fit the traditional concept of a family" (Pillay *et al.*, 2002: 8). Todes and Walker (1992) concur with this, by stating that personal biases of administrators and councillors also negatively impact women's access to public housing in South Africa.

Violence

The Declaration of the Elimination of Violence against Women (United Nations, 1993) states that violence against women means any act of gender-based violence that results in, or is likely to result in, physical, sexual or psychological harm or suffering to women, including threats of such acts, coercion or arbitrary deprivation of liberty, whether occurring in public or in private life. Violence against women by men is rampant in present-day South Africa, which has sought to develop a comprehensive response to gender-based violence that includes legislation, public awareness programmes and shelters for abused women. However, many women remain at risk as South Africa has one of the highest global rates of gender-based violence (Centre for the Study of Violence and Reconciliation, 2016. Violence against women in South Africa can be sexual, physical or psychological and it exists in many households, communities and institutions, and it cuts across race, class, ethnicity, religion and geographic locations. Domestic violence (violence perpetrated by an intimate partner) has become endemic in present-day South Africa and it has a profound effect on women's housing rights. Pillay *et al.* (2002: 9) catalogue the following impacts:

- Women staying in abusive relationships as they have nowhere else to go;
- Child care and custody of children in such cases vesting in the mother, resulting in a heightened need for secure housing;
- Loss of housing as a result of separation or divorce.

Pillay *et al.* (2002: 9) further argue that the fact that housing is usually in the name of the man makes women's housing situation particularly tenuous in instances of domestic violence, and fleeing from an abusive situation brings with it the impossible choice between homelessness and staying in an abusive relationship.

Findings and the way forward

The main finding that emerged from the desk research is that deep-rooted factors such as violence, patriarchy, culture, religion and economic status impact women's access to housing in South Africa. It also revealed that African women are the most affected by these factors thereby restricting their access to adequate housing. It is indicative in this study that engendering housing policies to increase women's access to housing is not enough.

There is a dire need to also shift mindsets, particularly those grounded in culture and religion. Ibhawoh (2000) states that formal legislative enactments alone cannot change pervasive cultural attitudes. He suggests that community involvement offers the best prospects for a culturally sensitive solution in resolving the conflicts between national human rights and cultural traditions. Efforts to change harmful traditions are most effective when they originate within the culture that practises them (Hersh, 1998). The government and other stakeholders should, therefore, enlist the cooperation of community, traditional and religious leaders to amend or eradicate discriminatory practices and beliefs. Meaningful conversations or dialogue, specifically those based on inheritance and housing rights, should be held with them to explore ways of working towards gender parity without overly compromising religious or cultural beliefs.

This chapter argues that if mindsets are shifted to allow for acceptance of gender equality and equal rights and opportunities for men and women, there will be an improvement in women's access to housing. Traditions that limit women's access to adequate housing must, therefore, be challenged. Furthermore, the state must create a viable condition to assist women who are financially constrained to be able to access adequate housing. Efforts should also be made by the government and other relevant stakeholders to provide women with more opportunities that will help them to overcome cultural, patriarchal and religious restrictions. Additionally, it is recommended that the government should embark on a policy of positive discrimination with regards to housing. This, in essence, means that that the South African government should give preference to women over men in all housing processes. These mindsets, change dialogues and other suggestions outlined should, however, be carried out alongside the implementation of gender-sensitive housing policies and legislations.

Conclusion

This chapter has provided a gendered discourse on women's access to housing in South Africa. It contextualised women's access to housing in South Africa and examined factors that limit South African women's access to housing using a gender lens. Additionally, it drew on an intersectional feminist framework to highlight that black women in South Africa experience the most challenges with regards to accessing housing. Finally, this chapter suggested possible ways in which women's challenges with regards to accessing adequate housing can be addressed.

References

Centre for the Study of Violence and Reconciliation, 2016. *Gender Based Violence in South Africa: a brief review*. Pretoria.

Charlton, S. 2004 *An Overview of the Housing Policy and Debates, Particularly in Relation to Women (or Vulnerable Groupings)*. Research report written for the Centre for the Study of Violence and Reconciliation. Johannesburg: CSVR.

Chenwi, L. and McLean, K. 2009. "A woman's home is her castle?" Poor women and housing inadequacy in South Africa. *South African Journal on Human Rights*, Vol. 25, No. 3, pp. 517–545.

City of Tshwane, UNISA, University of Pretoria and Tshwane Homelessness Forum, 2015. *Pathways Out of Homelessness*. www.up.ac.za/media/shared/249/ZP_Files/homelessness-report-2015.zp70613.pdf [accessed 27 August 2018].

Constitution of the Republic of South Africa, 1996. Bill of Rights. www.gov.za/documents/constitution/chapter-2-bill-rights#26 [accessed 17 August 2018].

Constitutional Court of South Africa, 2000. *Government of the Republic of South Africa and Others* v. *Grootboom and Others*. www.saflii.org/za/cases/ZACC/2000/19.html [accessed 18 August 2018].

Gandhi, N. 1987. Gender and housing. *Economic and Political Weekly*, Vol. 22, No. 47, pp. 1994–1997.

Hancock, A.M. 2007. Intersectionality as a normative and empirical paradigm. *Politics and Gender*, Vol. 3, No. 2, pp. 248–254.

Hennick, M., Hutter, I. and Bailey, A. 2011 *Qualitative Research Methods*. London: Sage Publications.

Henning, E., Van Rensburg, W. and Smith, B. 2004. *Finding Your Way in Qualitative Research*. Pretoria: Van Shaik publishers.

Hersh, L. 1998. *Giving Up Harmful Practices, Not Culture*. www.advocatesforyouth.org/publications/publications-a-z/521-giving-up-harmful-practices-not-culture [accessed 15 August 2018].

Holmes, J. and Marra, M. 2010. *Femininity, Feminism and Gendered Discourse.* A selected and edited collection of papers from the Fifth International Language and Gender Association Conference. Newcastle: Cambridge Scholars Publishing.

Ibhawoh, B. 2002. Between culture and constitution: evaluating the cultural legitimacy of human rights in the African state. *Human Rights Quarterly*, 22, pp. 838–860.

Lucke, A. 1996. Text and discourse analysis. *American Educational Research Association*, Vol. 21, pp. 3–17.

Maj, J. 2013. *The Significance of Intersectionality for Feminist Political Theory.* www.e-ir.info/2013/11/01/the-significance-of-intersectionality-for-feminist-political-theory/ [accessed 16 August 2018].

Maluleke M.J. 2012. Culture, tradition, custom, law and gender equality. *PER*, 15(1), pp. 1–22. www.saflii.org/za/journals/PER/2012/1.pdf.

Meth, P. and Charlton, S. 2017. Men's experiences of state sponsored housing in South Africa: emerging issues and key questions. *Housing Studies*, Vol. 32, No. 4. pp. 470–490.

Ministry in the Presidency Responsible for Women, 2015. *The Report on the Status of Women in South African Economy.* www.gov.za/sites/www.gov.za/files/Status_of_women_in_SA_economy.pdf [accessed 16 August 2018].

People's Environmental Planning, 2016. *Addressing the "Chronic" Housing Shortage in South Africa.* http://pep.org.za/2016/06/02/addressing-the-chronic-housing-shortage-in-south-africa/.

Pillay, K., Manjoo, R. and Paulus, E. 2002. *Rights, Roles and Resources: an analysis of women's housing rights – implications of the Grootboom case.* www.westerncape.gov.za/text/2003/womens_housing_rights.pdf [accessed 16 August 2018].

Public Service Commission, 2003. *Report on the Evaluation of the National Housing Subsidy Scheme*. Pretoria.

Raday, F. 2003. Culture, religion and gender. *ICoN*, Vol. 1, No. 4, pp. 663–715.

Rakoczy, S. 2004. Religion and violence: the suffering of women. *Agenda: Empowering Women for Gender Equity*, Vol. 18, Issue 61: Religion and Spirituality, pp. 29–35.

South African Human Rights Commission, 2002. *Right to Adequate Housing – Period: April 2000–March 2002.* www.sahrc.org.za/home/21/files/Reports/4th_esr_chap_2.pdf [accessed 16 August 2018].

Statistics South Africa, 2011. *Gender Statistics in South Africa.* Pretoria.

Statistics South Africa, 2017. *General Household Survey.* www.statssa.gov.za/publications/P0318/P03182017.pdf [accessed 17 August 2018].

Todes, A. and Walker, N. 1992. Women and housing policy in South Africa: a discussion of Durban case studies. *Urban Forum*, Vol. 3, Issue 2, pp. 115–138.

UN-Habitat, 2007. *Situational Analysis of Informal Settlements in South Africa: city of Durban (eThekwini), uMlazi and Kenville/ Sea Cow Lake.* Nairobi: United Nations Human Settlements Programme.

UN-Habitat, 2017. *Global Activities Report.* United Nations Human Settlements Programme 2017. https://unhabitat.org/wp-content/uploads/2017/02/GAR2017-FINAL_web.pdf [accessed 16 August 2018].

United Nations, 1948. *Universal Declaration of Human Rights.* www.jus.uio.no/lm/un.universal.declaration.of.human.rights.1948/portrait.a4.pdf [accessed 12 February 2019].

United Nations, 1966. *International Covenant on Economic, Social and Cultural Rights.* www.ohchr.org/en/professionalinterest/pages/cescr.aspx. [accessed 12 February 2019].

United Nations, 1993. *Declaration on the Elimination of Violence against Women.* www.un.org/documents/ga/res/48/a48r104.htm [accessed 18 August 2018].

Venter, A. and Marais, L. 2006. Gender and housing policy in South Africa: policy and practice in Bloemfontein. *Journal of Family Ecology and Consumer Sciences*, 34, pp. 69–79.

Venter, A. and Marais, L. 2010. IAHS housing policy and housing policy research. *Int. Journal for Housing Science*, Vol. 34, No. 4, pp. 249–264.

White Paper on Housing, 1994. www.gov.za/sites/default/files/16178_0.pdf [accessed 16 August 2018].

12 Climate change and housing

Implications for urban poor people in South Africa

Andrew Emmanuel Okem, Mdoda Davidson Zondo, Siyabonga Ntombela and Sarah Bracking

Introduction

The provision of housing for all South Africans has been a key policy priority of the ANC-led government since it took over the reins of power in 1994. Despite implementing various housing programmes in the past two decades, the housing backlog in South Africa, particularly in urban centres, remains an intractable challenge that is being worsened by the impacts of climate change. The impact of climate change on human settlement affects poor people disproportionately because of their vulnerabilities and their lack of/limited adaptive capacities. In this chapter, we argue that the frequency of climate change–related disasters and the vulnerability of resource-poor communities necessitates that the question of housing provision should move beyond the provision of physical dwelling units to explore the extent to which these are resilient to a changing climate. We begin with an overview of climate change followed by an exploration of the impact of climate change on human settlements. This is followed by a review of human settlements as a driver of climate change. Next, we examine the drivers of vulnerabilities in urban informal settlements in South Africa, before providing insights into how urban settlements can be positioned in a changing climate. We conclude the chapter by outlining the recommendations.

A review of climate change

Human activities including fossil-fuel-based development, deforestation and other forms of land use changes have led to a steep build-up of greenhouse gas (GHG) in the atmosphere since the industrial revolution (United Nations Human Settlement Programme, 2011; Minx *et al.*, 2013). According to a recent report by the Intergovernmental Panel on Climate Change (IPCC), these activities have resulted in about "1.0°C of global warming above pre-industrial levels, with a likely range of 0.8°C to 1.2°C" (Masson-Delmotte *et al.*, 2018: 4). The report further notes with high confidence that "warming from anthropogenic emissions from the pre-industrial period to the present will persist for centuries to millennia and will continue to cause further long-term changes in the climate system, such as sea level rise, with associated impacts" (Masson-Delmotte *et al.*, 2018: 7).

Around the world, global warming has been linked to various impacts on humans and ecosystems resulting in destruction of livelihoods and infrastructure, loss of lives, and damage to ecosystems and the services they provide. The impacts of climate change vary across different regions of the world because of the various feedback mechanisms in the climate systems. As such, different areas of the world are projected to experience different forms of weather extremes including heatwaves, precipitations and droughts (Gray and Mueller, 2012; Hoegh-Guldberg *et al.*, 2018; Masson-Delmotte *et al.*, 2018: 8) leading to multiple impacts including increasing food and nutritional insecurity (Masson-Delmotte *et al.*, 2018) with Africa bearing a high burden (Hoegh-Guldberg, *et al.*, 2018: 103). While the multiple impacts of climate change are being experienced in the current 1.0°C warmer world, the impacts are projected to be higher in a 1.5°C warmer world. The recent IPCC report noted with high confidence that the world is on track to reach said 1.5°C between 2030 and 2052 under the current emission scenario if drastic emission reduction measures are not implemented urgently (Masson-Delmotte *et al.*, 2018: 7).

Climate change–related impacts in a 1.5°C warmer world will result in many socio-economic challenges and will have implications for the global economy given the interlinkages of global trade in contemporary times (Fuchs *et al.*, 2011: 15). Global warming of 1.5°C above the pre-industrial level is projected to lead to the exposure of about 85 per cent of poor people in various regions including Africa to extreme drought. Such a scenario could also increase the number of people in Africa with limited access to adequate water (Waisman *et al.*, 2018: 10) and will erode the livelihoods of many dependent on rain-fed agriculture. Similarly, a report by the World Bank (2013) projected that global warming of 1.5°C by 2030 could lead to a loss of about 40 per cent of the land areas for maize production. Childhood malnutrition and related childhood health risks are projected to become more prevalent under such a scenario (Rogelj *et al.*, 2018).

Relatedly, global warming is projected to increase the burden of diseases. For instance, projections of the global distribution of malaria "confirm that weather and climate are among the drivers of the geographic range, intensity of transmission, and seasonality of malaria, and that the relationships are not necessarily linear, resulting in complex patterns of changes in risk with additional warming" (de Coninck *et al.*, 2018: 107).

There is an emerging body of studies supporting the claim that climate change contributes to migration (Berchin *et al.*, 2017; Freeman, 2017; de Coninck *et al.*, 2018). According to Berchin *et al.* (2017), climate change–induced migration is a form of forced migration in response to irreversible changes in the climate system and associated impacts. A study on drought and mobility in rural Ethiopia found "that men's labor migration increases with drought and that land-poor households are the most vulnerable" (Gray and Mueller, 2012: 134). Higher trends in climate-related migration are projected for the near future in response to climate change–related extreme events (Gray and Mueller, 2012). Droughts could potentially increase inter- and intra-group conflicts due to competition over constrained agricultural land (Hoegh-Guldberg, *et al.*, 2018: 113) and other livelihood opportunities. The pace of rural–urban migration will be heightened in such a scenario due to shrinking land-based livelihood opportunities in rural areas.

Repeated impacts of climate change–related extremes could undermine the resilience of human and natural systems resulting in the impoverishment of vulnerable groups thus increasing the poverty headcount (Hoegh-Guldberg *et al.*, 2018: 112). While the impact of climate change is a global phenomenon, different regions and communities respond differently because of their different adaptive capacities and vulnerability conditions. For instance:

> A global vulnerability index (27 indicators) in 181 countries found that countries with the lowest risk are found in western and northern Europe, central Asia, Canada, and New Zealand, while the highest sector risks are projected in Africa, the Middle East, South Asia, and SIDS [Small Island Developing States] in the Caribbean, Indian and Pacific Oceans.
>
> (Hoegh-Guldberg *et al.*, 2018: 110)

In the urban context, poverty coupled with rapid and sometimes uncontrolled urbanisation is increasing the number of human settlements exposed to the impacts of climate change.

The impact of climate change on human settlement: the global picture

In 2015, the global population was estimated at 7.3 billion. This is projected to increase to 9.7 billion by 2050 (European Environmental Agency, 2015). Associated with this rapid population growth is the rise in urbanisation with about 55 per cent of the global population currently living in urban areas. By 2050, urban areas are projected to be home to an additional 2.5 billion people mainly due to increased population growth and rural–urban migration. Projections indicate that Africa and Asia will experience 90 per cent of these projected changing urban dynamics (United Nations Department of Economic and Social Affairs, 2018). According to van Niekerk and le Roux (2017), urbanisation in most African states occurs with few changes to the built environment and human capacity to harness the process of sustainable and inclusive growth. Climate change exacerbates stresses on urban infrastructure (Ahammad, 2011: 503). Thus, poor people in urban areas tend to be the first affected by the adverse impacts of such imposed stresses.

Providing adequate housing for the burgeoning urban population remains an immediate and future challenge particularly in a changing climate. This is more so in the context of rapid urbanisation where a sizeable proportion of those that migrate from rural to urban areas reside in resource-poor and disaster-prone informal settlements (McGranahan *et al.*, 2007; Ahammad, 2011; Moser and Stein, 2011) on the periphery of urban centres for a number of reasons including a lack of employment opportunities (Campbell, 2010: 38). Such settlements are frequently characterised by infrastructure deficit, poor planning and limited or no government services. A combination of these factors increases the vulnerability of residents of informal settlements to climate change–related disasters (McGranahan *et al.*, 2007) including "heat waves, flooding, and diseases" (World Bank, 2013: xi). Campbell (2010: 38) therefore argues that migration to urban centres in search of livelihood opportunities may increase people's exposure to the impacts of climate change when compared to their exposure in the rural context from which they migrated.

Climate change will have significant impacts on human settlements irrespective of their sizes. However, vulnerability to the impacts of climate change vary because "different human settlement types and locations with varying vulnerabilities and capacities will experience the hazards associated with climate change to an unequal extent" with poor settlements bearing a disproportionately higher burden because of their limited adaptive capacity (van Niekerk and le Roux, 2017: 100). Resource-poor communities in informal settlements are often grounds for "the transmission of vector and water-borne diseases, such as cholera and malaria that are projected to become more prevalent with climate change" (World Bank, 2013: xxv). This re-emphasises that poor and vulnerable people are the most impacted by climate change.

Ahammad (2011: 503) argues that "rapid urbanization combined with the impacts of climate change is increasing human vulnerability in many cities in low-and-middle-income nations" with coastal cities projected to experience heightened storm surges (IPCC, 2007; Ahammad, 2011). In Asia, which is characterised by rapid urbanisation (estimated at 140,000 per day), many low-lying cities are projected to experience catastrophic impacts of climate change (Fuchs *et al.*, 2011: 14). Rising sea levels likely cause an "increase in the intensity of tropical cyclones, bringing higher winds, heavier precipitation, stronger storm surges and increased coastal flooding" (Fuchs *et al.*, 2011: 14). Similar challenges have been reported for urban centres in the Pacific (IPCC, 2007: 46), Africa (Salami *et al.*, 2017) and Europe (Dominik *et al.*, 2018).

McGranahan *et al.* (2007) argue that certain characteristics of urban settlements increase their vulnerabilities to the impacts of climate change. For instance, urban areas, by the very nature of their design, are concrete jungles with most of the surface areas covered by rooftops, paving, tar and concrete, which obstruct the natural flow of rainwater and its absorption by the soil. The obstruction and substitution of natural channels with drainage systems ensure water moves to rivers at a more rapid rate than under natural conditions thus increasing the risks of flooding and erosion (McGranahan *et al.*, 2007; Douglas *et al.*, 2008). McGranahan *et al.* (2007: 19) also note that "land compaction, subsidence due to groundwater withdrawal and reductions in the rate of sediment deposition (due to water regulation) can lead, in effect, to sea level rise, increasing flood risk (as well as creating various other problems)".

The destruction of natural surface cover in urban centres reduces albedo leading to urban heat islands (UHIs) (Sachindra *et al.*, 2016). Elevated temperatures due to UHIs taint air quality, and increase morbidity and mortality among urban dwellers (Corburn, 2008; Sachindra *et al.*, 2016). UHIs can warm urban areas about 3.5–4.5°C more than the neighbouring rural areas (Corburn 2008). Climate change, coupled with UHIs, increases the intensity and duration of heat waves in urban areas (Sachindra *et al.*, 2016). Douglas *et al.* (2008b) argue that as the city grows and UHIs increase, they experience heightened thunderstorms leading to flash floods. The impact of such storms disproportionately affects informal settlement dwellers since they are often located in flood plains, which are highly susceptible to flooding.

According to Ernstson *et al.* (2010: 531), "the city can be thought of as an agglomeration of contested spaces that generate a range of urban services, from transport, housing, and medical aid, to jobs and financial markets". Climate change is degrading the ability of cities and ecosystems to provide vital services. Ecosystem degradation and loss can amplify the impacts of climate change (McGranahan *et al.*, 2007; Roberts and O'Donoghue, 2013). This, along with poor planning, ageing/inappropriate infrastructure and rapid population growth in urban centres increases their vulnerabilities to the impacts of climate change (McGranahan *et al.*, 2007). In the human settlement sector, climate change affects various infrastructures including residential buildings, transport, water and sanitation as well as energy infrastructure.

Human settlement as a driver of climate change

Although human settlements are vulnerable to the impacts of climate change, they are also drivers of climate change (Gunnell, 2009: 3). For instance, unsustainable design makes human settlements energy intensive in meeting basic needs such as lighting, cooling, ventilation and heating (Abimaje *et al.*, 2013). According to the International Energy Agency (2016, cited in Pablo-Romero *et al.*, 2017: 341), the "residential sector represents around 25% of global energy consumption, and 17% of global CO_2 emission". However, the pattern of household energy consumption differs by countries with households in developed economies such as the United States of America consuming 50 per cent of the energy (Salami, 2012, cited in Abimaje *et al.*, 2013: 124).

In South Africa, households consume 17 per cent of the country's energy (Witi and Stevens, 2014), 77 per cent of which is generated from coal-fired plants (Department of Government Communication and Information System, 2018). Between 2000 and 2010, GHG emission from residences increased from 7,100 Gg CO_2eq to 24,817 Gg CO_2eq. The increase was attributed mainly to population and economic growth (Witi and Stevens, 2014: 108). Despite this reality, energy-related GHG emission "is unlikely to change significantly in the next two decades owing to the relative lack of suitable alternatives to coal as an energy source" (Department of Government Communication and Information System, 2018: 8) because of a number of factors including the abundance of coal supply, the contributions of the coal industry to the country's gross domestic product and employment, with the coal mining industry being the third largest employer (Statistics South Africa, 2015).

The housing sector accounts for 12 per cent of fresh water consumption (Abimaje *et al.*, 2013: 125). In addition, the construction of human settlements entails the exploitation of various forms of natural resources that often has negative impacts on the environment. In the Philippines, for instance, wood consumed by the human settlement sector saw a 40 per cent increase in just one decade (1990–2000) while 60 per cent of wood in Chile is consumed by human settlements. The unstainable harvesting of wood for human settlement has negative impacts on the environment including "deforestation with the attendant environmental degradation such as landslides, top soil erosion, desertification and so on" (Abimaje *et al.*, 2013: 124). Deforestation also reduces the services provided by the forest as a carbon sink and other ecosystem services provided by forests.

The production of cement for human settlement construction also contributes to GHG emission. A study by Robbie (2018: 195) found that "global process emissions in 2016 were $1.45 \pm 0.20\,GtCO_2$, equivalent to about 4 per cent of emissions from fossil fuels. Cumulative emissions from 1928 to 2016 were $39.3 \pm 2.4\,GtCO_2$, 66 per cent of which have occurred since 1990". Similarly, Gunnell (2009: 3) notes that the building sector in South Africa "accounts for 23 per cent of greenhouse gas emissions, while emissions from the manufacture of the major materials for the building sector amounts to around $18\,mtCO_2$ per year, or around 4 per cent of total CO_2 emissions".

The location of human settlements and associated transport infrastructure also contribute to climate change due to transport-related GHG emission. Globally, transportation accounts for 23 per cent of CO_2 emission (Agarana *et al.*, 2017) with private cars accounting for nearly 75 per cent of transport-related CO_2 emission (Gopaul, 2015: 12). Transport-related emissions are considerably higher when human settlements are located far from economic centres.

Drivers of vulnerabilities of South African human settlements to climate change

Urban centres in South Africa, like those in other parts of the world, are vulnerable to the impacts of climate change. The impacts are felt across multiple systems, including urban infrastructure, and the related services that they provide. Various health-related impacts have also been reported in South Africa with growing concerns about diseases due to a warming climate. For instance, rodent infestation and the spread of diseases have already been reported as a growing public health concern in many South African urban areas (Department of Health, 2014: 17). Similarly, the Center for Disease Control (2017) identifies temperature increase as a contributing factor to the reported rise in the incidence of malaria-related mortality in certain parts of the world.

Coastal cities in South Africa are projected to be negatively affected by climate change. These "cities are vulnerable to sea level rise, increased sea surface temperature, increased storm intensity and storm frequency, which may pose severe threats to coast urban and peri-urban populations" (Department of

Health, 2014: 15). These climate change–related impacts threaten economic and livelihood opportunities with agriculture and tourism being the most vulnerable. Hope (2009: 651) reports that "the combination of sea level rise, degraded coastal zone, extreme high tides, and altered frequency and intensity of storm events threaten tourism revenue, public infrastructure, and real estate to the value of the equivalent of US$500 million–US$6 billion" across a period of slightly over two decades.

The vulnerability of human settlements in South Africa is worsened by the phenomenon of informal settlements, which, because of their temporal nature, are not resilient to extreme weather events (Department of Health, 2014). This reality is one of the legacies of the many segregationist policies of the apartheid era. In that regard, the Department of Environmental Affairs notes (2016: 10):

> Apartheid spatial planning has shaped urban settlements in maladaptive ways, particularly with respect to spatial planning, as poor, historically disadvantaged households are relegated to the urban periphery far from economic opportunities. This increases the percentage of their income that poor households must spend on transport, which is exacerbated by the fact that their transport options are often neither safe nor affordable.

Rural–urban migration, driven mainly by socio-economic factors, is increasing demand for housing in and around urban centres with the Gauteng Province (see Figure 12.1) attracting the highest number of migrants (Statistics South Africa,

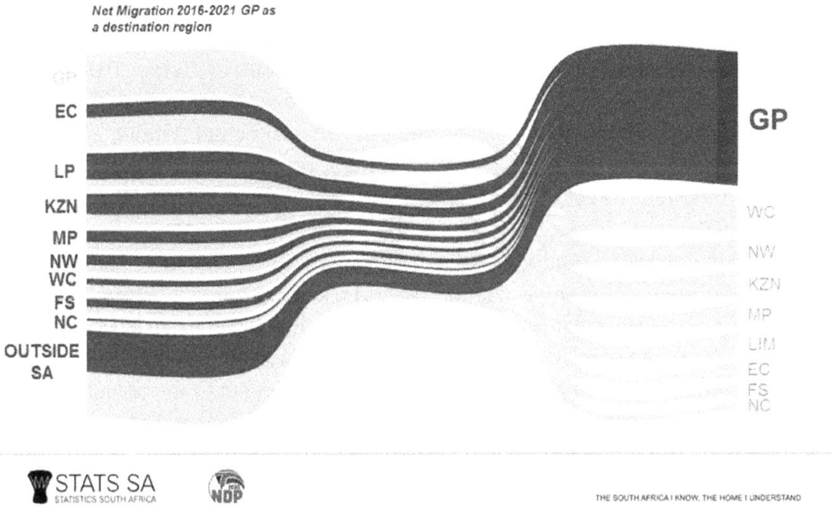

Figure 12.1 Gauteng receives the highest number of in-migrants for the period 2016–2021. The economic strength of Gauteng influences it attractiveness to migrants.

Source: Statistics South Africa, 2018.

2018). The lag between the demand and the supply of housing leads to housing backlogs, resulting in the growth of urban sprawl with people migrating to already overstressed urban areas, living in dangerous areas characterised by the lack of/limited infrastructure and absence of basic services (United Nations Human Settlement Programme, 2011). In South Africa where urbanisation is at 64 per cent (van Niekerk and le Roux, 2017), "between 1.1 and 1.4 million households, or between 2.9 and 3.6 million people lived in informal settlements in South Africa" in 2011 (Socio-Economic Rights Institute of South Africa, 2018: 7). The report also notes that this number could be higher considering that most informal settlements have insecure tenure as well as the temporal nature of these settlements. The report also noted that "over two million children live in backyard dwellings or shacks in informal settlements; over 40 per cent of these children are within the particularly vulnerable 0–5-year age group" (Socio-Economic Rights Institute of South Africa, 2018: 7).

Informal settlements are often constructed on undesirable and unsafe land using highly flammable building material. In addition, they often depend on highly flammable sources of energy. The combination of these factors makes them vulnerable to fire (Department of Environmental Affairs, 2016; van Niekerk and le Roux, 2017). The Fire Protection Association of Southern Africa (2018) reported that there were "5,283 informal dwelling fires recorded by municipalities" in 2016/2017 resulting "in an estimated loss of about R179,513,324".

Despite the location of some informal settlements on unsuitable lands, they are often the main target of the provision of government subsidised housing programmes (Department of Human Settlements, 2004). This programme, however, has been plagued with problems as the houses are maladaptive and are often made of low-quality material which makes them vulnerable to extreme weather and climate-related damage (Department of Environmental Affairs, 2016). These social housings are in most instances located on land far from urban centres thus contributing to GHG emission (Department of Environmental Affairs, 2016).

With a drier future projected for South Africa, drought extremes and flooding remain a persistent threat (Department of Environmental Affairs, 2013; Davis-Reddy and Vincent, 2017; van Niekerk and le Roux, 2017). The recent drought in Cape Town during which the city almost ran out of water only re-emphasises the vulnerabilities of urban centres in South Africa (Barnes and Shippey, 2017). In the past, several urban centres in South Africa have experienced severe drought. These are projected to worsen with a warmer climate. While the response of the city of Cape Town, as well as the residents to the recent drought episode, has been commended for averting a "day zero", it is unlikely that other resource-poor (both human and financial) cities will respond effectively to such large-scale drought incidence. While non-governmental organisations have been instrumental in addressing experiences of climate change in certain parts of South Africa, experiences in some cities (such as Cape Town) have demonstrated reliance on the non-governmental sector (Baudoin *et al.*, 2017; Gift of the Givers, 2018), but the ability of this sector to respond to wide-scale drought in multiple cities is unknown.

Positioning human settlement in a changing climate: policy options for South Africa

According to UN-Habitat. the issue bearing on urbanisation and climate change is that unlike urbanisation during the twentieth century in developed countries, the fastest rates of urbanisation are currently taking place in the Global South (United Nations Human Settlement Programme, 2011). Therefore, responding to the realities of climate change particularly in urban centres in the Global South such as South Africa requires urgency. The impacts of climate change are projected to become more severe in the near and distant future if current emissions and the associated global warming trajectory remain unabated.

Reducing the pace of global warming requires deep emission reduction beyond the commitments of the Paris Agreement (Masson-Delmotte *et al.*, 2018). In addition to climate change mitigation, responding to present impacts remains an important policy response globally and locally. Hence, while climate change mitigation is important, the impact of climate change is unavoidable and, thus, adaptation becomes an important climate change response strategy (Serrao-Neumann *et al.*, 2015). This is particularly important in the context of the Global South where there is a deficit of adaptive capacity. Bearing this in mind, it is critical that cities, particularly those in developing contexts such as South Africa, take proactive adaptation and mitigation measures. Addressing this requires that cities, as centres of GHG emission and as vulnerability hotspots, take such measures to simultaneously reduce their GHG emission while bolstering their climate change adaptive capacities. Doing this requires new forms of urban governance that are inclusive of stakeholders both locally and internationally, recognising the international dimension and the interconnectedness of cities at the global level (Masson-Delmotte *et al.*, 2018). Along the same line, Ernstson (2010: 531) argues that "urban governance needs to harness social networks of urban innovation to sustain ecosystem services, while nurturing discourses that situate the city as part of regional ecosystems". This is important in the context of South Africa where there are immense political pressures to address the thorny issue of housing backlogs but there is an absence of clear policy on land, which is a critical component of housing provision (van Niekerk and le Roux, 2017). In addition, the government also lacks the capacity to meet housing needs with different levels of government being unable to spend money allocated to them for housing provision (van Niekerk and le Roux, 2017). This lack of capacity to provide proper housing makes it difficult for the government to evict people who settle illegally in areas prone to climate change–related disasters. This usually means relocating communities to areas with fewer economic opportunities and people usually return to these biophysically vulnerable areas shortly after being evicted or settled in areas far removed from economic opportunities with significant transportation costs for the residents (Department of Environmental Affairs, 2016).

Improving the energy efficiency of urban areas is another important climate change mitigation strategy (Pablo-Romero, *et al.*, 2017: 341). Evidence from countries such as Sweden, Canada and the Czech Republic demonstrates the importance of a state-led approach since the return on investment comes over a long time horizon, which is likely to be unattractive for the private sector (Nieboer, *et al.*, 2012: 243). The state can facilitate the engagement of the private sector through the introduction of policies that enforce energy efficiency in both new and existing buildings.

Applying the concept of green building in new human settlement projects (Gunnell, 2009) as well as retrofitting of energy inefficient buildings are both important energy efficiency strategies (Department of Health, 2014). Green building provides an important mitigation opportunity particularly in the context of urban centres that are yet to be characterised by lock-in technologies (Hetz and Bruns, 2014). Many climate change mitigation response options in the context of cities have been reported including solar water geyser and solar lighting (Bulkeley *et al.*, 2014). Energy efficient buildings could improve the comfort levels/experiences of their inhabitants (Harris and Krueger, 2005: 39). A further benefit is the reduction in the cost of energy, which could thus be part of a poverty alleviation initiative (Okem and Bracking, 2019). In the South African context, enhancing the implementation of the Energy Efficiency and Demand Side Management programme is critical to reducing energy demand (Boyd *et al.*, 2014) and hence reducing GHG emissions.

Improving urban transportation networks is another important strategy in reducing GHG emission. In a study in Beijing, for instance, Wang *et al.* (2015: 217) found that the "development of rail transit and further limitation on cars could assist in reducing 4.39 million tonnes CO_2 emission". This potential is high in many developing countries that have not locked in carbon-intensive transportation systems. Besides, pollution from urban transportation is the cause of about 49,000 deaths in Sub-Saharan Africa (Agarana *et al.*, 2017). The location of new housing developments close to urban centres along with employment opportunities and improved public transport connections will reduce the distance of daily commute and the related GHG emission (Dodman, 2009: 69). This could also provide some health benefits in the form of a reduction of respiratory diseases and related mortality (Martine, 2009).

Climate change mitigation and adaptation remains a relatively new idea for many cities and therefore does not constitute an important component of their planning (Fuchs *et al.*, 2011; Hetz and Bruns, 2014). In addition, responding to climate change competes with other priorities of elected officials, who must also prioritise issues that contribute to increasing their political capital. This is because:

> elected officials with short time horizons – may understandably be tempted to consider these risks as "distant thunder" and give higher priority in resource allocation to the very certain and immediate problems of housing, transport and provision of basic urban services.
>
> (Fuchs *et al.*, 2011: 16–17)

This is more so in the context of South Africa where high levels of poverty and inequality remain key priorities for elected officials. Linking these elements to climate change response options, therefore, is critical to ensuring that they make their way to the agenda of elected officials (Boyd *et al.*, 2014: 1).

Conclusion

The provision of housing for all South Africans has been a key policy priority of the ANC-led government since it took over the reins of power in 1994. However, housing provision remains a key challenge with rapid urbanisation and climate-related disaster increasing this challenge. Despite implementing various housing programmes in the past two decades, the housing backlog in South Africa remains an intractable challenge that is being worsened by the impacts of climate change. In this chapter, we note that the frequency of climate change–related disasters and the vulnerability of resource-poor communities necessitate that the question of housing provision for urban poor people should move beyond the provision of physical dwelling units to explore the extent to which these are resilient to a changing climate. This is particularly important given South Africa's vulnerability to climate change and its poverty and inequality extremes.

Moving people from temporary structures in informal settlements to permanent structures remains an important adaptation response. However, this should consider key issues including ensuring that such buildings are climate smart, located within transportation routes and located in close proximity to economic opportunities. In addition to being an adaptation strategy, this will also assist in reducing transport emissions.

There is a need to integrate resilience in infrastructure development to increase the recovery potential of communities after devastating weather disasters. We conclude by arguing that adaptation to climate change needs to be viewed as an integral part of the broader development challenges facing South African human settlements and the housing backlog.

Acknowledgement

The initial draft of this chapter was supported by the South African Research Chairs Initiative of the Department of Science and Technology and National Research Foundation of South Africa (Grant No. 71220 held by Professor Sarah Bracking). The contents of this work are the sole responsibility of the authors and can in no way be taken to reflect the views of the National Research Foundation or Department of Science and Technology.

References

Abimaje, J. and Akingbohungbe, D.O. 2013. Housing and climate change in the Nigerian built environment. *Journal of Environment and Earth Science*, 3(4), pp. 122–129

Agarana, M.C., Bishop, S.A. and Agboola, O.O. 2017. Minimizing carbon emissions from transportation projects in Sub-Saharan Africa cities using mathematical model: a focus on Lagos, Nigeria. *Procedia Manufacturing*, 7, pp. 596–601. doi: 10.1016/j.promfg.2016.12.089.

Ahammad, R. 2011. Constraints of pro-poor climate change adaptation in chittagong city. *Environment and Urbanization*, 23(2), pp. 503–515. doi: 10.1177/0956247811414633.

Barnes, A. and Shippey, K. 2017. *Provincial Drought Update and Impacts*. Cape Town. www.wcpdf.co.za/workshops/western_cape_water_crisis/Provincial drought update and impacts.pdf.

Baudoin, M.-A. *et al.* 2017. Living with drought in South Africa: lessons learnt from the recent El Niño drought period. *International Journal of Disaster Risk Reduction*, 23, pp. 2212–4209. doi: http://dx.doi.org/10.1016/j.ijdrr.2017.05.005.

Berchin, I.I., Vogel, C., Nortje, K. and Naika, M. 2017 Climate change and forced migrations: an effort towards recognizing climate refugees. *Geoforum*, 84, pp. 147–150. doi: 10.1016/j.geoforum.2017.06.022.

Boyd, A., Coetzee, K.I.M. and Boulle, M. 2014. What does the current NAMA-space in South Africa look like ? www.erc.uct.ac.za/Research/publications/14Boyd-etal-Current_NAMA_space.pdf.

Bulkeley, H., Luque-Ayala, A. and Silver, J. 2014. Housing and the reconfiguration of energy provision in Cape Town and São Paulo: making space for a progressive urban climate politics? *Political Geography*, 40, pp. 25–34. doi: 10.1016/j.polgeo.2014.02.003.

Campbell, J. 2010. Climate change and population movement in Pacific island countries. In B. Burson (Ed.), *Climate Change and Migration South Pacific Perspectives*. Wellington: Institute of Policy Studies.

Center for Disease Control, 2017. *Malaria in South Africa 2017: an update*. Communicable Diseases Communiqué. www.nicd.ac.za/wp-content/uploads/2017/05/Malaria-update.pdf.

Corburn, J. 2008. *Collaborative Research and Practice for Healthy and Equitable Urban Development*. American Public Health Association (APHA) 136th Annual Meeting.

Davis-Reddy, C.L. and Vincent, K. 2017. *Risk and Vulnerability: a handbook for Southern Africa climate*, 2nd edn. doi: 10.1016/B978-0-12-801477-6.00003-4.

de Coninck, H. and Revi, A. 2018 *Global Warming of 1.5C: an IPCC special report on the impacts of global warming of 1.5C above pre-industrial levels and related global greenhouse gas emission pathways, in the context of strengthening the global response to the threat of climate change*. http://report.ipcc.ch/sr15/pdf/sr15_chapter4.pdf.

Department of Environmental Affairs, 2013. *Long Term Adaptation Scenarios: together developing adaptation responses for future climates*. Pretoria. www.sanbi.org/sites/default/files/documents/documents/ltassummary-policy-makers2013high-res.pdf.

Department of Environmental Affairs, 2016. *Climate Change Adaptation Perspective on Urban, Rural and Coastal Human Settlements in South Africa*. Pretoria.

Department of Government Communication and Information System, 2018. *South Africa Yearbook 2017/2018, Science And Technology*. Pretoria. doi: 10.1177/0047117813517911.

Department of Health, 2014. *National Climate Change and Health Adaptation Plan*. Pretoria.

Department of Human Settlement, 2004. *Breaking New Ground: a comprehensive plan for the development of sustainable human settlements*. Pretoria.

Dodman, D. 2009. Urban form, greenhouse gas emissions and climate vulnerability. In J.M. Guzmán, K. Alam, M. Machenda, Y. McDonnel, and C.J. Mclean (Eds.),

Population Dynamics and Climate Change. United Nations Population Fund and International Institute for Environment and Development.

Dominik, P., Vousdoukas, M., Morales-Nápoles, O., Jonkma, S and Feyen, L. 2018. Compound flood potential in Europe. *Hydrology and Earth System Sciences Discussions*, 132.

Douglas, I. *et al.* 2008. Unjust waters: climate change flooding and the urban poor in Africa. *International Institute of Environment and Development*, 20(1), pp. 187–205.

Ernstson, H. van der Leeuw, S.E., Redman, C.L., Meffert, D.J., Davis, G., Alfsen, C. and Elmqvist, T. 2010. Urban transitions: on urban resilience and human-dominated ecosystems. *Ambio*, 39(8), pp. 531–545. doi: 10.1007/s13280-010-0081-9.

European Environmental Agency, 2016. *Population Trends 1950–2100: globally and within Europe*. www.eea.europa.eu/data-and-maps/indicators/total-population-outlook-from-unstat-3/assessment-1.

Fire Protection Association of Southern Africa, 2018. *Informal Settlement Fires 2018*. www.fpasa.co.za/140-informal-settlement-fires-2018.

Freeman, L. 2017. Environmental change, migration, and conflict in Africa: a critical examination of the interconnections. *Journal of Environment and Development*, 26(4), pp. 351–374. doi: 10.1177/1070496517727325.

Fuchs, R., Conran, M. and Louis, E. 2011. Climate change and Asia's coastal urban cities: can they meet the challenge? *Environment and Urbanization Asia*, 2(1), pp. 13–28. doi: 10.1177/097542531000200103.

Gift of the Givers, 2018. *Fullarton Farmers Receive Fodder*. 05 October 2018. www.giftofthegivers.org/index.php?option=com_content&view=category&id=1165.

Gopaul, A. 2015. *Operational Greenhouse Gas Emmissions of Public Transportation in the eThekwini Municipality*. Master of Science in Engineering. Master's thesis, University of KwaZulu Natal.

Gray, C. and Mueller, V. 2012. Drought and population mobility in rural Ethiopia. *World Development*, 40(1), pp. 134–145. doi: 10.1016/j.worlddev.2011.05.023.

Gunnell, K. 2009. *Green Building in South Africa: Emerging Trends, Earth*. www.academia.edu/29569417/Green_Building_in_South_Africa_Emerging_Trends.

Harris, H.C. and Krueger, D.L.W. 2005. Implementing energy efficiency policy in housing in South Africa. *Journal of Energy in Southern Africa*, 16(3), pp. 38–44. www.eri.uct.ac.za/jesa/volume16/16-3jesa-harris.pdf.

Hetz, K. and Bruns, A. 2014. Urban planning lock-in: implications for the realization of adaptive options towards climate change risks. *Water International*, 39(6), pp. 884–900. doi: 10.1080/02508060.2014.962679.

Hoegh-Guldberg, O., Jacob, D. and Taylor, M. 2018. *Global Warming of 1.5°C: an IPCC special report on the impacts of global warming of 1.5°C above pre-industrial levels and related global greenhouse gas emission pathways, in the context of strengthening the global response to the threat of climate change*. http://report.ipcc.ch/sr15/pdf/sr15_chapter3.pdf.

Hope, K.R. 2009. Climate change and urban development in Africa. *International Journal of Environmental Studies*, 66(5), pp. 643–658. doi: 10.1080/00207230903367955.

Martine, G. 2009. Population dynamics and policies in the context of global climate change. In J.M. Guzmán, G. Martine, G. McGranahan, D. Schensul, C. Tacoli (Eds.), *Population Dynamics and Climate Change*. United Nations Population Fund and International Institute for Environment and Development.

Masson-Delmotte, D. *et al.* 2018. *IPCC Special Report on the Impacts of Global Warming of 1.5 °C: summary for policy makers*. www.ipcc.ch/report/sr15/.

McGranahan, G., Balk, D. and Anderson, B. 2007. The rising tide: Aasessing the risks of climate change and human settlements in low elevation coastal zones. *Environment and Urbanization*, 19(1), pp. 17–37. doi: 10.1177/0956247807076960.

Minx, J., Baiocchi, G., Wiedmann, T., Barrett, J., Creutzig, F., Feng, K., Förster, M., Pichler, P., Weisz, H. and Hubacek, K. 2013. Carbon footprints of cities and other human settlements in the UK. *Environmental Research Letters*, 8(3), p. 35–39. http://stacks.iop.org/1748-9326/8/i=3/a=035039.

Moser, C. and Stein, A. 2011. Implementing urban participatory climate change adaptation appraisals: a methodological guideline. *Environment and Urbanization*, 23(2), pp. 463–485. doi: 10.1177/0956247811418739.

Nieboer, N., Tsenkova, S., Gruis, V. and van Hal, A. 2012. *Energy Efficiency in Housing Management Policies and Practice in Eleven Countries*. Oxon: Routledge, pp. 232–246.

Okem, A. and Bracking, S. 2019. The poverty reduction co-benefits of climate change-related projects in eThekwini Municipality, South Africa. In B. Cobbinah and M. Addaney (Eds.), *The Geography of Climate Change Adaptation in Urban Africa*. Cham: Palgrave Macmillan, pp. 275–304. doi: https://doi.org/10.1007/978-3-030-04873-0.

Pablo-Romero, M. del P., Pozo-Barajas, R. and Yñiguez, R. 2017. Global changes in residential energy consumption. *Energy Policy*, pp. 342–352. doi: 10.1016/j.enpol.2016.10.032.

Robbie, M.A. 2018. Global CO_2 emissions from cement production. *Earth Syst. Sci. Data*, 10, pp. 195–217. https://doi.org/10.5194/essd-10-195-2018.

Roberts, D. and O'Donoghue, S. 2013. Urban environmental challenges and climate change action in Durban, South Africa. *Environment and Urbanization*, 25(2), pp. 299–319. doi: 10.1177/0956247813500904.

Rogelj, J., Shindell, D. and Jiang, K. 2018. *Global Warming of 1.5°C: an IPCC special report on the impacts of global warming of 1.5°C above pre-industrial levels and related global greenhouse gas emission pathways, in the context of strengthening the global response to the threat of climate change*. http://report.ipcc.ch/sr15/pdf/sr15_chapter2.pdf.

Sachindra, D.A., Muthukumaran, S., Ng, A. and Perera, B.J.C. 2016. Impact of climate change of urban heat island effect and extreme temperatures: a case study. *Quartely Journal of the Royal Meteorological Society*, 142, pp. 172–186.

Salami, R.O., Von Meding, J.K. and Giggins, H. 2017. Urban settlements' vulnerability to flood risks in African cities: a conceptual framework. *Jàmbá: Journal of Disaster Risk Studies*, 9(1), pp. 1–9. doi: 10.4102/jamba.v9i1.370.

Serrao-Neumann, S. Schuch, G., Harman, B., Crick, F., Sano, M., Sahin, O., van, Staden, R., Baum, S., Low Choy, D. 2015. One human settlement: a transdisciplinary approach to climate change adaptation research. *Futures*, 65, pp. 97–109. doi: 10.1016/j.futures.2014.08.011.

Socio-Economic Rights Institute of South Africa, 2018. *Informal Settlements and Human Rights in South Africa*. www.ohchr.org/Documents/Issues/Housing/InformalSettlements/SERI.pdf.

Statistics South Africa, 2015. *The Importance Of Coal*. www.statssa.gov.za/?p=4820.

Statistics South Africa, 2018. *Migrants Flock to Gauteng*. www.statssa.gov.za/?p=11331.

United Nations Department of Economic and Social Affairs, 2018. Sixty-eight per cent of the world population projected to live in urban areas by 2050. News. www.un.org/development/desa/en/news/population/2018-revision-of-world-urbanization-prospects.html.

United Nations Human Settlement Programme, 2011. *Global Report on Human Settlement: cities and climate change*. London.

Van Niekerk, W. and le Roux, A. 2017. Human settlement. In C.L. Davis-Reddy and K. Vincent (Eds.), *Climate Risk and Vulnerability Risk: a handbook for Southern Africa*, 2nd edn. Pretoria: Council for Scientific and Industrial Research, pp. 100–110. www.csir.co.za/sites/default/files/Documents/SADCHandbook_Second Edition_full report.pdf.

Waisman, H., Bangalore, M., Cartwright, A., Ellis, N., Gupta, M., Huppmann, D., Massera, O., Newman, P., and Hinge, D. 2018. *Global Warming of 1.5°C: an IPCC special report on the impacts of global warming of 1.5°C above pre-industrial levels and related global greenhouse gas emission pathways, in the context of strengthening the global response to the threat of climate change*. http://report.ipcc.ch/sr15/pdf/sr15_chapter5.pdf.

Wang, Z., Chen, F. and Fujiyama, T. 2015. Carbon emission from urban passenger transportation in Beijing. *Transportation Research*, Part D 41, pp. 217–227.

Witi, J. and Stevens, L. 2014. *GHG Inventory for South Africa: 2000–2010, Educational Forum*. doi: 10.1080/00131724509340472.

World Bank, 2013. *Turn Down the Heat: climate extremes, regional impacts, and the case for resilience*. Washington: The World Bank. www.worldbank.org/content/dam/Worldbank/document/Full_Report_Vol_2_Turn_Down_The_Heat_ Climate_Extremes_Regional_Impacts_Case_for_Resilience_Print version_FINAL.pdf.

Index

Page numbers in *italics* denote figures, those in **bold** denote tables

Abimaje, J. 178
Abolition of Racially Based Land Measures Act (1991) 36–7
activism, women's 100–1
adequate housing: defined 161; right to 18, 72, 81, 101, 147–8, 150–1, 160, 164
Afesis-Corplan 104
African National Congress (ANC) 1, 4, 39, 42, 62, 67, 80, 93, 112, 115, 150, 160–1
African National Congress Women's League 100
African Union 14
Ahammad, R. 176
Ajam, T. 113
Allmendinger, P. 129
ANC *see* African National Congress (ANC)
Angola 121
apartheid era: housing and land dispossession policies 29–37, **31**, 60–1, 82, 101, 117, 132–3; urban livelihoods and housing 54–7
Association of Building Societies 36

Baken, R.J. 130
Bantu Housing Board 33, 36
Bantu Investment Corporation Act (1959) 55
Beall, J. 54
Berchin, I.I. 174
Binns, T. 80
"Black Spot Removals" 30, 31, **31**, 133
Bragg, W.G. 64, 65
Breaking New Ground (BNG) policy 3, 62, 80, 81, 84, 85, **135**, 152, 155; Cornubia Housing Project 84, 86–94
Bricknell, L. 83–4
Build Your Own House 34
Built Environment Support Group 104
Burke, R. 83, 84
Businesses Act (1991) 56

Campbell, J. 176
Cape Town: drought 180; informal settlement upgrading 44; street vending regulations 55–6; women's access to housing 100
cement production 178
Chambers, R. 53
Charles, A. 21
Charlton, S. 45, 123, 162–3, 164, 166, 168
Chatiza, K. 23
Chaudhuri, S. 123, 125
Chenwi, L. 165
Chile 65, 66, 73
Cities Alliance 19
climate change 173–83; human settlement as driver of 177–8; impacts on human settlements 175–7; policy options for South Africa 181–3; vulnerabilities of South African human settlements 178–80, *179*
Clos, J. 15
Coelho, V. 123
CohoUsing 85
cohousing 85
Collier, P. 15
Collins, P.H. 102
comfort and discomfort, spaces of 24
Community Residential Units (CRU) programme 47, 81, 136
Comprehensive Plan for Sustainable Human Settlement *see* Breaking New Ground (BNG) policy

Constitution, South African 3, 61, 81, 101, 115, 147–8, 164, 166–7
Constitutional Court 161
cooperative housing 45, 83
Cornubia Housing Project, eThekwini Municipality 84, 86–94
Cornwall, A. 123
Croese, S. 121
Croucamp, P. 113
CRU *see* Community Residential Units (CRU) programme
culture, women's access to housing and 166–7

de Coninck, H. 174
de Smidt, M.B.P. 54–5
Declaration of the Elimination of Violence against Women 168
deforestation 178
de-housing 31, 149, 156
demand-driven approach to housing delivery 65, 66, 75, 85
dependency and underdevelopment approach to development 64–5
dependency culture 64–5, 68, 71, 72, 74, 75–6, 102, 129, 142
desperation, theory of 23–5
Development Action Group 44, 104, 167
development approaches 64–5
development rights agreements **138**
developmental state concept 112, 113–15
disabled people 74, 122
discourse analysis 162
diseases, climate change and 174, 178
domestic violence 168–9
donation agreements **138**
Draai, E. 93
drought 174–5, 180
Dugard, J. 3
Durban (eThekwini): Cornubia Housing Project 84, 86–94; gender-related workshops 104; land challenges for low-income housing 136–41, **138**; Piesang River, iNanda 98–9, 105–8; state of housing in 82–3

eligibility criteria for government housing subsidy 4, 70–4, 92–3, 163
Ellis, F. 53
emergency housing assistance 46–7, 70, 81
energy efficiency strategies 181–2
Engels, F. 149
Enhanced Extended Discount Benefit Scheme 46
enhanced People's Housing Process (ePHP) 98, 104–8, **135**, 154
Ernstson, H. 177, 181
Escobar, A. 117
eThekwini Municipality (Durban): Cornubia Housing Project 84, 86–94; gender-related workshops 104; land challenges for low-income housing 136–41, **138**; Piesang River, iNanda 98–9, 105–8; state of housing in 82–3
expectant stakeholders 84
Expropriation Act (1975) 138

Fabre, E.A. 15
Fawcett, B. 23
Federation of South African Women 100
Federation of Urban Poor (FedUP) 98, 99, 104, 105, 106, 108
feminism 102; intersectional 162–3, 164, 166, 167; postmodern 102
Finance Linked Individual Subsidy Programme (FLISP) 46, 89
financial programmes 46
foreign aid programmes 64
Foucault, M. 115
Fox, S. 148
Fox, W. 84
Freire, M.E. 20, 48
Fuchs, R. 176, 182

Gandhi, N. 163
gap housing market 46
Gaventa, J. 122, 123
gender and development (GAD) approach 102
gender equality 104, 161–2, 164, 166–7
Gender Policy Framework for Local Government (2007) 104
gender-based violence 168–9
gendered nature of housing delivery *see* women's access to housing
Gigaba, Malusi 48–9
global reformism development approach 64
global warming *see* climate change
Goodfellow, T. 148
Goonewardena, K. 116
Gordhan, Pravin 43
government subsidised housing 1–4, 60–76, 81, 134–5, **136**, 152–6; constraints 48–9; demand-driven approach 65, 66, 75, 85; eligibility criteria 4, 70–4, 92–3, 163; individual housing subsidy 44–5, 46, 89, 153, 154;

government subsidised housing *continued* informal settlement upgrading 4, 43–4, 98, 142, 151, 154, 156; institutional housing subsidies 153; Jozini rural housing subsidy project 117–25; naming of rural subsidy schemes 119–20; number of households *63*; patrimonialism in 121–2; policy intention vs enactment 67–8; rural housing subsidy 47–8, 117–25, 134–5, 154–5; Slovas informal settlement case study 68–74, *69*; subsidy amount 153; supply-driven approach 61, 62, 64, 65–6, 74–6, 85; traditional leaders' involvement 119–23; *see also* Breaking New Ground (BNG) policy; National Development Plan (NDP)
governmentality 115–17
Gramsci, A. 116
Gray, C. 174
green building 182
greenhouse gas (GHG) emissions 173, 177, 178, 181, 182
Grindle, M.S. 131
Group Areas Act (1950) 31, **31**, 35, 55, 82, 133
Gunnell, K. 178
Gunter, A. 49, 148, 156

Habitat for Humanity 17–18, 19
Habitat III conference 12–23
Haffner, M. 3–4
Hancock, A.M. 162
Hart, D. 117–18
Hart, H. 148
Harvey, D. 129, 130, 149
HDA *see* Housing Development Agency (HDA)
health, climate change and 174, 178
heat waves 177
hegemony 116, 119–20; localised 148, 156
Heller, P. 123, 125
Hendriks, S. 40, 41
Hennick, M. 162
Hodkinson, S. 149
Hoegh-Guldberg, O. 175
Hoekstra, J. 3–4
Holmes, J. 162
homeless people 151, 161; *see also* housing backlog
homeownership rights *see* property ownership rights
Hope, K.R. 179
Housing Act (1920) 29, 132
Housing Act (1957) 33
Housing Act (1997) 3, 63, 81, 103, 134, 148, 151
housing allocation 3–4; eligibility criteria 4, 70–4, 92–3, 163; patrimonialism in 121–2; *see also* women's access to housing
Housing Amendment Act (1979) 36
Housing at the Centre approach 160
housing backlog 3, 62, 81, 83, 135, 151, 180, 181, 183
Housing Consumer Protection Measures Act (1998) 151
Housing Development Agency (HDA) 135–6, 141
housing loans 33, 34, 36, 149
housing microfinance 19, 81
housing policies 81, 133–6, **135**, **136**, 150–3; enhanced People's Housing Process 98, 104–8, **135**, 154; historical context 28–37, **31**, 60–1, 82, 101, 117, 131–3; Inclusionary Housing Policy **135**; National Housing Code 70–4, 93, **135**; neoliberal 129–31; People's Housing Process 104, **135**, 142; Reconstruction and Development Programme 3, 39, 61, 62, 81, 85, 98, 118, 133–4, **135**, 150–1; Social Housing Policy 81, **135**, 154; White Paper on Housing (1994) 3, 81, 134, **135**, 151, 160–1, 164; *see also* Breaking New Ground (BNG) policy; government subsidised housing
housing projects/programmes 43–8, 81–2, 152–6
Housing Strategy (1997) 104
Huchzermeyer, M. 44
human capital 53
human rights *see* right to adequate housing
Human Settlements Development Grants (HSDG) 89

Ibhawoh, B. 169
Inclusionary Housing Policy **135**
incompatibility, theory of 156–7
Independent Development Trust 133, **134**
indigenous knowledge systems 120
individual housing subsidy 44–5, 46, 89, 153, 154
individual sovereignty 156
informal economic sector, apartheid era 54–7
informal settlements 1, 3, 49, 82, 155–6, 161; apartheid era 32, 35, 36; climate

change and 175–6, 177, 179, 180, 183; eThekwini Municipality 82–3; fire 180; New Urban Agenda and 16, 17–18, 19–20, 22, 23; upgrading 4, 43–4, 98, 142, 151, 154, 156; women and 100, 101, 163, 165
Ingonyama Trust Board (ITB) 137, **138**
Institute of Architects 34–5
institutional housing subsidies 153
integrated human settlement approach 84; Cornubia Housing Project 84, 86–94
Integrated Residential Development Programme (IRDP) 81, 118, 153
Intergovernmental Panel on Climate Change (IPCC) 173
International Covenant on Economic, Social and Cultural Rights 160
International Monetary Fund 21
interpretivist paradigm 162
intersectional feminism 162–3, 164, 166, 167
invited spaces 122–3
IRDP *see* Integrated Residential Development Programme (IRDP)

Jacobs, S. 82–3
Jenkins, P. 129
Joffe, H. 49
Johnson, K. 82–3
Jozini rural housing subsidy project, KwaZulu-Natal 117–25
Juli, G. 53
Juta, L.B. 93

Kanji, N. 54
Kapoor, I. 125
Karam, A. 44
Keivani, R. 130
Kenya 64
Kipfer, S. 116
Kloosterboer, M. 20
Kloppers, H.J. 29, 30, 31
Kollmair, M. 53
Koma, S. 113
KPMG 87, 90–1
Kuye, J. 113
KwaZulu-Natal 104; Jozini rural housing subsidy project 117–25; Slovas informal settlement, Mfolozi Municipality 68–74, *69*; *see also* eThekwini Municipality

Lall, S.V. 49
land acquisition agreements 137–8, **138**
land audit 137
land availability agreements **138**
land challenges for low-income housing 128–43; conceptual framework 129–31; in Durban 136–41, **138**; historical context 131–3; post-apartheid policies and 133–6, **135**, **136**
land dispossession policies 28–37, **31**, 60–1, 82, 131–3
land expropriation process 138
land invasions 133, 141
Lang, M. 64
latent stakeholders 84
le Roux, A. 175, 176
leasehold tenure restrictions 30, 36, 133
Lee, R. 100
Lefebvre, H. 116–17, 124
Leftwitch, A. 113
liberalism 148
Licensing and Business Hours Ordinance (1973) 55
livelihood activities, apartheid era 54–7
loans, housing 33, 34, 36, 149
local territorial allegiance 156
Lombard, J.J.G. 30, 133
Lucke, A. 162
Lupton, M. 35

Maasdorp, G. 54–5
Macedo, J. 80, 106
McGranahan, G. 176
McGregor, A. 84
McLean, K. 165
malaria, climate change and 174, 178
Maluleke, M.J. 167
Mamdani, M. 119–20
Manase, G. 23
Mandela, Nelson 3
Marais, L. 162, 163, 164
Marra, M. 162
Marx, A.W. 34
Marx, K. 148
Maserumule, M. 113
Masson-Delmotte, D. 173
Maylam, P. 31, 132
Mayo, M. 85–6
Mbeki, Thabo 3
Merrifield, A. 116
Meth, P. 123, 162–3, 166, 168
Mfolozi Municipality 68–74, *69*
microfinance, housing 19, 81
migration, climate change and 174–5, 179–80, *179*
Millennium Development Goals 1, 14, 152, 155

mining 131–2
modernisation approach to development 64
Morreira, S. 16
mortgages 19, 149, 156
Mueller, V. 174
Mukorombindo, Y. 155
Muller, G. 32
Muller, J. 43
Municipal Systems Act (2000) 134
Murphy, S. 35
Mzolo, N.P. 92

"naked women's protest" 101
National Building Research Institute 31–2, 34
National Development Plan (NDP) 39–50, **42**; housing projects/programmes 43–8; opportunities and constraints 48–9
National Housing Code (2009) 70–4, 93, **135**
National Housing Commission 33, 36
National Housing Finance Corporation 46
National Housing Forum 61, **134**
National Housing Fund 33
National Party 30, 100, 132; *see also* apartheid era
National Planning Commission (NPC) 39, 40, 41
National Policy on Women and Youth in Housing 103–4
National Upgrading Support Programme (NUSP) 43–4
National Water Act (1998) 139
Native Building Workers Act (1951) 32
Native Services Levy 32, 33
Native Trust and Land Act (1936) 29
Native Urban Areas Act (1923) 29, 100, 133
Natives Land Act (1913) 28–9
natural capital 53
NDP *see* National Development Plan (NDP)
Nene, Nhlanhla 43
neoliberalism 4, 5, 61, 129–31
Nesvag, S.I. 55
New Growth Path (NGP) 39, 40
New Urban Agenda and Sustainable Development Goals 1, 12–23; constraints 22–3; guiding principles 14–15; opportunities 20–1; recommendations for achieving 18–20; theory of desperation and 23–5
NGP *see* New Growth Path (NGP)
NPC *see* National Planning Commission (NPC)
NUSP *see* National Upgrading Support Programme (NUSP)

oppression, spaces of 24

Pan-African Banks 21
panopticism 124–5
Parnell, S. 117–18
participatory democracy 114–15, 118, 123, 125
participatory exclusion, spaces of 24–5
participatory planning theory 102–3
partnership approach to housing delivery 85–7; Cornubia Housing Project 84, 86–94
Partnership for Action on Green Economy 22
Passenger Rail Agency of South Africa (PRASA) 141
Patel, Ebrahim 40
Paterson, A. 67
patriarchy, women's access to housing and 56–7, 123–5, 162–3, 164, 168
Peck, J. 131
People's Environment Planning (PEP) 44, 48–9, 161
People's Housing Process (PHP) 104, **135**, 142; *see also* enhanced People's Housing Process (ePHP)
Peru 73
Pheko, L.L. 56–7
Phillips, R. 80
PHP *see* People's Housing Process (PHP)
physical capital 53–4
Pienaar, G.J. 29, 30, 31
Piesang River, iNanda, Durban 98–9, 105–8
Pillay, K. 163, 165, 167, 168, 169
Pillay, N. 54–5
polygamy 167
postmodern feminism 102
power decentralisation 102–3
PRASA *see* Passenger Rail Agency of South Africa (PRASA)
Prevention of Illegal Eviction from and Unlawful Occupation of Land Act (1998) 3, 134, 142, 151
Prevention of Illegal Squatting Act (1951) 32
Prieur-Richard, A.-H. 20
private sector involvement 21, 22, 46, 64–5, 66, 133, **134**, 150, 151, 165; *see also* public–private partnerships

property ownership rights: de-housing and 149, 156; historical context 28, 30, 32–3, 35–6, 56–7, 133; leasehold tenure restrictions 30, 36, 133; meanings of 147–9; as sovereignty 148, 156; theory of incompatibility 156–7; women 56–7, 162–3, 167, 168
Public Service Commission 164
public transport 43, 182
public–private partnerships 21, 86–7; Cornubia Housing Project 84, 86–94
Pugh, C. 129, 130, 131
purchase and sales agreements 137, **138**

Raday, F. 167
Rakoczy, S. 168
RDP *see* Reconstruction and Development Programme (RDP)
Reconstruction and Development Programme (RDP) 3, 39, 61, 62, 81, 85, 98, 118, 133–4, **135**, 150–1
religion, women's access to housing and 167
rental housing 45–6, 47, 83, 133, 136, 155–6
restricted choices and constrained opportunities, spaces of 24
right to adequate housing 18, 72, 81, 101, 147–8, 150–1, 160, 164
right to culture 166–7
Ripstein, A. 148
Robbie, M.A. 178
rural housing subsidy 47–8, 134–5, 154–5; Jozini rural housing subsidy project 117–25; naming of schemes 119–20; traditional leaders' involvement 119–23
rural–urban migration, climate change and 175, 179–80, *179*

savings club 106–8
Scheepers, E.Y. 44, 45, 46
Scholtz, L. 45–6
sea level rise 176, 178
self-help housing 1, 65, 66, 117; apartheid era 34–5, 36, 101, 117; enhanced People's Housing Process (ePHP) 98, 104–8, **135**, 154; People's Housing Process (PHP) 104, **135**, 142
self-reliance approach to development 65
self-territorial determination 156
Sexwale, Tokyo 67
Shabangu, Susan 168
Shai, L. 93
Sikota, Z. 45, 156
Simone, A. 116, 124
Slovas informal settlement, Mfolozi Municipality 68–74, *69*
Smit, D. 133, 150, 152
Smith, C. 30
Smith, H. 129
social and economic facilities 46, 154
Social and Rental Housing Programme (SRHP) 45–6
social capital 54
social contract 103
Social Facilities Accessibility Model 83, 140
Social Housing Act (2008) 45
Social Housing Policy 81, **135**, 154
South African Cities Network 137–8
South African Constitution 3, 61, 81, 101, 115, 147–8, 164, 166–7
South African Development Trust 29
South African Housing Council 133, **134**
South African Institute for Race Relations 49, 155
South African Native Trust 29
sovereignty, property ownership as 148, 156
spatial triad 116–17
SRHP *see* Social and Rental Housing Programme (SRHP)
stakeholder participation in housing delivery 83–94; Cornubia Housing Project 84, 86–94; theorising 83–5
Stallard principles 60, 132
state subsidised housing *see* government subsidised housing
structural adjustment programmes 129, 130
subsidised housing *see* government subsidised housing
supply-driven approach to housing delivery 61, 62, 64, 65–6, 74–6, 85
Sustainable Development Goals (SDGs) *see* New Urban Agenda and Sustainable Development Goals
Sustainable Livelihoods Framework (SLF) 52–4

Taylor, D. 93
Thaver, D. 87
theory of desperation 23–5
theory of incompatibility 156–7
Thomas, C.G. 30, 32, 33, 34
Tickell, A. 131
Tissington, K. 3, 4, 22, 104, 155
title deeds 2, 43, 107, **138**

Todes, A. 163, 165, 168
Tomlinson, M.R. 150
Tongaat Hulett Developments (THD) 86, 87, 88, 90–2, 93
traditional leaders and institutions 119–23
transportation systems 43, 54; climate change and 178, 182
Turner, J.F.C. 129

UN-Habitat 15, 17, 128, 160, 181
United Nations Development Programme (UNDP) 18, 22
Universal Declaration of Human Rights 160
Upgrading of Informal Settlements Programme 4, 43–4, 81, 98, 142, 151, 154, 156
Urban Areas Act (1923) 29, 100, 133
Urban Foundation 36, 133, **134**
urban heat islands (UHIs) 176–7
urban land challenges for low-income housing 128–43; conceptual framework 129–31; in Durban 136–41, **138**; historical context 131–3; post-apartheid policies and 133–6, **135**, **136**
urban livelihoods, apartheid era 54–7
urbanisation 15–16, 49, 128, 142, 154, 175, 176, 180, 181; *see also* New Urban Agenda and Sustainable Development Goals
uTshani Fund 99, 104, 105, 106, 107

Van der Linden, J.J. 130
Van Dijk, H. 113
van Niekerk, L. 44
van Niekerk, W. 175, 176
van Noorloos, F. 20
Venter, A. 162, 163, 164
Venter, R. 83–4
violence against women 168–9

Walker, C. 30
Walker, N. 163, 165, 168
Wang, Z. 182
Ward, P. 131
welfarist policy frameworks 64–6
Werna, E. 130
White Paper on Housing (1994) 3, 81, 134, **135**, 151, 160–1, 164
Wilkinson, K. 155
Wilkinson, P. 60, 132
Wolpe, H. 30, 34
women's access to housing 97–109, 112, 160–70; culture and 166–7; economic issues 165–6; enhanced People's Housing Process (ePHP) 104–8; historical overview of 56–7, 97, 99–101, 163–4; informal settlements 100, 101, 163, 165; Jozini rural housing subsidy project 122, 123–5; livelihood activities under apartheid and 56–7; panopticism and 124–5; patriarchy and 56–7, 123–5, 162–3, 164, 168; patrimonialism and 122; property ownership rights 56–7, 162–3, 167, 168; religion and 167; theoretical framework 101–5; violence and 168–9; women's activism and 100–1
World Bank 82, 100, 129, 130, 174, 176

Zanetta, C. 131
Zuma, Jacob 40

For Product Safety Concerns and Information please contact our EU representative GPSR@taylorandfrancis.com
Taylor & Francis Verlag GmbH, Kaufingerstraße 24, 80331 München, Germany

www.ingramcontent.com/pod-product-compliance
Ingram Content Group UK Ltd.
Pitfield, Milton Keynes, MK11 3LW, UK
UKHW011013180926
475701UK00004B/709
* 9 7 8 1 0 3 2 1 7 7 5 0 2 *